The Dynamics of Residential Treatment
A Social System Analysis

The Dynamics
of Residential Treatment

A Social System Analysis

by
Howard W. Polsky *and* Daniel S. Claster
with the collaboration of
Carl Goldberg

The University of North Carolina Press
Chapel Hill

For Zita and Jill

Acknowledgments

Our first debt of gratitude is to the youth and staff of Fairline, Hearthstone, and Concord, who generously welcomed us into their cottages and graciously permitted us to come and go at our convenience.

The following administrators and supervisors of the Jewish Board of Guardians and Hawthorne Cedar Knolls School helpfully paved the way for us to conduct our research: Herschel Alt, Dr. Jerome Goldsmith, Morton Helfer, Harry Krohn, and Vito Sabia.

Robert Falcier and Howard Schwartz, research assistants, made substantial contributions to our theoretical framework and research methodology. Mrs. Alice Jackman, Helen Cardellino, and Barbara Bertine turned in superb clerical performances.

This study was supported by Grant 02121 from the National Institute of Mental Health, and publication was assisted by a grant from the Jewish Board of Guardians.

Contents

Appendixes

Tables

Figures

Introduction

The origins of the therapeutic milieu, or therapeutic community, as it is sometimes called, lie in the "moral treatment" approach to mental illness popular during the last century[1] and the "total push" emphasis preceding World War II.[2] However, the unique aim of milieu therapy—to structure patients' relationships with all staff members and with each other in ways that are conducive to rehabilitation—began during World War II and achieved recognition in the post-war period. It has taken various forms with diverse inmate populations—victims of war neurosis,[3] severely withdrawn adult psychotics,[4] emotionally disturbed children,[5] and adult and juvenile offenders.[6]

1. J. Sanborne Bockoven, "Moral Treatment in American Psychiatry," *Journal of Nervous and Mental Disease*, 124 (1956), 167-94, 292-321.

2. Abraham Myerson, "Theory and Principles of the 'Total Push' Method in the Treatment of Chronic Schizophrenia," *American Journal of Psychiatry*, 95 (1939), 1197-1204.

3. Maxwell S. Jones, *Social Psychiatry* (London: Tavistock Publications, 1952).

4. Paul Sivadon, "Techniques of Sociotherapy," *Psychiatry*, 20 (1957), 205-10.

5. Bruno Bettelheim and Emmy Sylvester, "A Therapeutic Milieu," *American Journal of Orthopsychiatry*, 18 (1948), 191-206.

6. J. C. Spencer, "Problems in Transition: From Prison to Therapeutic Community," in Paul Halmos (ed.), *Sociological Studies in the British Penal*

The principles underlying the creation of a therapeutic milieu have proved difficult to transmit from one practitioner to another. Administrators of institutions vary in the emphasis they give to personal qualities of staff members or to organizational structure, to managing discrete interactions or to planning daily programs. Efforts to lay down general principles, moreover, fail to provide concrete guidance for creating therapeutic milieux. Accounts of particular therapeutic communities do not present the rationale for therapeutic goals and practices in a form that can be adapted to other settings.

The present study examines residential cottages at the Hawthorne Cedar Knolls School, a treatment center for emotionally disturbed and delinquent boys and girls, by viewing specific situations, interactions, and behavior patterns within a theoretical scheme appropriate for characterizing social systems.

This research is part of an ongoing series of investigations conducted over the last decade at Hawthorne Cedar Knolls School.[7] Previous studies relied mostly on qualitative modes of studying peer organization: participant observation, focused interviews, and filmed interaction of resident groups.[8] In this study, both general observation and systematic quantitative procedures are employed.

Findings from the earlier studies provided compelling evidence for the critical significance of cottage life in the lives of youngsters. Nevertheless, a gap persisted in the institution between professional personnel and the child-care staff in the cottages. Psychiatrists and psychiatric social workers have considerable training, high pay, and the reputation for making the essential contribution to the child's rehabilitation. Cottage personnel have little training, low pay, and a reputation for exerting at best a benign influence on children. Three child-care staff members in each cottage are

---

Services: Sociological Review Monograph No. 9 (Keele: University of Keele, 1965), pp. 13-30.

7. These and other approaches to residential treatment are reviewed in Howard W. Polsky, Daniel S. Claster, and Carl Goldberg (eds.), *Social System Perspectives in Residential Institutions* (East Lansing, Mich.: Michigan State University Press, 1968).

8. Leon Tec, "A Psychiatrist as a Participant Observer in a Group of 'Delinquent' Boys," *International Journal of Group Psychotherapy*, 6 (1956), 418-29; Howard W. Polsky and Martin Kohn, "Participant Observation in a Delinquent Subculture," *American Journal of Orthopsychiatry*, 29 (1959), 737-51; Howard W. Polsky, *Cottage Six: The Social System of Delinquent Boys in Residential Treatment* (New York: Russell Sage Foundation, 1962); Howard W. Polsky, Irving Karp, and Irwin Berman, "The Triple Bind: Toward a Unified Theory of Individual and Social Deviancy," *Journal of Human Relations*, 11 (1962), 68-87.

entrusted with the care of eighteen or nineteen highly unstable youngsters. Although supervised by a trained social case worker, child-care staff are by and large isolated from the sophisticated theory and practice of psychoanalytically oriented therapy. They have to work out their own modus operandi for managing the inevitable individual and group disruptions. Despite these limitations and in the face of the residents' collective pathology, cottage counselors often do manage to introduce elements of a therapeutic milieu.

The institution's administrators had long been aware of the potential contribution that well-selected and trained cottage staff members might make toward realizing the goal of a "total treatment environment." Therefore, when funds were made available through a research-demonstration grant from the National Institute of Mental Health to introduce trained professionals as child-care workers into the Senior Boys' Unit, the administration welcomed the opportunity for a research team to observe differences in cottage-care orientation and management modes and their consequences for the peer-group organization. This study is a systematic theoretical and empirical record of the experiment.

The cumulative development and assessment of residential treatment, in particular, has been hindered by the lack of a social-system conceptual framework. But we believe that such a framework, once formulated, can be extended beyond this setting to other types of resident facilities outside of or in the larger community. Although the following analysis and interpretation are based fundamentally upon a comparison of three cottage systems in one institutional setting, it is our hope that the empirical work is formulated on a sufficiently broad theoretical base to be applied with minimum variation to small group systems in diverse other settings as well.

The Dynamics of Residential Treatment
A Social System Analysis

I. Setting and Conceptual Framework

The point of departure of this study is the analysis of cottage life in residential treatment. We concentrate on the cottages, the basic living units of the institution, in order to study the dynamics of day-to-day living relationships between staff and residents as actors in a complex social system.

Fairline, Hearthstone, and Concord are pseudonyms given to three cottages selected for analysis. They constitute the Senior Boys' Unit at Hawthorne Cedar Knolls School, a treatment center twenty-five miles from New York City. A brief overview of the institution, with emphasis on the life of the older boys, will serve as background for the study.

The Setting

Hawthorne Cedar Knolls School contains 205 emotionally disturbed boys and girls, ranging from the ages of nine through eighteen. About 160 boys occupy three divisions—the Junior, Intermediate, and Senior units—each of which contains three cottages. All nine boys' cottages are located on one side of the campus, and three girls' cottages are on the other side. Interaction among the boys within a cottage is much greater than between cottages, and boys in the Senior Unit interact much more frequently with each other than with boys in other units. The institution does not encourage intercottage visiting nor interdivision mingling.

Boy-girl contacts are discouraged. Each youngster is accounted for at every minute of the day. Within this general setting, however, much permissiveness obtains. There are no locks and keys, walls or fences, but the resident must have a pass in order to go from one place to another on campus. Weekend home visits are permitted every six weeks; except for these times, only a privileged few boys are allowed off grounds without adult supervision.

A daily schedule, with some variation on weekends, holidays, and during the summer, governs the life of each youngster. Counselors awaken the boys at 7:00 A.M. and prod them to dress and get to the common dining hall, where each cottage has its own alcove, by 7:45. Housekeeping tasks are performed in the cottage after breakfast, and all boys attend school on grounds from 9:00 A.M. to 3:00 P.M., with time out for lunch. After school, boys return to cottages unless they join special after-school activities. The evening meal is at 5:00, after which the boys return again to the cottage, although a few boys participate in evening clubs. Because of the working conditions of the staff, these restless boys must retire early—about 10:00 P.M. Thus, going to bed at night is a chronic problem. In general, it appears that fostering compliance with routines consumes a great deal of staff energy.

A quota of 18 boys in each cottage is held to as rigidly as possible, since a loss of money to the institution is accrued when a bed is empty. As soon as one boy is discharged, his bed is taken by an applicant from an ever-present waiting list for the institution. Discharge dates are not established at intake; they are determined in large part by the recommendations of boys' social case workers and may occur at any time throughout the year, although an effort is often made for discharge to coincide with the end of a school term. The average stay is about a year and a half, but this varies widely.

Not enough systematic knowledge has been gathered about the attitudes of the boys before entering Hawthorne. By and large, these boys could not be contained in the community. About half are referred to Hawthorne through the Family Court for minor delinquencies—truancy, unmanageableness, theft—and the other half, by agencies and private psychotherapists. These boys, in a word, have been in revolt against authority. They have been proved inadequate to the task of managing normally within family, community, and school systems. Many have been in chronic conflict with inadequate parents. Frequently, they come to Hawthorne after attempts at outpatient psychotherapy have been unsuccessful.

Although most of the boys are of Jewish background, many have only one parent who is Jewish. Their Jewish training and education is generally minimal. Approximately 15 per cent of the residents are non-Jewish.

It is important to point out that the residents are not hard-core delinquent boys with extensive histories of gang activities. On the contrary, many youngsters were extremely isolated in the community; many have severely restricted ego capacities—poor judgment, little self-awareness, inability to control their impulses. Although a minority of senior boys show neurotic guilt and anxiety symptoms, the largest group manifest character disorders; they are boys who have acted out their own inadequacies and conflicts and cannot maintain a viable adjustment in the community.

The staff system has two major components. A professional subsystem centers around institutional management, individual treatment, and the school program. It is run by professional administrators, social workers, psychiatrists, and teachers. Reliance on various professional technologies makes this component quite different from the cottage subsystem, where very few specific goals for cottage treatment have been formulated. Often the main task within the cottage centers on controlling the youngsters, for which the non-professional staff have to devise *ad hoc* methods. Lacking a systematic technology, they have to employ a variety of techniques, often arbitrary, for containing the youngsters. Punishments for infractions predominate over rewards for compliance. For example, a day's smoking prohibition is given for minor infractions, revocation of a home visit for more serious ones. "Privileges" are not special rewards so much as reinstatement of normal gratifications. An implicit exchange system operates whereby the staff permits these "privileges" in return for the boys' compliance with cottage and institutional rules.

The Conceptual Framework

To analyze a cottage within a residential institution as a social system requires conceptualizing and finding indicators of the major types of behavioral exchange that compose cottage life. The social-system theory of Parsons, Bales, and their colleagues, with emphasis on the functional imperatives of small social systems, has been adapted for this purpose.[1]

It is useful to review briefly the origins of this theory. Two major system roles emerged from Bales's experimental studies of small groups at Harvard. The major distinction is between instrumental and expressive behaviorial patterns. Instrumental behavior characterizes the group member who has the best ideas and who does the most to help the group achieve its objectives. An expressive function is carried out by the best-liked individual (the sociometric star), who is most sensitive to the tensions and personal needs of the group members. Usually expressive and instrumental leadership are carried out by different participants in a given group, although there are exceptions to this pattern.

The instrumental-expressive axis is further subdivided according to a distinction developed by Homans in *The Human Group*. Homans conceives of systems as consisting of external and internal dimensions. The external system is "a set of relations among the members of the group that solves the problem: how shall the group survive in its environment?"[2] The external-system tasks are activities that the group must accomplish in order to maintain itself in its environment. The internal system is composed of informal relations, based principally on common sentiments which arise in the course of the group's activities in the external system.

It took the genius of Parsons to see the strengths and limitations of both Bales's and Homans' models and to develop a theory of human systems at a more general level of abstraction. Bales's laboratory groups were given specific circumscribed goals to achieve under quite severe time limitations. The instrumental leader was seen as "adapting" primarily to this external given so that the emergent informal (internal) system was primarily "expressive" with very little indigenous goal attainment. A group that has more opportunity to create its own group goals might indeed require a

1. Talcott Parsons and Robert F. Bales, "The Dimensions of Action-Space" and Parsons, Bales, and Edward A. Shils, "Phase Movement in Relation to Motivation, Symbol Formulation, and Role Structure," in Parsons, Bales, and Shils, *Working Papers in the Theory of Action* (Glencoe, Ill.: Free Press, 1954) pp. 63-110 and pp. 163-269; Robert F. Bales and Philip E. Slater, "Role Differentiation in Small Decision-Making Groups," in Talcott Parsons and Robert F. Bales, *Family, Socialization and Interaction Process* (Glencoe, Ill.: Free Press, 1955) pp. 259-306; and Talcott Parsons, "General Theory in Sociology," in Robert L. Merton, Leonard Broom, and Leonard S. Cottrell, Jr. (eds.), *Sociology Today* (New York: Basic Books, 1959), pp. 3-38.

2. George C. Homans, *The Human Group* (New York: Harcourt, Brace, 1950), p. 93.

different kind of leadership role that would have to integrate more both the instrumental and expressive modalities.

Homans viewed the internal system as an integrative force within the group that increased its solidarity to counter excessive demands made upon it by external pressures. His theory underplays the instrumental phases that mold the informal internal system, although his discussion of the Bank Wiring Room provides many examples of this function.

A human system not only adapts to the supersystem but creates its own goals and is generally much more expressive in the latter phase and more neutrally affective (controlled expressiveness) in the former. The boys in the cottage are much more excited about planning and implementing a camping trip than devising a more adequate system for cleaning up the cottage. The quality of these two objectives is quite different and the boys will not be permitted to exercise their initiative in planning their own goals unless minimally adequate standards prescribed by the institution for the cottage are maintained.

Contrariwise, within the internal system the integration of the group is often threatened by individual or subgroup deviations or breakdowns that require special attention and support. Such activity in the internal system may be regarded as instrumental in healing solidarity and promoting the group's integration.

Parsons visualizes both the external and internal systems as containing means-ends developmental phases. We also see both the internal and external systems undergoing instrumental-mean phases to attain the more "expressive" ends of goal attainment in the environment and integration in the group. Parsons' term "consummatory" (rather than "expressive") complements more adequately the instrumental phase within both the external and internal systems by connoting the goals toward which the instrumental cycles converge.

The new synthesis of external and internal systems with instrumental and consummatory activity resulted in the following fourfold functional imperatives.[3]

	Instrumental	*Consummatory*
External	Adaptation	Goal attainment
Internal	Pattern maintenance and tension management (latency)	Integration

3. Talcott Parsons, "General Theory in Sociology," p. 7.

1. *Adaptive function*: members' regulation to physical and social facilities and authorities external to the system, including manipulation of outside forces, groups, and individuals, which result in a favorable balance between the system and its external environment.

2. *Goal-attainment function*: accomplishment and enjoyment of goals that emerge from within the system and are enacted in the environment.

3. *Integration function*: activities directed to the adjustment of the relations of members to each other within the system.

4. *Pattern-maintenance and tension-management (latency) functions*: activities directed toward maintenance of motivation of individual members to the system, affirmation and identification with group values.

According to system theorists, the above paradigm can be used for any durable pattern of social interaction. This paradigm is our point of departure for analyzing the transactions and diverse structures that emerge from the interaction of adults and youths in adaptation to the larger institutional field.

Cottage System and Institution

Each cottage is a separate building occupied by eighteen or nineteen youngsters and three or four staff members (two are normally on duty at a time). Although the cottage staff is given prescriptions of how the cottage should function, they do have some autonomy within this structure to develop their own procedures, in effect, to evolve distinctive subcultures. In this treatment center, however, much more attention and prestige is conferred upon the psychiatrists and psychiatric case workers, who see individual youngsters throughout the week in a clinic removed from the cottage, than upon the staff in the cottages.

The function the administration regards as most salient is supervision of custodial routines, which have been worked out in detail for cottage workers. As monitors, cottage staff must keep constant track of the children. They wake them in the morning and put them to bed at night. Their numerous responsibilities include preparing snacks during the evening, mending and laundering clothes, supervision of canteen and allowance, and punishment and deprivations for violations.

In order to manage the cottage, the staff evolves a custodial structure based upon the routines and sanctions prescribed by the institution. We would be seriously amiss, however, to abridge the total functioning of the cottage system by concentrating solely on the custodial or adaptive function. The fourfold functional system comprehends other significant activities performed by staff with the youngsters, activities that can be visualized as follows:

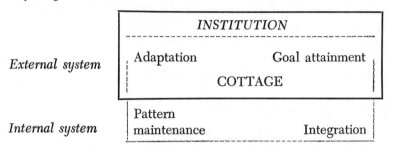

	INSTITUTION	
External system	Adaptation	Goal attainment
	COTTAGE	
Internal system	Pattern maintenance	Integration

Adaptation and goal attainment refer to the activities that the cottage performs in what Homans calls the "external system." The adaptational sphere comprises activities and routines incumbent upon the cottage to perform by virtue of membership in the institution: cleaning up, wearing appropriate dress, adherence to the time schedule, general conformity with institutional regulations. We also include in this category punishment, often the withdrawal of privileges, of youngsters who have violated institutional rules.

The cottage, however, does not merely respond to institutional rules. In addition to being molded by the institution through all of its adaptive adjustments, the youngsters, with the cottage staff, devise many activities of their own. Cottage activities not directly sponsored by the institution and generated from within the cottage we place in the goal-attainment sphere. This includes activities such as ping-pong and chess, singing groups, auctions, camera clubs, card-playing, record groups, and so forth. Needless to say, the cottages vary in the kind and complexity of group activities and autonomous goals formulated, participated in, and attained by the youngsters with counselor guidance and inspiration.

In addition to the two external functions are two internal functions. Pattern maintenance and tension management (latency) refers to any activity in which the staff member gives direct emotional or psychological support to a youngster or group. This ranges from the expression of sympathy for a youngster with a physical injury to structured individualized private counseling sessions carried on in two cottages by the two professional head counselors. By pattern maintenance we mean direct assistance to the individual of a "bucking up" character. Mostly it is directed at youngsters who are in a temporary state of depression, rebellion, or general confusion.

The final function, integration, refers to the informal relationships of staff with youngsters not especially goal-oriented, related to fulfilling an adaptive task, or, directly psychologically supportive. The informal interplay of staff and youngsters in general conversations and bull sessions is integrative because we think that the major function of this kind of interchange is cementing internal relationships along specific values and themes.

The Cottage-Care-Worker Role

To the disturbed delinquent youngsters who must be contained within the setting, the cottage-care worker is the chief representative of the institution. He must control the residents but do so "therapeutically." He is, to be sure, so outnumbered by youngsters in constant turnover that highly unstable boys are always entering the cottage and challenging its stability.

The cottage-care-worker role is undergoing a transition because its functions are now being modified and redefined. At one time, the major function of the worker was custodial. He kept the cottage clean and managed an orderly physical plant. He punished boys for violations. With the permeation of therapeutic principles throughout the institution, the counselor's role in the cottage has now shifted. He is now expected to become part of the rehabilitation team rather than merely an overseer of cottage life.

It is also true that in the past cottage parents emphasized the nurturing, comforting, and sympathizing function. Most youngsters in institutions have been severely emotionally deprived in their early childhood years. Much of their deviancy is regarded as a reaction to the lack of tender loving care in these earliest years. Cottage control was easier to achieve with younger children than with older ones because the older children possessed a greater need for independence. A worker could not easily control older boys by being unduly permissive and understanding. The child-care role underwent many vacillations between emphasis on structure and control, and permissiveness and relaxed discipline. Gradually, the ideal child-care person came to be seen as a unique combination of a rough but loving "parent" who balanced his custodial and nurturing functions.

The four major roles of the worker correspond to the functional imperatives of the cottage social system:

FUNCTIONAL ROLE[4]	SYSTEM PHASE
1. Nurturer, comforter, supporter	Pattern maintenance and tension management
2. Counselor, guide, teacher	Goal attainment
3. Mediator, integrator, friend	Integration
4. Custodian, monitor, supervisor	Adaptation

The cottage-care worker is in charge of a large group of youngsters in a total living-in arrangement, which automatically brings into play all of the above functions. The child-care worker is at times supporter, guide, integrator, and monitor. He must be able to choose and emphasize the appropriate role at the proper time and situation.

This complement of role segments complicates the child-care worker's position in the institutional setting. The role is ridden with potential conflict. The child-care person is encouraged, for example, to allow for individual development in the cottage, but he also must maintain control. He is supposed to inculcate in the youngsters pride in taking care of the cottage and punish them when they are not properly fulfilling this task, and he is also supposed to be a playmate and counselor. He is encouraged to be affectionate and loving but also to induce independence and initiative. For the fulfillment of all these complex responsibilities, the child-care person receives very little training.

Uncovering the complex interplay of functions underlying an apparently unitary role enables us to develop a more comprehensive picture of the dynamics, conflicts, and potentialities of the cottage worker's role. We probe beneath the label "residential worker" to examine the actual demands and responsibilities placed upon this pivotal position. If we can uncover the interplay of functional activities in the role, we can begin to develop the appropriate training program for persons in charge of this complex system. A valid portrayal of the diverse functions within the overall role may enable us to develop a more effective treatment approach to cottage and institutional life.

4. The terms that will be used throughout this study to generally characterize each of these four functional role segments are "supporter," "guide," "integrator," and "monitor."

II. The Functions of
Residential Care in Cottage Life

In this chapter the four functions of child care in the cottages —monitoring, guidance, support, and integration—are illustrated with examples from the research observers' recordings.[1] These examples serve two purposes: they amplify our definitions of the functions with corresponding detailed descriptions of behavior, and they introduce the staff members[2] of Fairline, Hearthstone, and Concord cottages.

The Counselor As Monitor

Child-care workers monitor the boys' behavior to meet institutional demands, but this in turn enables the group to pursue autonomous goals. In this sense, monitoring is an instrumental function. Three aspects may be distinguished: cottage housekeeping, relationships with other cottages and subsystems in the institution (for example, doing school homework or securing a pass to see a therapist), and meeting broader standards of the

1. A full account of observation procedures will be found in chap. iii, below.
2. The names of all counselors are pseudonyms.

institutional community (wearing appropriate dress, using appropriate language, restraining aggressive impulses).

The first example of monitoring is from Fairline cottage. Fairline's head counselor is Joe Strickland, a thirty-five-year-old West Indian Negro with a doctoral degree in education. He had been in charge of the cottage about nine months at the time of the study. He conceives of his role as maintaining strict standards in the cottage while emphasizing fairness and impartiality in dealing with the youngsters. His full-time female assistant, Jamie Rowe, is a recent college graduate with very little experience in residential care. They are the two main figures in the cottage, although several counselors occasionally spell them on a part-time basis.

An example illustrates how Strickland begins the cottage day.

Joe Strickland awakened the boys in the morning. He snapped on the lights in each room and briefly said, "Gentlemen, it is time to get up." He said a couple of more words to individual boys, snapped off the light, and went on to the next room. In some rooms he pulled the covers off boys who did not stir. One boy complained about not having slept well. The head counselor replied that it did not matter. He checked off the boys who made their beds before breakfast.

Minky came downstairs and Strickland blocked him. He told him that he could not go to breakfast without making his bed. The boy was defiant, but the counselor answered determinedly that it was the rule. The boy said that he wouldn't go to breakfast. Joe indicated that he had to make his bed anyway; finally the boy went back upstairs to make his bed.

Cottage and institutional regulations enforced by counselors range from breaking up fights to inducing a boy to do his homework in the cottage.

Joe went into the living room where several boys were studying and asked them if they had done their homework, Silverstein in particular. Seedman asked Joe to check his chemistry homework. Joe did and went off to look at somebody else's homework.

The counselor regulates the boys' general appearance and behavior:

A boy started to go out of the cottage without a shirt. Joe made him go upstairs and put on a shirt. He came down with a half-opened, untucked shirt. Joe went out and spoke to him and the boy buttoned up the shirt.

New counselors are not often as successful as veteran counselors in inducing boys to conform to cottage rules, as the following event illustrates:

Bill Philler kept putting his feet on the desk and Jamie, new on the job, kept coming over to him to tell him to get his legs down. Philler would kid around with her and take his feet off as she left. Then, as she returned to her seat, he would put his feet right back up.

Jamie vacillated between coming back to Bill or sitting in her place and telling him to take his feet off; after a little while she would stand up, come over to Bill and tell him sternly to put his feet down. This byplay continued until the boys went to supper.

There is a different quality to the monitoring function in Hearthstone, largely attributable to the individuals who staff that cottage. Mike Littleton, a non-professional middle-aged Negro who has been at Hawthorne many years, is in charge of Hearthstone. Mrs. MacDougall, a very motherly middle-aged widow, has come to Hawthorne only a few months ago, although she has had experience in other residential child-care settings. They are the two main counselors in Hearthstone and, like the Fairline staff, are relieved on occasion by "roving counselors" who also spend time in other Hawthorne cottages.

This observation illustrates how boys occasionally do assist the counselor in controlling the cottage:

Littleton told two boys that they could not go to one of the Intermediate Division cottages to play ball, but would have to stay in back of Hearthstone. They agreed to this. A few minutes later Muckler reported to Mike that two boys from the cottage were playing over at Concord. Mike became angry, put on his cap, picked up a little stick and went out stomping, saying, "Now those guys are really going to get it!" He returned shortly and indicated that he had made the boys return to the cottage area. Littleton said that the boys expected to get canteen tonight but he thought that they should not for what they had done.

Occasional delinquent accommodations in the adaptational sphere between head counselor and the youngsters were observed.

Littleton (Hearthstone) yelled to Schaffer asking him why he wasn't taking the garbage out. The boy came halfway down the stairs and said that it wasn't his job. Littleton asked whose job it was and the boy answered, "Levy." Littleton yelled up to Levy to get the garbage out and Levy came down and began stuffing paper into the cans. Some boys were milling around and Littleton picked up a reference among the boys about Levy having "sold jobs" or paid other boys to do his cottage chores. Littleton said to Levy with seemingly mock seriousness, "I wondered where you got all that money." Levy replied, "You'll never find it." Littleton rebutted good-humoredly, "You got to sleep sometime." The repartee continued a little longer and Levy completed his garbage detail.

Whenever the boys do not conform, the custodial mode of monitoring is to threaten extra chores:

Joe Skiller, the recreation director, entered Hearthstone and called the boys into the living room. The boys started horsing around, going into all sorts of football formations in the lounge. Littleton quietly said that it looks like the boys want some generals to do, and the boys quickly sat down. The recreation director spent about 15 minutes discussing after-school activities and had the boys mark down their choices.

The custodian-oriented counselor uses his authority to trade conformity for privileges:

Franklin encountered Balboa (a relief counselor) outside and said, "I am going to the gym." Balboa indicated to him that he should say "May I go to the gym?" When Franklin said it in this way, Balboa let him go.

The performance of adaptational tasks is sometimes seen as an opportunity to teach the boys. Here is Littleton talking to an observer in private:

The kids are weaker. The cottage is far different than what it used to be. In the past we had stronger kids who were also wilder. It is reversed in a way. Today they are weaker and can't seem to do anything. They don't even know how to pick up a broom or a mop. Every one of them that comes into the cottage today has to be taught. Whether they are faking it or not, that is something we have to find out, the majority don't know the first thing about sweeping or mopping a floor or even making their beds. So I say that they are weaker today than they were in the past.

Yet another mode of monitoring is apparent in Concord cottage, which is headed by Manny Reisner, a young graduate social group worker, who has been at Hawthorne almost two years and in charge of this cottage for nearly a year. He is assisted by two female assistant counselors: Mrs. Murphy, a middle-aged cottage parent who has been in residential work for many years and who has in the past primarily emphasized the housekeeping function, and Mrs. Pepper, a younger, extremely spontaneous person, who does not work full time, but whose boundless energy makes her presence intensely felt in the cottage. She is the wife of one of the senior administrators of the institution. Relief counselors are needed less frequently in Concord cottage than in Fairline or

Hearthstone because Mrs. Pepper supplements the regular full-time complement of one male and one female.

One distinctive uncontrolled fact applies to Concord cottage. Unlike the other two senior cottages, it is a one-story structure, only a few years old, whereas the other cottages are older two-story buildings not unlike large private houses. All cottages, however, are similar in quantity and utilization of space—a living room, a recreation room, kitchen, six or seven bedrooms with two or three boys in each, and a staff office and living quarters.

Boys in each cottage must carry out certain housekeeping duties each day and perform a more thorough "general" once a week. Concord cottage was observed on "general" day.

Upon entering the cottage, the observer was greeted by Mrs. Murphy who immediately told him that this was the time of day "we really earn our money." Almost everybody was actively doing a household chore except two boys who were sitting in the recreation room laughing over a letter that one of them had received. The noise level in the cottage was low as the boys were busy working.

A few minutes later Mrs. Murphy walked into Filmore's room with another counselor and complained to him that Filmore's room was really filthy. Macy was also in the room. Mrs. Murphy called Filmore, who was at the other end of the corridor sweeping. He replied by saying, "What?" For the first time that morning, the observer heard Mrs. Murphy raise her voice. She said to Filmore, "When I call you, you come and you don't say 'what' but you come to me." He quickly came over and apologized. She said, "Don't bother apologizing to me, just learn some manners next time."

Dakeman came into the kitchen and asked if it was all right if he could take a shower. Mrs. Murphy asked him if he had cleaned his room yet. He said that it wasn't his turn to clean the room and it didn't need a cleaning. She answered, "You can't tell me that there is a room down there that couldn't stand a general cleaning." Dakeman replied that the room was one of the best "pigsties" in the place. They continued the conversation until Dakeman finally asked her if she "was going to take a look at the room." Mrs. Murphy indicated that she would be down to look at it in a few minutes.

Mrs. Pepper's approach to custodial routines contrasts markedly with the other counselors and is vividly portrayed in the following record:

Mrs. Pepper came out of the kitchen and said sweetly, "Ronnie, you didn't get all that stuff underneath the table." The boy replied that the hall area directly in front of the kitchen and around the telephone table were not his assigned areas. Mrs. Pepper came forward, joked and laughed as she swept the dust into the area that the boy had designated was his area. The boy stood there and joined in the cleaning. He completed the job without further objection or discussion.

A few minutes later, Mrs. Pepper confronted Foreman about his shaving. He said that he really didn't need a shave. She indicated that he really did need one, saying, "Why not, is it against your religion?" He hesitated momentarily and said, "Seriously, I really can't, I have a bad pimple." Mrs. Pepper gripped his chin in a roughly affectionate gesture, indicating facetious concern. He went off to take a shave.

Another contrasting mode in carrying out the monitoring function is illustrated in the group worker's (Manny Reisner) orientation. The extract below gives the flavor of extreme reluctance to impose rules or conformity upon the boys:

The head counselor in Concord was walking around the cottage with a list in his hand describing the various house jobs. As he was making his rounds, he noticed a boy lying on his bed. The head counselor asked if the boy was tired. The boy said he wasn't. The head counselor looked at his sheet to see what his job was for the moment. The head counselor saw it was sweeping the rec room. The head counselor mentioned that this was pretty easy work and maybe he should give the boy more work. Without waiting for a reply the head counselor turned and left.

At another time he looked into a boy's room and saw that it was quite dusty. He saw the boy who was responsible for the room sitting and reading in the living room. He asked him if he had done his house job. The boy said he had. The counselor asked him to come with him to his room. They looked at the room. The counselor said nothing and the boy went to the hall closet, took out a broom, and dusted the room.

The Counselor As Guide

Each cottage not only conforms to institutional rules but develops "an innovative posture" toward its environment. Cottages have varying relations with the institution depending upon their ability to generate autonomous goals. Concord, for example, had more activities off grounds than the other cottages. Once a stable pattern of relations with the institutional environment evolves, the cottage attains what Parsons calls a "consummatory" or "maximum-gratification state." The cottage system strives to maintain the closest approximation to a satisfactory consummatory state. This is what is meant by the tendency of the system to attain goal states. Many courses of action are open to each cottage, potentially oriented to a plurality of goals.

The function of guidance refers to the counselor's role in encouraging such innovation. An example of goal innovation initiated by a relief counselor is the following:

Mr. Balboa(in Concord) was working around the kitchen and told the observer to make believe that he wasn't there. He "was on by himself" so had to really keep on his toes. He showed the observer corn that he had grown and was now preparing for the boys.

About 10 minutes later, Shoenstein and Hawkes came in and shortly afterward Balboa announced that fresh corn was now ready. This broke up all ongoing activity and the boys rushed in. The observer participated in the corn fest. A real sense of friendliness and joking pervaded the room as the boys, Balboa and the observer indulged themselves in eating the corn.

Counselors vary greatly in their ability to join boys in spontaneous activities:

Jamie (Fairline) walked into the living room and sat down near Stanby, Silverstein, and Miller. They were singing. She suggested in an unenthusiastic voice that the other boys join in and harmonize with them. "Come on you boys, sing."

The boys ignored her. Those who were harmonizing did not even bother to turn around and look at her and just went on singing as before. She did not have any effect at all upon the boys.

The clearest example of a child-care worker in the capacity of recreation and guidance counselor is the group worker in Concord. The other counselors in the cottage followed his ideas and method of working, which resulted in high participation of the residents in many diverse events. One such event, a huge auction sale, was held and over $200 was collected. For several months the boys were engaged in collecting and repairing items for the sale. The group worker and his assistants were fully involved in the activity:

Manny's room became the center of activity. Manny sat in the middle of the room amidst a clutter and sorted out auction items according to the way they were to be sold. Apparently, a number of small items were to be sold at one-half to one-third of retail price on a rummage-sale basis and major items were to be auctioned. Two boys sat on the floor with him and assisted in the selection, sorting, and tentative pricing. The price at which these items could be sold was agreed upon through consensus of the three.

The boys would contemplate each item, arrive at a price, and place it in an appropriate carton containing items within a given price designation. There was a chatty informal atmosphere and the boys had minor disagreements on some price evaluations. A good give-and-take ensued, Mrs. Murphy joining in and making comments and evaluations about the prices.

The main activities in the other cottages were occasional parties for boys who were leaving, a singing trio in Hearthstone, and a variety of games in all three cottages: ball-playing, gardening, chess, and ping-pong. The head counselor, Joe Strickland of Fairline, participated frequently in the latter two games.

The Counselor As Supporter

The two dimensions of the internal system are support and integration. As Parsons points out, it is possible for individuals to adhere to a group and participate in its activities, but not be attached to it as a focal center of attention and striving. Such a person can be described as *in* the group but not *with* it.

Since Parsons' pattern-maintenance functions refers to the state of the units within the social system, our counterpart function, support, concerns meeting emotional needs of individual residents as a prerequisite for participation in the cottage system.

Counselors vary in the amount of attention to individual residents, which is, of course, greatly dependent upon the saliency and seriousness of the residents' ailments. The observations below consist of supportive activities by different counselors in the three cottages:

A fat boy approached Mike (Hearthstone) for some chocolate. Mike did not send him away abruptly, as he often does in this kind of a situation, but began talking to him seriously about eating chocolate and putting on too much weight. He emphasized this was bad for the boy's health.

A boy who had had his foot in a modified bandaged cast came by and Mike reacted to his limping by saying, "Say, that's good, Bristol. You seem to be able to put a lot more weight on it. How does it feel?" The boy responded in an equivalently friendly way, said it was getting better and it was all right going upstairs but he had a hard time coming down.

Mike Littleton returned to his desk and gnawing at his pipe said, in a kind of mumbling way, "It is always hard coming down because of putting more weight on the foot at each stair." This was Mike's characteristic way of talking to the boys, starting off directly addressing them but then chattering in a mumbling way more to himself as if the listener couldn't really hear him.

The clearest examples of support are responses to the boys' physical ailments:

Feldman came into the kitchen and Mrs. Murphy (Concord) asked him how he was feeling. He said he wanted an aspirin and then he would go to bed. Mrs. Murphy was very concerned because he had not eaten supper. Mrs. Murphy asked him if he wanted some soup or tea. He said that he would like some tea. She felt his forehead solicitously and remarked that she thought he was getting a temperature. She went to the phone and called the nurse. The latter said that she would be over at 8:30 to see him. Over the phone she asked if it was all right to give the boy an aspirin. She did not have a thermometer to take his temperature. The nurse replied that it was all right and Mrs. Murphy gave the boy an aspirin. She also prepared tea for him.

Ashe walked in looking quite depressed. He told Mrs. Murphy about his father being in a federal penitentiary. Mrs. Murphy expressed the feeling that he was the nicest kid around. The boy wanted to know whether he should write his father's address as the federal penitentiary. Another boy came in and asked for three bandaids for his toe which Mrs. Murphy immediately gave him.

A good example of supporting a group of boys is the following observation in Concord.

Mrs. Murphy went into the kitchen and several boys there mentioned that they had just found out that Skippy was shipped today. The boys indicated anxiety and depression about this. Mrs. Murphy tried to reassure them by saying that he needed medication that could be given only at the hospital. He wanted to be hospitalized because he felt he couldn't make it here. She also indicated that he had recently shown many anxiety symptoms.

The Counselor As Integrator

The cottage in many respects is like a family and a small tribe. Those activities that are focused primarily on harmonizing relations among the residents, and between them and the staff, fall in the functional sphere of integration. Although integration often refers to promoting cohesion where no relationships exist, it also applies to breaking up hostile interaction patterns; for example, counselors exhort residents to act considerately toward one another, or they simply step into a fight. These two aspects of integration call on child-care workers to carry out two separate roles, at one time "judge," at another "friend." In the judicial role the counselor is called upon to mediate youngsters' relations with each other and with other cottage staff, whereas in the friendship role he assumes an informal "man-to-man" orientation, a give-and-take as "one of the boys." The extracts below illustrate these roles.

The "Judge" Role / For a very short period, Manny Reisner (who later was head counselor in Concord) was an assistant counselor in Fairline.

Manny was addressing Miller: "Look, for a couple of months you were one of the biggest pricks in this cottage. Would you like it if the guys treated you like you were a prick or rather they treated you with understanding?" Miller nodded to the latter statement. The other concurred.

Manny then addressed himself to Breckler. He told him he was a prick and asked him to show some understanding. "How would you like it if Joe Strickland or myself treated you in that way?" Breckler said, "You wouldn't because you are adults." Manny said, "That's right, that's right, but you still know the difference." The boy was overwhelmed by the argument, and by the shake of his head seemed to agree with Manny.

Mrs. Murphy was often sensitive to the boys' relationships:

Wurzberg came in and said to Adler that he needed a chisel and hammer. He wanted to get it from Simmons and Adler said, "Well, you better not ask Simmons because he doesn't like you and he won't give it to you." Mrs. Murphy heard this and said, "Is that any way to talk to your roommate?"

The entrance of group worker Reisner into Concord as head counselor resulted in several innovations, among which was the way he mediated conflicts among the boys:

A boy talked to the group worker about the fact that he and another, who then came in, had not been able to get along. The group worker asked them to stay in his office and talk about their problems and see if they couldn't work it out between themselves. He discussed a topic with them for a minute or two, left and closed the door behind him so the two boys could discuss this problem themselves.

The group worker indicated to the boys his faith in their ability to work out the problem by themselves.

In a somewhat similar way, he mediated conflicts between residents and staff members.

Harvey came in to chat informally with the group-work counselor in Concord. He complained about a new young staff member who was very insistent upon making him in particular, and the boys in general, do a lot of things(such as combing their hair, brushing their teeth, etc.) which they have always been doing without being told to do so.

Harvey appealed to Manny: "Don't you think it's an awful bore, an awful pain to have someone constantly telling you to do things that you have been doing right along anyway?" As presented, the counselor would not concede the boy's point and avoided answering the question directly. His acknowledgment was implicit; it was to some extent expressed by his quasi-apology for the staff member's newness. To some extent Manny's tone and manner implied that Harvey should be big enough to let these things pass without unduly bothering him.

The Counselor As Friend / The isolated incidents below, illustrating counselors temporarily shedding their authoritative positions *vis-à-vis* the youngsters, are representative of broader integration patterns in the cottages that will be discussed in later chapters.

One of the most uninhibited counselors in the integrative sphere was Mrs. Pepper in Concord.

Greta Pepper was busying herself over the stove in the kitchen. She was moving quickly back and forth and giving brief directions to several boys in the room. Odler appeared at the kitchen entrance and Greta called to him, "Hey, what's doing, pussy cat?"

Now she advanced toward him at the entrance in a samba-like motion, meeting him at the door. Odler was smiling broadly as she approached him. She said something in a low tone and they both began to laugh.

Simultaneously he started to dance backward in a retreating movement while she advanced slowly but deliberately after him. Smiling broadly, he raised his fists in a feigned sparring pose, which she reciprocated with a gesture of the same kind, advancing more rapidly toward him. Finally he turned tail and ran toward the rear door at the end of the corridor. Mrs. Pepper took off in pursuit, chasing him right out of the door but going only as far as the door. She made a noisy over-sized gesture of closing the door and locking him out. She started back along the corridor with a feline grin. Odler burst in through the entrance saying in a mocking, teasing, way, "Hey, Mrs. Pepper, don't lock me out."

Mrs. Murphy frequently joined Mrs. Pepper in gab fests around the kitchen table.

An observer walked into the kitchen where Mrs. Pepper was vivaciously telling Mrs. Murphy a story. Mrs. Murphy was smiling. A group of boys were also in the kitchen sitting all around. A warm feeling pervaded the room. Several members told stories. Mrs. Murphy told a story about California, how she got onto a throughway and wanted to get off at Pasadena but she ended up in San Diego. Her story was met with a ripple of laughter. Mrs. Murphy told a story about a man dressed as a gorilla and the shock on people's faces when they saw him. One of the boys told a story of how he was watching TV and a home finance commercial came on. Right after the commercial on a news broadcast the same finance company was reported as robbed. Everybody broke up.

In Fairline the head counselor, Joe Strickland, permitted quite a bit of horseplay and was able to take it good naturedly, often joining in for short periods:

A number of boys were fighting quite boisterously upstairs in the cottage. The head counselor separated them and indicated his disapproval but did not take it all very seriously. Although he felt it should be discontinued since it was apparently getting out of hand, he did not misinterpret it as any more than horseplay. He seemed to enjoy getting in the middle of the pushing and holding and hollering and separating the boys from each other.

An example of an assistant counselor who was the target of hostility during an "integrative" activity is the following:

Shortly later in the dining hall the boys continued teasing Jamie. Some of the boys began to holler about how awful the table top smelled. They began to howl about what kind of rag was used to clean off the tables and whether it was washed first. One of the boys yelled to get a rag which prompted another boy to yell, "Get her a rag!" The counselor sat quietly through this, not exerting any disciplinary or corrective action. This counselor and another on duty tended to permit the boys to dominate and control each other. A tough boy, Lockholtz, sat down and told another boy to get him a setting. The other boy, with a look of terror in his eyes, quickly got up and brought back a setting. The counselors did not intervene.

Integrative periods in Hearthstone between Mike Littleton and the boys consisted of considerable rough-house kidding.

Alvin walked down the stairs and paused at the landing. He took a long look at Mike across the room. Mike with a perfectly straight face and in his usually facetious gruff manner said, "Do you want to make something of it?" Alvin didn't answer but reciprocated with a playful gesture of his forearm and elbow at Mike.

A discussion ensued between Alvin and Mike about the latter's job. Littleton put his arm first around the boy's shoulders and then his large hand around the boy's neck and directed him to the bulletin board. Here he leafed through several pages of job assignments to show the boy his job.

Then Mike stepped outside with Alvin on the steps to shoot the bull.

A boy walked out of the room into the hall and saw Mike, the head counselor. In a loud voice he said, "This place is turning into a Ringling Brothers Circus, look at all the animals we have roaming around here." He was referring to the counselor's dog and the two kittens in the cottage that morning. Mike in a loud voice, said, "I know a candidate for the side show." The boy walked on into the bathroom.

We are aware of the complex and rapidly shifting interplay of functional transactions between counselors and residents in the cottage. A good example of how one counselor shifted from monitoring to integration is the following:

Mrs. MacDougall (Hearthstone) said to a boy who had just finished eating a sandwich: "Anytime you do a job, you should always clean up afterwards. I am sure," she added, turning to another boy, "he will help you."

"Nope, I am not going to do it," the boy replied. "He [pointing to the other boy] has been sitting around while I have been making the sandwiches. I made the snacks. I don't have to clean up too." The counselor withdrew defeatedly, but with apparent conscientiousness about the matter, reversed herself and said, "Well, I guess that is really fair."

This last example illustrates the complexity of functions that are compressed into transactions between counselors and residents. In the next chapter we shall turn our attention to procedures for ordering these complex observations.

III. The Method of Cottage Observation

The research model for this study is based on cottage comparisons. Modes of staff functioning in each of the three cottages are compared; individual counselors' methods are contrasted; differences among cottage peer groups are assessed; and, finally, these different levels of comparison are interrelated.

The analysis in Chapters III through VI is based on systematic observation; in later chapters our attention turns to the results of questionnaires administered to the boys. The systematic observation in the three Senior Unit cottages consists of research observers' perceptions of counselor-resident transactions called "events." The basic analysis rests on classification of each event according to its primary function. The proportions of events are compared for cottages and counselors.

Most studies of interaction in treatment centers rely on questionnaires or rating scales filled out by staff members or residents. These methods are generally impaired by reporters' biases. Neither residents nor counselors can be objective under the best of circumstances; both groups are influenced by feelings, values, and perceptions connected with the roles they play in the institution.

We therefore introduced research observers into the cottages who would play no other role. They would be less subject to bias, and even more important, they would be able to concentrate exclusively on the task of observation and thus be able to apply their observer training to rigorously sampled, clearly circumscribed segments from the stream of behavior that transpires in the cottages.

The feasibility of direct observation by an adult in the cottage setting was demonstrated in a previous investigation.[1] Our analytical attention to staff modes of cottage care and greater emphasis on objective quantification in this study required new observation procedures especially designed for these purposes.[2]

Development of Observation and Coding Procedures

The final procedures for coding and observation grew out of experimentation with a variety of methods over a two-year period. The research staff was in continuing contact with the senior cottages. Initially, observation was confined to one cottage in order to validate a sociometric questionnaire of peers' interaction and roles. As the scope of the study expanded to include all three senior boys' cottages, observers spent periods of time varying between ten minutes and an hour in a cottage, trying out various observational procedures.

At no time did observers take notes in the presence of the boys. During the exploratory phase they returned to the research office after each observation period to dictate behavior descriptions and comments. As an observation schedule began to develop, trial forms were filled out as well as brief descriptions of staff-resident interaction. Dictation became more structured as difficulties in demarcating and classifying "events" were ironed out. Thus, our earliest reports consist of very general accounts of cottage behavior which observers highlighted during an observation period. "Events" at one stage lasted five minutes, at another, thirty minutes. We also experimented with different ways of demarcating events by functional emphasis and by participating actors.

The examples of the functional imperatives in the previous chapter are taken from these dictated observations. They serve both to clarify our formulation of the systematic procedures and to illustrate and amplify our presentation.

1. Howard W. Polsky, *Cottage Six: The Social System of Delinquent Boys in Residential Treatment* (New York: Russell Sage Foundation, 1962).
2. Although direct observation is seldom used as a source of quantitative data except with young children, the procedure can be carried out with measurable reliability. See Herbert F. Wright, "Observational Child Study," in Paul H. Mussen, *Handbook of Research Methods in Child Development* (New York: Wiley, 1960), pp. 71-139.

When coding was first attempted, our schedule was essentially atheoretical, with items recording number of actors, location, and time, verbal or non-verbal interaction, form of verbalizations, etc. From this we moved to a schedule informed by the theory of social-group work practice. Here we concentrated on indicators of staff behavior that included promoting cohesiveness by increasing boys' awareness of their group membership, recognizing autonomous needs of individuals within the group, making use of discussions, administering rewards rather than punishment in enforcing adherence to institutional expectations, and directing boys' energy toward constructive group goals.

Altogether, the observation schedule was revised more than a dozen times; four or five versions were substantially different from each other, with varying theoretical orientations, units of behavior, methods of observer behavior, and classification schemes. The successive pilot procedures led at last to what we felt was a methodologically sound procedure of gathering the data most relevant to our theoretical interests. This final procedure prescribes how to carry out observation in the cottages, how to separate the stream of behavior observed into events that can be classified, and how to perform the classification.

The Procedure for Systematic Observation

The observer's job was defined as entering the cottage at a specified time, seeking out a particular staff member who was known beforehand to be scheduled for duty at that time, and remaining in his vicinity for thirty minutes or until the observer felt he would be able to record nine events. Thereupon the observer returned to the research office to fill out an observation schedule for each event observed. Except for the training period, only one observer was assigned to a cottage at a time. Observers were instructed to interact as little as possible, without risking loss of rapport, with boys and counselors. They learned to greet anyone present quite casually on first approach to the cottage, not to initiate discussion or interaction, and in fact to discourage efforts by staff or boys to include them as significant actors in the situation. When asked anything about the purpose of the research, the observers were to respond in very general terms: they were members of a research project concerned with learning something about cottage life, and the purpose was to learn how things at the institution might be improved in the future. They were explicitly cautioned to avoid giving the impression that their reports would provide a basis for any direct evaluation of staff functioning or boys' behavior.

Since we did not wish to reveal to counselors or boys that we were specifically interested in staff-resident events, observers did not literally follow staff members everywhere they went but stayed close enough to see and hear practically everything within the counselor's purview. If a staff member moved to another room, the observer followed after a minute or two. This compromise resulted in some slight loss of material, but we felt that still closer observation would have resulted in such lack of rapport that the validity of our data would have been adversely affected.

Time Schedule of Observation

Our systematic data are based on observations carried out within the three senior boys' cottages and adjacent areas. They were scheduled Monday through Friday between 3:15 and 9:30 P.M., from May 26 through June 19, 1964. During this four-week period, the schedule was arranged so that the same number of observations was made for every half-hour period in each cottage at the same time of day and same day of the week. Insofar as working schedules permitted, counselors were observed at equivalent times and observers were systematically rotated among cottages.

Thus, the observation data constitute a systematic sample of a large segment of cottage life, the weekday afternoon and evening periods. This included considerable "free time" as well as some required activities, such as cottage housekeeping. The time period of observation is probably intermediate between two periods of cottage life not systematically sampled—the early morning, which is almost exclusively devoted to housekeeping, and weekends, when cottage activities are most unstructured. A further limitation on the generality of our observations is the time of the year; different findings might have been obtained had we observed in the dead of winter or during the school holiday in August.

Selection and Training of Observers

Five young men, four graduate students and one advanced undergraduate, were recruited to spend five weeks as observers in the cottages, one week for orientation and training followed by four weeks of data gathering. The first week was used for two purposes: introducing observers to the cottages and encouraging them to establish rapport by informally talking to staff and boys, and training them to carry out the systematic observation and coding procedures.

At the beginning of the orientation week either the director or co-director of the study introduced each observer as a research staff member to the counselors and boys in each cottage. We allocated several hours a day for observers to become acquainted with boys and staff.

We also met with them daily for training in systematic observation. We reviewed observation protocols, recording procedures, and a manual of instructions for the observation schedule.

After two days of studying and discussing procedures and informally observing in the cottages, the observers began systematic training observations. Pairs of observers were assigned to a counselor at the same time. Upon completing an observation stint in a cottage, the pair returned to the research office and coded it independently. Then they and other observers not currently carrying out or coding observations and the project directors discussed at length three main areas: general observation procedure, demarcation of events, and comparisons of observers' coding of events.

If in these discussions substantial disagreement about what happened arose, or if one observer saw and heard a transaction that another observer did not, our discussions centered on procedures for entering a cottage and assuming favorable positions from which staff members could be observed effectively. When problems in demarcating events arose, we discussed the observation period in relation to our definition of event boundaries.

When observers demarcated essentially the same transaction, the codes assigned to each item were compared; we focused on ambiguities and discrepancies in observations recently coded and fresh in the observers' minds. In many cases, the discussion referred back to the coding instructions and their interpretation. However, when a problem not anticipated in the instructions did arise, notes were kept so that they could be referred to when future problems of the same kind arose. Of course, we did not permit changes to be made in codes following discussion of dual observations since we wanted to analyze these data quantitatively for reliability. As in the discussion of demarcating events, the focus was always on improving future observations.

Actual training continued beyond the first week. Whereas during the first week all observations to be coded were carried out in pairs, for the next four weeks of data-gathering each observer's weekly assignment of twenty observations included three dual observations. These ongoing dual observations were treated in the same way as those carried out during the training week: independent coding, followed by group discussion of discrepancies and other problems.

At the end of the four weeks of data-gathering (after all the observations had been carried out), both investigators met together with each observer. In tape-recorded discussions, we probed the observer's overall impressions of the cottages and staff members. The observer was first asked to describe and compare the cottages generally and in terms of the functional imperatives. Then, more specifically, we went down the list of functional imperatives for each cottage and asked which staff member assumed major responsibility for each function in that cottage. We then probed how each staff member carried out each function.

After interviewing each of the five observers, we brought them all together in a group discussion that followed a similar line of inquiry. Here we had an opportunity to explore differences in overall impressions among observers. Selected transcriptions of these discussions are used in the following chapter to illustrate and interpret our quantitative results.

Demarcation of Events

An event is the basic unit of counselor-resident interaction employed in this analysis. Our demarcation of these events rests in the middle ground between arbitrary units that can be very reliably established, such as five-minute time periods, and observer options that permit considerable latitude in determining the connectedness of behavior constituting an event, such as Schwartz[3] used in his qualitative observation. The first extreme was rejected as too artificial for our purposes and the second as too unreliable. Since our analysis was to concentrate on comparisons between counselors—as staff groups and as individuals—a preliminary event boundary consisted in centering on a specified adult during each period of observation. Within this limit imposed by the restriction of observer's attention to a given staff member, each observation period was divided into events according to three criteria: (1) when there was a change of youngsters involved, (2) when the functional

3. Morris S. Schwartz and Charlotte G. Schwartz, "Problems in Participant Observation," *American Journal of Sociology*, 60 (1955), 343-53.

situation presented by youngsters changed, or (3) when ten minutes of the previous event had elapsed.

The first criterion for demarcating events was adopted in order to differentiate among patterns that counselors may have evolved for interacting with particular youngsters or groups. We wanted separate events for interactions involving different youngsters. Thus, the manual of procedure indicated to observers that, when half or more of the boys with whom the adult was interacting changed, the ensuing interaction was to be regarded as a new event. For example, if one boy was involved with a staff member and another boy joined the group, or the first boy left, the previous event was considered terminated and a new event recorded. Similarly, if two boys were in interaction with a staff member and two more boys joined the group, a significant enough change in actors was presumed to have occurred so that the transaction following this change would be coded as a new event. However, if two boys were talking to a staff member (or if the staff member was talking to two boys) and a third boy joined the group, a new event had not begun.

Just as we wanted to preserve differences in staff responses to different youngsters, the demarcation of an event was used also to indicate variations of different functional situations, so that a change in function by youngsters in the adult's presence signified the beginning of a new event. Here, function refers to the four functional imperatives: monitoring, guidance, support, and integration. The procedure for coding events in this way is presented later in this chapter.

Finally, we chose an arbitrary time limit of ten minutes as the maximum boundary for any event, after which observers were instructed to regard that event as finished and to code ensuing behavior as a separate event. There were two reasons for this: first, to provide additional weight for longer transactions when events were aggregated for analysis; and second, to alert observers to re-evaluate the content of extended transactions after they were well underway so that they could note gross or subtle changes occurring after the initial encounter.

The Structure of an Event

In order to code a given event, it was necessary to provide observers with a way of structuring their perception of it. Each transaction had to be divided into two parts in the observers' minds—the situation presented by boys and the response of the counselor—so that each part could be coded independently. The starting point of an event occurs when the counselor begins to interact directly with residents in his field. Mentally, the observer codes the primary function that is enacted by the counselor. Simultaneously, he determines the functional activity residents are engaged in immediately prior to the counselor's interaction with them. The basis for coding counselor behavior is all of his activity within an event; for boys, on the other hand, coding is restricted to behavior immediately preceding the counselor's intervention.

The Observation Schedule

The final observation schedule consists of five mimeographed pages containing thirty-one items. The schedule, amplified in an instruction manual with specific guidelines for demarcating and coding events, pinpoints criteria for making coding distinctions, and illustrations.[4] All items on the schedule, except for one requiring a very brief description of the event, are pre-coded.

The schedule is divided into three sections. The first section, "Identifying Data," includes the date, location, and time of observation, the name of the observed staff member, and space for two or three sentences outlining the content of the event.

The second part of the schedule, "Situation Confronting Staff Member," consists of items describing boys' behavior. Here, observers recorded the number of boys in the staff member's field and the number actively confronting the staff member; the degree of interaction among boys and the object toward which boys' behavior is directed; the peer-group functions apparent in this situation prior to intervention by the staff member; and the role content of boys' behavior.

The third section, "Staff Behavior," indicates the staff member's intervention and participation or lack of response to the residents. Items in this section include the number of boys addressed by the staff member; the system function he emphasized; the staff member's method of control; his manner of responding to requests; and his affect in the interaction. Other items consist of observer's ratings of the authority assumed by the counselor; the counselor's use of evaluation; the role in which he cast residents; and the basis he indicated for his actions, if any. Finally, a judgment is made,

4. The schedule is included in Appendix A, pp. 179-84.

for the observation period as a whole rather than for each event, of the proportion of that period spent by the adult in interaction with residents.

Functional Emphasis by Boys and Counselors

Although the functional imperatives have been illustrated with examples in Chapter II, their central position in our analysis requires some explanation here of how they were translated into coding categories.

The relevant items are numbers 15 and 20 in the observation schedule.[5] Item 15 assesses the function addressed by boys, and item 20, the function addressed by staff; coding categories are virtually the same in each case.

The function of monitoring, or enactment of the custodial role, is worded in the schedule as "meeting institutional, staff requirements." For our purposes, we saw institutional expectations and power carried out in the cottage primarily by staff members. Thus, behavior that is prescribed by institutional policy, such as time of arising and going to bed, is included in this category. In addition, staff behavior that did not purely apply formal institutional rules but appeared oriented toward carrying out more informal institutional expectations was included here.

Guidance is defined as "organizing for and carrying out peer-group or subgroup goals." This includes such activities as cottage building projects, informal athletic, social, and cultural activities, and money-raising projects. The instructions pointed out a major distinction between goals that were known to have been originated by the peer group, a subgroup within it, or staff (and which are coded as goal attainment), as opposed to goal activities that the institution imposed or offered to the youngster (to be coded as adaptation). Support is defined as "satisfying [the boys'] own individual needs." We side-stepped the problem of determining whether satisfaction of a boy's need did in fact help to maintain the group pattern by making the assumption that any individual need satisfied within the cottage context would generally reinforce the individual's attachment to the group.

Finally, "promoting harmonious relations among boys" was the operational category corresponding to the integration function. As distinguished from the instrumental function of support, where group solidarity was presumed to derive from an individual's satis-

5. See Appendix, pp. 180-82.

fying his needs within a group context, this category represents behavior directly involving the establishment of good feeling, reduction of conflict, or stabilization and harmonization of relationships among group members.

Reliability of Systematic Observation and Coding

Reporting the reliability of systematic observation has two parts: reliability in selecting events, and reliability in coding content of events for which there was agreement in selection. For the 218 dual-observation events, just 108, or 50 per cent, represent the same transactions between staff members and residents; this figure indicates the degree of reliability in selection. For coding events which correspond between observers, reliability ranged from 57 per cent to 98 per cent for different items, with a median of 69 per cent.

The items for which higher observer agreement was attained, above 90 per cent, were those involving a minimal amount of inference, such as identifying location and duration of events.

Items that entailed greater leeway for observers' judgments were coded less reliably. Items 15 and 20, which required observers to assess the event's major functional emphasis—monitoring, guidance, support, or integration—were coded with 57 per cent agreement for boys' behavior, and 59 per cent for staff behavior. Although this agreement is considerably better than chance when there are five categories (including "no function") to choose among, it reflects the difficulties inherent in such complex judgments. Nevertheless, we do not regard this level as the maximum attainable with these categories. Evidence for this belief is derived from separating dual observations carried out during the data-gathering phase into a beginning, a middle, and a final segment, and then computing separate reliability percentages for each. During the initial phase, agreement was 50 per cent on item 20, the function emphasized by staff. It reached 75 per cent during the middle phase, but fell off to 56 per cent for the last segment. Whether the final drop can be explained by fatigue, loss of morale, or lapse in attention, we do not know. But it seems likely in retrospect that our efforts to sustain reliability were not sufficient; we probably did let up somewhat in emphasizing the importance of following written criteria explicitly, discussing all disagreements, etc. On the basis of this experience, we would emphasize the need for greater sustained attention to the reliability of the observations than was maintained in this study.

IV. Systematic Observation in the Three Cottages

Analysis of Combined Observations

To provide a context for understanding the relations between counselors and boys in the Hawthorne Senior Unit, we shall begin by analyzing the combined observations for all three cottages.

The residents' predominant behavior is gratifying their individual needs, 49 per cent, with each of the other spheres falling below one-fifth of their total activity (Figure 1).[1] In short, youngsters in the counselors' presence predominantly carry out activity of a personal character. In 18 per cent of their events, the young-

---

1. Percentages add to slightly more than 100 per cent in some cases, since double coding was permitted on certain items if two categories were inextricably interwoven within an event. See Appendix B, page 188. However, observers were instructed to select the single predominant function (or other category) insofar as possible and to employ double coding sparingly. The observers adhered to these instructions, so that only a small fraction—never more than a few per cent—of events were in fact double coded. The problem of double coding in chi-square computation was dealt with by using corrected frequencies. The formula is:

$$\text{corrected frequency} = \text{uncorrected frequency} \cdot \frac{\text{number of events}}{\text{number of codes}}$$

Figure 1.   Functions Boys Were Engaging in, for All Cottages Combined.

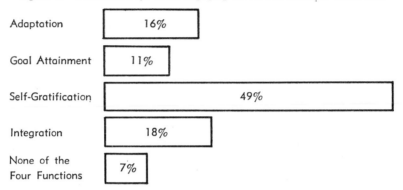

sters participate in non-goal-oriented (group-integrative) activity; in 16 per cent, the boys turn their attention to cottage routines; and in 11 per cent, they are involved in working toward their own group goals. Perhaps the youngsters' relatively great proportion of attention to their own individual needs derives from the institutional emphasis on individual treatment, reflected in the prestige of one-to-one psychotherapy at Hawthorne.

As for cottage workers, Figure 2 reveals that even within this permissive treatment-oriented residential center, staff in the Senior Unit devote about half of their activity to monitoring rules and routines and one-fourth to supporting boys' individual needs. This leaves a relatively small proportion of time for functioning in the role of guide to group goal-attainment, 9 per cent, and integrator, only 5 per cent. Comparing the totals in Figures 1 and 2,

Figure 2.   Functions Staff Members Emphasized, for all Cottages Combined.

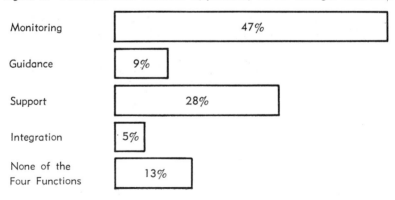

we see that youngsters' functional emphasis contrasts markedly with that of staff. In almost half the recorded events, counselors were occupied with monitoring, whereas the boys addressed the adaptation function in only one-sixth of them. Inversely, residents were engaged in self-gratifying activity half the time, whereas staff were devoting just over one-fourth of their efforts to those needs. The boys emphasized integration in 18 per cent of the events; the staff, in 5 per cent. Only in goal attainment were youngsters and staff nearly alike: 11 per cent for residents, 9 per cent for counselors.

Counselors' emphasis on monitoring and support both have compelling sources within the institutional setting. Custodial emphasis is, of course, derived from the administrative mandate that cottage workers oversee the youngsters' conformity with institutional regulations, and the individual gratification emphasis reflects the clinical investment of this treatment-oriented center, as well as the press of youngsters' demands. Moreover, the absence of correspondingly structured requirements for attention to promoting indigenous group goals and stimulating informal interaction in the cottage explains the finding that cottage staff pay proportionately little attention to these functions.

Fairline, Hearthstone and Concord Compared

Now, what of the possibility that each cottage has a distinctive pattern of functional emphasis? Turning to cottage comparisons,

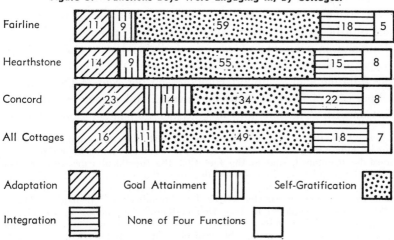

Figure 3. **Functions Boys Were Engaging in, by Cottages.**

we shall see that the aggregate Senior Unit percentages just noted mask wide variation among cottages.

In the category of residents' self-gratification behavior, Figure 3 shows that considerable differences[2] underlie the 49 per cent average noted above. Most marked is the difference between Concord, on the one hand, and Fairline and Hearthstone on the other. Whereas Fairline and Hearthstone boys devote 59 per cent and 55 per cent of their activity to satisfying their own individual needs, such conduct comprises only 34 per cent of resident activity in Concord.

Adapting to cottage and institutional requirements engages 23 per cent of Concord boys' attention, 14 per cent of the attention of Hearthstone boys, and 11 per cent for boys in Fairline. Goal attainment represents 14 per cent for Concord events and 9 per cent of events in both Fairline and Hearthstone. Integration activity ranged from 15 per cent at Hearthstone to 22 per cent in Concord, with Fairline, 18 per cent, intermediate between the other two.

Generally, it appears that for the boys, the function of self-gratification is most prominent in each cottage, although it is relatively less important for Concord than Fairline or Hearthstone boys. Concord boys' activities tend toward greater balance:[3] all three of the (quantitatively) lesser functions—adaptation, goal attainment, and integration—show proportionate increments for Concord compared to the other cottages, at the expense of individual need fulfilment.

Turning to staff activity, we find Joe Strickland's Fairline team most actively engaged in the monitoring function: it receives 53 per cent of their attention, compared with 45 per cent at Hearthstone and 43 per cent in Concord. Individual support is most apparent in Hearthstone, where Littleton and Mrs. MacDougall are the full-time staff. Support composes 33 per cent of their events, 26 per cent of Fairline counselors' events, and 25 per cent of those in Concord. The functions of guidance and integration, although

2. When "differences" are noted in the text, they are supported by chi square tests with $p < .05$. However, here a word of caution in interpretation must be mentioned, due to the fact that the functional categories are not coded independently. In cases of this sort, the "reader should understand category by category comparisons to be the equivalent of viewing interrelated data from different perspectives." Fred L. Strodtbeck and Richard D. Mann, "Sex Role Differentiation in Jury Deliberations," *Sociometry*, 19 (1956), 7.

3. "Balance" here refers to equal emphasis on all functions. No implication that "balance" is a desirable goal of child care is intended.

Figure 4. Functions Staff Members Emphasized, by Cottages.

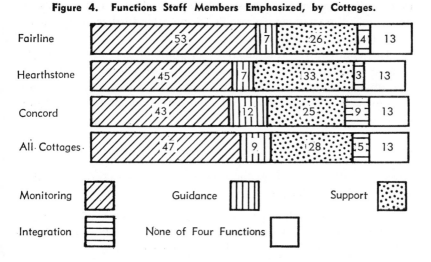

relatively neglected in all cottages, are less so in Concord, headed by group worker Reisner. He and his staff give 12 per cent of their attention to guidance, compared with 7 per cent for the other two cottages, and 9 per cent to integration, against less than 5 per cent in Fairline and Hearthstone.

Thus it appears that a balance among functions, as the term is used above to describe Concord boys' more equal proportions of attention to all functions, applies as well to Concord staff. For the boys' activity, self-gratification predominates in all three cottages, but less so in Concord; in the case of counselor emphasis, monitoring occupies a less substantial role in Concord than in Fairline. While Hearthstone staff do little more monitoring than staff in Concord, they devote their residual attention primarily to support, which is not notably understressed in the other cottages. By no means does the Concord staff's emphasis on guidance and integration approach the other two functions, yet their greater attention to these functions is distinctive when contrasted with the other two cottages.

Looking again at the question of functional balance in the three cottages among residents and staff, we note a curious paradox. That cottage, Concord, which manifests the least staff attention to monitoring also shows the most resident initiative in fulfilling cottage routines. Concord staff have to pressure the boys least to perform cottage chores, which apparently are most accepted by the residents. This enables Concord staff to direct more energy to other cottage spheres and to stimulate youngsters in other kinds of activities. We shall return to this theme after further comparative inspection of the three cottages.

The comparative functional description of the three cottages can be understood and pictured better with selected excerpts of the observers' qualitative impressions. In what ways are the various functions carried out and what is the climate in each of the cottages?

Observers' Qualitative Impressions of the Three Cottages

After spending a month in the cottages, one research observer described them as follows:

> Fairline comes closest to what you would think of being an institution cottage. Hearthstone reminds me of an orphanage; Concord could almost be a camp group. . . .

Another characterization was based on the family model. Observers described Hearthstone as best approximating a traditional family, with Mike Littleton playing the role of an authoritarian father and Mrs. MacDougall the role of a very nurturant mother. Concord was described as least like a family, more like a camp. Fairline also fell short of an ideal typical family in that Jamie, the young female counselor, failed to fulfil the maternal role—"Jamie Rowe is a person who listens to people, she just listens."

The observers saw Fairline and Hearthstone as less sophisticated and intellectually oriented than Concord. Fairline was the most fragmented: it exhibited the most tension among subgroups and had the least cottage-wide spirit. Concord was regarded as the cleanest, Hearthstone next, and Fairline, the least cleanly kept of the three cottages.

The cottages' formal and informal group activities were described as follows:

> In Concord, Mrs. Pepper and Mrs. Murphy are friendly and affectionate people who build up considerable *esprit de corps.* Mrs. Pepper, especially, stimulates the boys to interact both among themselves and with her. Concord has the most group activity. Fairline is the most "neutral," in that counselors do not play an active role in stimulating group activities. Hearthstone had even less activity than Fairline largely because of the negative influence of Mike Littleton with his dominant authoritarian bearing.

> Hearthstone, compared to both Fairline and Concord, and especially the latter, does not engage the boys in rational discus-

sions about their responsibilities in the cottage. Concord, and especially the head counselor, Manny, is the most rational and reasonable with the youngsters.

Concord has the most cottage feeling in the kids' sense that it is good for them to be there. In Fairline and Hearthstone, the spirit is less. Especially in Hearthstone, I get the feeling that the cottage is a place to sleep in. Fairline is in between Hearthstone and Concord.

From the kids' point of view, Concord is definitely the nicest place to live in. There is just so much a kid can do in Concord. The books look like they have been used, and the cottage on the whole is much cleaner than the others. Youngsters also have more access to staff rooms and there is a feeling of more freedom in the cottage.

The monitoring function was taken for granted in Concord.

If a kid comes to Manny with a pass which is signed, he just looks at it. In Hearthstone and Fairline there is a different attitude. In Hearthstone there would be, 'Oh, you are going there!'

The observers felt that there was much more suspicion and distrust between the boys and the counselors in Hearthstone and Fairline than in Concord. Apparently, in Concord the boys were able to manage much more autonomously; they took responsibility themselves for many cottage routines that had to be supervised by the workers in Hearthstone and Fairline.

Comparison of Chief Counselors

In each cottage the counselor in charge was a male, although the superiority of his position was perhaps less formally sanctioned for Littleton than for Strickland or Reisner. In any event, we might expect the entire tone of the cottage to be strongly influenced by the man in charge. We should therefore expect a comparison among male counselors' events to highlight the overall cottage differences just described.

Whatever tone the chief counselor sets must have an impact on residents, so that their activities in his presence give us some clues to this tone. Concord boys initiated more adaptational activities in the head counselor's field, 28 per cent, than boys in Fairline, 18 per cent, or Hearthstone, 9 per cent. In contrast, the youngsters in the latter two cottages devoted more than half of their events to self-gratification: 55 per cent and 59 per cent, compared to 31 per cent for Concord. One-fourth of the events in

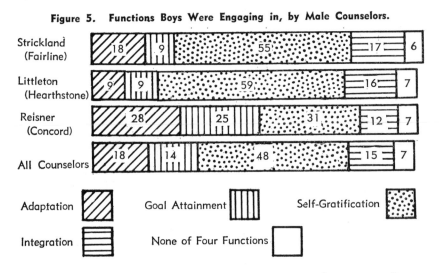

Figure 5. Functions Boys Were Engaging in, by Male Counselors.

Concord entailed boys' working toward group goals, compared to 9 per cent each in the other two cottages. Here again we see more balance in Concord boys' behavior, although the balance in Reisner's presence differs from the total Concord staff picture by its greater stress on goal attainment and less on integration. In disproportionate attention to self-gratification, the other two cottages once again closely resemble each other.

Figure 6 indicates that a comparison of functions emphasized by different head counselors does indeed highlight the cottage varia-

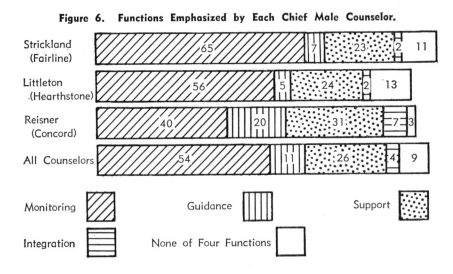

Figure 6. Functions Emphasized by Each Chief Male Counselor.

tion found in total staff emphasis. This is clearest for the monitoring function. We noted previously a range of 10 per cent—from a low of 43 per cent in Concord to a high of 53 per cent in Fairline—in proportion of events given primarily to overseeing rules and routines by the aggregate of counselors in each cottage. The range among male counselors, however, is fully 25 per cent, with Joe Strickland devoting 65 per cent of his time and energy to monitoring, Mike Littleton, 56 per cent, and Manny Reisner, 40 per cent.

Less striking are differences in emphasis on support, with Reisner showing 7 or 8 per cent more than the others. The integration function is addressed by him 7 per cent of the time, and by Strickland and Littleton, only 2 per cent each. Guidance, however, which is a rather minor activity for Strickland, 7 per cent, and Littleton, 5 per cent, receives much more of Reisner's attention—20 per cent.

Overall, the similarity between Fairline and Hearthstone, in contrast with Concord, is brought into sharper relief by comparing the activity of their chief counselors. Strickland and Littleton provide models of primary emphasis in monitoring, whereas Reisner's attention to rules and regulations is less conspicuous. He mitigates it with almost as much individual support and, relative to the other counselors, appreciably more guidance toward goals that residents have in common.

We feel it is important to "personalize" our quantitative data with the observers' impressions of each head counselor's style in the three cottages. Here too emerges a plausible interconnection between the quantitative functional emphasis in the cottage-care role and the manner in which each chief counselor performs his role in the cottage system.

Observers' Impressions of Head Male Counselors

Joe Strickland (Fairline) / The head counselor in Fairline, Joe Strickland, was described by the observers as a strong figure of authority, who dealt with the boys in a fair and impartial manner.

If a boy thought he was not getting something he justly deserved, or was entitled to, he would feel free to go to Joe.

The observers were impressed with Strickland's consistency:

If a boy does not do what he was supposed to do, he has to reckon with Joe, and sometimes they do press their luck but not often, because Strickland really lays down the law.

Strickland's authority was decisive:

When Joe decides that there is going to be order, he gets order. Certainly, when Joe speaks, the boys obey. I don't see anyone going against Joe's word or anything like that, when important rules are involved. There is a definite respect for Joe.

However, when Strickland was absent from the cottage, his reign was not maintained:

I think there is order when he is around, but when he leaves it is a situation sort of like a bank robber. When the cop is around, he behaves but when the policeman is away, the robber goes right back and robs the bank. The boys do all the wrong things. . . . When Joe himself is not present the youngsters tend to act up.

The following extract captures the main characteristics of Strickland's management of Fairline: control, authority, fairness, and discipline.

Joe is close to a "complete counselor" if I can use the phrase. In a pinch, he would be capable of running the whole cottage by himself. . . . boys can't battle against Joe because he can slap them down. . . . he is a big guy, a powerful guy. Joe knows judo. Joe tries to be fair, he always is very careful about the things he says and exerts a tremendous amount of self-control. He can get involved in competitive games with the boys and loses like a man.

Joe shows the boys sportsmanship by examples—showing the boys how to conduct themselves as men. He practices what he preaches and I think the boys can see this. . . . He takes an interest in everything that goes on in the cottage. . . . As far as keeping boys in line and making sure that they do their jobs and deciding who will be allowed to go anywhere—Joe does an excellent job.

More than any other counselor, Joe managed the custodial tasks with a view toward teaching traditional middle-class values.

Joe seems to go by the book pretty much. He was giving boys money to go home and he gave them just enough. Joe said he wanted to teach the boys thriftiness and he knows that this is a battle between them. They try to get as much as possible and he tries to give them as little as possible. He seems to be the only one who consciously tries to teach them little things like thrift, honesty, and things like that. Joe makes a point of teaching a lesson, for example, around giving the boys money for home leave. According to Joe, boys at Hawthorne are supposed to be thrifty and honest. . . . because he acts this way he appears to be stricter. He conforms to the rules more strictly than other counselors.

Mike Littleton (Hearthstone) / Mike Littleton, Hearthstone's head counselor, first impressed the observers as gruff and short-tempered, but after a week or two they came to see that Mike was not all "ice"; underneath the gruffness was considerable warmth for the boys.

On the surface, he seemed generally removed from the boys:

Mike does the very minimum; he doesn't initiate anything. When he tells a kid to clean up, he doesn't interact very much with him.

In contrast with Strickland, he came across as less rational and more dogmatic. The observers stressed Littleton's negative authoritarian control of the cottage:

His authoritarian overbearing attitudes tend to minimize the things that kids could do.

His occasional feelings of warmth were expressed in this way:

He pats boys on their heads. I have seen him do this a few times. This is certainly a sign of warmth. I saw him discuss a problem with one of the boys for about a half-hour. He is the authoritarian father but also has compassion which comes out now and then when he feels that it is necessary.

His good-humored moments are limited in several ways.

Mike doesn't mind a certain amount of sauciness if it comes from the right kid. . . . But if Mike is down on a kid. . . . He will be treated pretty badly. I think punishments are out of proportion to what the youngsters violate.

More than any other counselor, Littleton was described as being derogatory toward the residents. Often the derogation takes the form of "good fun."

Mike does pick on some boys. . . . His remarks show his superiority over them. Last night, for example, he picked out two boys and told them that they didn't have a brain, etc. One of the boys who had a little trouble hearing was made fun of by other boys and were led by Mike. Mike sanctioned this kind of fun.

His apparent aims are summarized as follows:

He doesn't want fooling around or yelling or fighting upstairs. He wants to keep peace in the cottage. He wants to see everything that happens. I don't think he sets a positive tone at all. He has to make sure everything is under control. His attitude is a damper on the cottage. . . .

He likes to sit down and read a paper. For long periods he tends to ignore what is going on around him.

Manny Reisner (Concord) / The observers described Manny Reisner as the "ultimate authority" in Concord, but the way in which he used his authority was quite different from Strickland's or Littleton's. Reisner was described as not participating "in giving orders" too much. Yet the boys responded to Manny's authority with the least resistance.

If Manny says something, the kid does it, and he does not complain about it either.

Thus, Reisner seemed to be "using his authority behind the scene." He has authority but does not express it directly or in an authoritarian manner, as do the head counselors in Fairline and Hearthstone.

The observers cited his fairness and his understanding of the boys. He frequently helped youngsters with practical problems, such as school work. Moreover, as a trained social worker, he undertook to deal with problems eschewed by non-professionals. "Many of the deeper problems of the youngsters were referred to Manny by the other counselors." On the surface, the method was not distinguishable from traditional casework interviewing. All the observers noted that Reisner conducted frequent individual counseling sessions with residents in his office—but with this difference: he simultaneously had administrative responsibility for the living unit.[4]

Manny Reisner's other main activity lay in formal group projects. He seemed to have the most authority in directing these activities but also delegated major responsibilities to youngsters. Whereas other counselors also undertook group projects on occasion, Reisner was unique in continually re-emphasizing that the residents' participation was necessary in achieving cottage goals.

Provisional Interpretation of Staff Functioning

At this juncture in our quantitative and qualitative descriptions of the Senior Unit and its three cottage systems, we can provisionally interpret staff functioning as follows: the major staff activity is monitoring institutional rules, whereas the boys pursue predominantly individual self-gratification in the counselors' presence.

4. For a similar example, see Lloyd E. Ohlin, "The Reduction of Role Conflict in Institutional Staff," *Children,* 5 (1958), 65-69.

Staff, however, are also responsive to the boys' press for individual attention. In all, 75 per cent of counselor activity is occupied with the combination of gaining the boys' conformity to the rules and, to temper the custodial emphasis, supporting individual boys' needs for self-gratification.

In the Senior Unit, staff spend very little time interacting informally with groups of youngsters, 5 per cent, and only 9 per cent encouraging residents to develop their own goals. The residents, however, devote 18 per cent of their activity to informal group interaction and 11 per cent to pursuing indigenous group goals.

The analysis of the three cottage systems reveals important differences in interrelated emphases on the four functions among staff and chief counselors. Fairline and Hearthstone staff show the most emphasis upon monitoring, and the boys, least initiative in fulfilling cottage routines. Joe Strickland, the chief counselor in Fairline, carries out this function vigorously and impartially. His philosophy of child training reflects this behavorial emphasis, for he believes that cottage routines are an excellent proving ground for developing character.

Hearthstone staff tempers custodialism with more individual support to youngsters than Concord or Fairline. This is reflected in the chief counselor's (Mike Littleton) style of requiring that minimum housekeeping standards be maintained and tempering his custodialism with a gruff big-brotherly relationship. The boys show the least initiative in carrying out routines in his presence.

Concord staff as a whole and its chief counselor, Manny Reisner, in particular, also devote most of their energy to monitoring, placing secondary emphasis on supportive activity; however, they show appreciably more activity than the other two cottages in guiding boys in indigenous cottage goals and informal, expressive group activity.

In the next chapter we examine the roles of the female assistants and total staff functioning in each cottage.

V. Staff Variability in the Three Cottages

Although the head counselor's position of authority in each cottage is an important source of influence in shaping the cottage climate, his female subordinates affect the climate very significantly too. As in the natural family, where the dominant parent's effect on children cannot be adequately gauged without understanding the less powerful spouse's role, so we must spell out the patterns of child care by assistant counselors to see how they reinforce, weaken, or counter-balance the emphasis of the men in charge.

Therefore, the patterns of boys' activities in the presence of each female counselor and her relative functional emphasis will be examined. We shall be especially concerned with how they are related to the functional emphasis of the dominant male worker in her cottage.

When Jamie Rowe is present, Fairline residents engage in self-gratifying behavior 66 per cent of the time. What conclusion can we draw from this observation? To begin with, we might conceive self-gratification conduct to be expected of these boys when they are not stimulated to engage in other activities influenced by staff inducements. Jamie, then, appears least influential of the women, for the boys' attention is limited to their own needs in her presence more than in the presence of any other counselor. Mrs.

Figure 1. Functions Boys Engaged in, by Female Counselors.

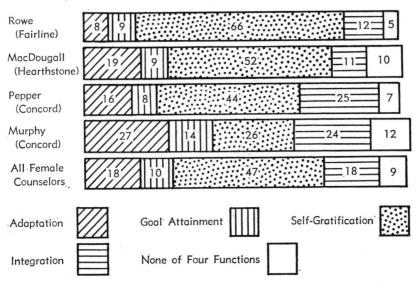

Rowe
(Fairline)

MacDougall
(Hearthstone)

Pepper
(Concord)

Murphy
(Concord)

All·Female
Counselors.

·Adaptation   Goal· Attainment   Self-Gratification

Integration   None of Four Functions

Murphy and Mrs. Pepper are faced with more adaptational behavior by boys, and Mrs. Murphy most of all the females, 27 per
cent. The latter also encounters more goal-oriented activity, 14
per cent, than the other women. Both Concord women, Mrs.
Pepper and Mrs. Murphy, exceed the others in proportion of
events with boys engaged in informal activity, 25 per cent and 24
per cent respectively.

Turning to the functions emphasized by female counselors, we
can see that their aggregate patterns shown in Figure 2 differ
somewhat from the aggregate male pattern noted in Figure 6 in
the preceding chapter. The greatest difference is in the monitoring
function, comprising 54 per cent of head counselors' events and 41
per cent of the events of their female assistants. The women give
31 per cent of their attention to individual support and the men,
5 per cent less. But men and women counselors differ by only 2
per cent in average attention to the other functions, with each
sex devoting about one event in ten to guidance and one event in
twenty to integration.

Now, beyond the overall comparison of female assistants with
head counselors, we see significant variation among the female
counselors in the three cottages. Mrs. MacDougall, the female
counselor in Hearthstone cottage, differs most markedly from
the other females in relative attention to monitoring and support,

Figure 2.   Functions Emphasized by Female Counselors.

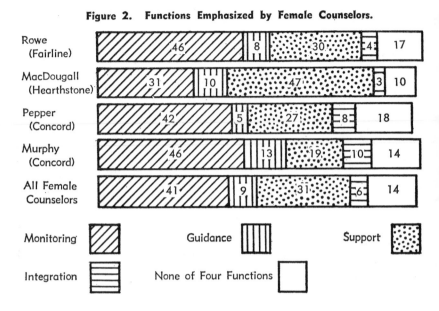

Monitoring   Guidance   Support

Integration   None of Four Functions

the functions that compose the major portion of all counselors' activities. Unlike the other female counselors, or for that matter any male counselor, Mrs. MacDougall devotes more attention to giving boys individual support, 47 per cent of her events, than to monitoring rules and regulations, 31 per cent.

This case highlights the importance, in comparing female counselors, of counter-posing their functional patterns against the chief male counselors'. Their own individual experiences, philosophies, and values influence their ways of working, to be sure, but in each case these factors are mediated by the mandate each male counselor conveys, by word and example, to his female subordinates.

Mrs. MacDougall's primary attention to support rather than to monitoring, the case in point, can thus be seen in relation to the modality established by her head counselor, Mike Littleton (Figure 3). For it is precisely Littleton's custodial emphasis that frees Mrs. MacDougall from the monitoring task so that she can provide support for the residents of Hearthstone.

This is the profile for old-line cottage care: the authoritarian male and the nurturant female. Mike devoted 56 per cent of his events to institutional requirements, but Mrs. MacDougall, only 31 per cent of her time. But fully 47 per cent of her events reflect primary concern with gratifying boys' individual needs, twice the proportion of Littleton's concern with them. Then, too, Mrs.

Figure 3. Functions Emphasized by Hearthstone Counselors.

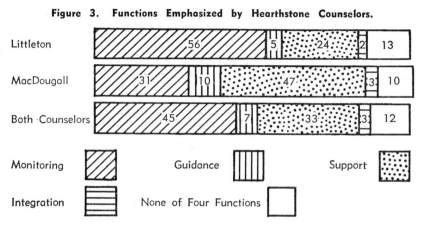

MacDougall spent twice as much time with autonomous goal activity as did Littleton—10 per cent to his 5 per cent. Each devoted little attention to group integration: 3 per cent for her, 2 per cent for him.

Qualitative observations reflect the ways in which this old-line division of labor worked out.

Mike tends to do more ordering and sees that boys follow the rules. In general, he doesn't have any prolonged interaction with the boys. He will tell the boys what chores have to be done.

Mrs. MacDougall is very important in the cottage because she supplies the motherly love. . . . The boys need someone to love them like this in a motherly way; they need it more than the boys in the other cottages.

The part of the routines that do not require authority are done by Mrs. MacDougall, the minor everyday things, laundry, snacks, picking up the place. When someone does something wrong, Mike handles it. Mrs. MacDougall is not the person to put someone on deprivation. In fact, whenever there is a question about a boy leaving the cottage Mrs. MacDougall refers him to Mike.

Mike and Mrs. MacDougall's relationship is cogently summarized in the following extract:

Mrs. MacDougall is a unit unto herself. She operates pretty much by herself. In fact I have never seen Mike and Mrs. MacDougall deal with a situation together. I have never seen them together at all. Mike may be watching TV and Mrs. MacDougall may be sitting at the desk—they really don't operate as a team as such. . . . In this cottage the kids don't try to play one of the counselors against the other.

Jamie Rowe in Fairline, however, does not provide a foil for her chief counselor's emphasis on monitoring, as Mrs. MacDougall does in Hearthstone. In fact, Jamie gives more emphasis to monitoring than to support, even though her chief counselor, Joe Strickland, pays more attention to monitoring than any other staff member. The difference lies in the different ways Strickland and Littleton performed the custodial function. Strickland was continually expressing dissatisfaction with the level of adherence to rules and regulations by Fairline boys. He therefore stressed to Jamie the importance of uniform pressure on the boys to conform to stiff standards, no matter who the counselor on duty was. Although Strickland did want Jamie to assume a nurturant feminine role, his expectation of this was unrealistic, because he expected simultaneously a high degree of attention to monitoring.

The pattern that she shows in Figure 4 appears to reflect her efforts to follow Strickland's instructions to give preference to monitoring activities over individual support. Fully 46 per cent of her events focus on rules and regulations. Although this proportion falls short of Strickland's nearly two-thirds attention to monitoring, she seems to take his example seriously. To the nurturant function Jamie devotes 30 per cent of her events. She surpasses Strickland in this and thus to a degree meets his expectations in this sphere. But the discrepancy between these counselors is only 7 per cent, as compared with the 23 per cent by which Mrs. MacDougall surpasses Mike Littleton's attention to support in Hearthstone.

As in Hearthstone, both consummatory functions are relatively eschewed by both Fairline counselors. With 8 per cent of her

Figure 4. Functions Emphasized by Fairline Counselors.

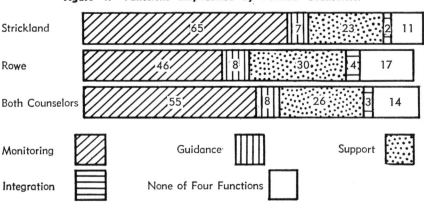

events falling under group guidance, Jamie is similar to Strickland, who has 7 per cent in this sphere. Her attention to integration—4 per cent—is little more than Strickland's 2 per cent. Thus, the distinctive emphasis here, as in Hearthstone, must be understood in terms of the balance between monitoring and support.

Observers' qualitative descriptions indicate how Joe Strickland set the tone. Jamie was regarded as a very passive counselor who, dominated by Strickland, was "a listening ear" rather than a "helping hand." She tried very hard to maintain his standards for the cottage and follow his method of management, but whenever any major resistance to performing routines arose among the boys, it was Joe who had to clamp down.

If the kids don't dress properly, Joe will tell them. Jamie will be there but Joe gives the orders. Jamie notices but she won't say much about these kinds of things.

She was often frustrated in her attempts to make the boys conform to rules:

Jamie was in the cottage and she wanted to write down the names of the boys who wanted to go swimming. They completely ignored her and she let them go without getting their names.

The observers describe Jamie as not fulfilling "the woman role" in the cottage. As one observer phrased it, she functioned more as "a big sister." She was not able to minister to many of the residents' needs, mending clothing, special snacks, and so forth.

I never saw Jamie prepare anything. She doesn't fulfil the woman role in the cottage. She might arrange furniture or something like that but as far as the mother role is concerned, she does not fulfill this.

On the other hand, in spite of having to absorb some provocative teasing with sexual undertones, she got along well with the residents without becoming intensely involved.

Jamie is friendly. . . . I have seen her talking to the kids and exchange views and opinions. However, she is not much older than the kids. She is pleasant with the kids. There is nothing fake about her. She seems to be liked by the boys.

Strickland, too, was seen to be on friendly terms with the boys and often joined in activities, but his effectiveness as an integrator seemed to be hampered by the disciplinary emphasis he adopted.

Joe won't get involved. He will play horseshoes, but he is the one to discipline. He won't be a part of the group so much but he will be around. If a kid has problems, I think he goes more often to Joe than to any one of the other counselors.

Residents are often most adept at perceiving the niceties of differential staff power in residential treatment institutions, and the fact that they sought him out when they had problems, in spite of Jamie's friendliness and willingness to help and in spite of his disciplinary posture, reflects the impact of his superordinate position in Fairline.

How then, do these configurations compare with Manny Reisner's child-care philosophy and practice in Concord, as reflected in Mrs. Pepper's and Mrs. Murphy's functional emphasis? To begin with, Reisner conveyed a different notion of responsibility for the monitoring function. Figure 5 indicates that monitoring duties in Concord are more equally shared among counselors than in the other cottages; it is less a male-dominated activity. In fact, Mrs. Pepper's attention to monitoring, 42 per cent, and Mrs. Murphy's, 46 per cent, slightly exceed Reisner's 40-per-cent emphasis on that function.

When monitoring requirements are more widely distributed among counselors, it becomes possible for each one to pay greater attention to other functions. The way in which these residual events are distributed for each Concord counselor reflects both Reisner's administrative direction in general emphasis and per-

Figure 5. Functions Emphasized by Concord Counselors.

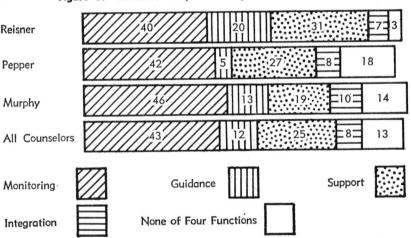

sonal predilection. Keeping in mind that Reisner devoted greater attention to individual support than the other counselors, it is not surprising that his assistants in Concord needed to emphasize this less, although they differed considerably between them. Neither approached Mrs. MacDougall's 47 per cent, but Mrs. Pepper, with 27 per cent, is near the level of Jamie Rowe, whereas Mrs. Murphy, with only 19 per cent, has a lower proportion in this category than any other counselor.

In guidance, Reisner's considerable attention to this function does not set a consistent example. Mrs. Murphy does more group guidance than anyone else save Reisner, 13 per cent, but Mrs. Pepper shares with Mike Littleton the least attention to this function, 5 per cent.

Integration, however, does reflect the impact of Reisner's attention to it. Unlike monitoring, it is relatively more emphasized rather than less emphasized in Concord, but the Concord integration pattern is, like its monitoring, rather evenly distributed among its members. Mrs. Pepper, with 8 per cent, and Mrs. Murphy, with 10 per cent, both exceed Reisner's 7-per-cent participation in informal group-cohesive activity, and no other counselor gives more than 4 per cent of his attention to this activity.

Thus, the Concord pattern of counselor emphasis reflects not only the greater balance among all functions noted previously, but within monitoring, support, and integration, in the distribution of emphasis among counselors as well. But in spite of the relative balance Concord showed in comparison with Fairline and Hearthstone, observers' comments reflect variations suggested by the quantitative data.

The everyday running of Concord, the routines, center around Mrs. Pepper and Mrs. Murphy although, at one time or another, every counselor is involved in this activity. When it comes to just talking, in passing the time of day, either Mrs. Murphy or Mrs. Pepper is in the kitchen and the boys are always welcome there. Manny was someone whom the boys talked to when they had serious problems. They would go to the staff room with Manny and he would shut the door and have an extended talk with them. Manny is the person in the cottage with the greatest amount of respect. He commands the most authority without being tough at all. Manny is also involved with cottage goals. I was impressed with the rummage sale and how Manny carried it off. The boys all went to him with the questions and he is the one to whom all the boys looked up.

Mrs. Pepper, the wife of a high-ranking administrator in the institution, was seen by the observers as "the most striking person" in the cottage:

I think she feels free to do whatever she wants. She is the only counselor who will show outward signs of affection, terms of endearment. She banters and plays with the boys all the time. Two boys once had a sweater and she was trying to get it from them as they threw it back and forth. She is the only counselor who has nothing to fear and can do anything she wants. . . . I don't think she has to be on her guard about what is appropriate or what isn't.

Another observer described her as being the focal person around whom everything seemed to revolve. All of the boys seemed to be influenced by her: "She is a center not only for seeing that housekeeping tasks are fulfilled but also for general conversation. . . ."

One observer commented on her manner of working in the cottage as follows:

She jokes and makes wise cracks which is her way of controlling the boys. She will tell a boy to do something, but instead of ordering him, she threatens in a joking tone, that she will chop his head off or something similar. The boy winds up doing it. In this way she exerts control and yet is friendly at the same time. She is extremely active and energetic. In the kitchen she fairly flies, talking to one boy, making sandwiches, joking with others. . . . The whole pattern in the kitchen seems to reflect her energy.

Mrs. Murphy, in contrast, was seen as much more authoritarian than Mrs. Pepper. She was very strict on cleanliness in the kitchen and the boys had to conform to her standards. She was not regarded as being as intimate with the boys as Mrs. Pepper. Mrs. Murphy was seen as exercising more discipline. However, Mrs. Murphy plays various informal games with the boys and was also frequently involved in general informal discussions with them:

She is a little bit authoritarian but she is a woman and does kid around with the boys at times, and they do come to her with problems.

Mrs. Murphy was described as participating extensively in activities around the cottage:

She plays shuffleboard and cards. When the kids are playing the piano, she will go in and listen. In the cottage Mrs. Murphy is with the kids. She either watches or participates in activities with them. In the garden the other day she was really pulling weeds out with another kid. Although she is older, she gets in with the kids.

The female counselors in Concord were compared as follows:

Women don't worry about what they are doing or whether they are going to get fired from the job. Mrs. Pepper does play favorites. She doesn't seem to discriminate against boys so much as to have favorites among them. Mrs. Murphy is much more quiet and not nearly so feminine as Mrs. Pepper or Mrs. MacDougall. There is almost at times a masculinity tone about her. She seems to have authority over the boys although the boys know that if Mrs. Murphy says something they can stall her. Mrs. Murphy will let things drop if there is enough protest. I can also think of plenty of times when she gets personally involved with boys in a motherly manner. Both Mrs. Murphy and Mrs. Pepper are not as strong motherly types as Mrs. MacDougall. They care for the boys but not so much in a motherly way.

The observers saw Mrs. Murphy and Mrs. Pepper performing the routine adaptational tasks more often than the head counselor, which was in marked contrast to Fairline and Hearthstone. All the counselors were described as extending sympathetic support to youngsters. Mrs. Pepper was more effusive than Mrs. Murphy, who was also sympathetic albeit somewhat more impersonal.

The relationship between youngsters and these three counselors was summarized by one observer as follows:

Manny Reisner is the counselor for whom the boys have the most respect and whom they go to with personal problems; Mrs. Pepper is someone who the boys seem to be more relaxed with and Mrs. Murphy is someone in between. She is somewhat authoritarian but also kids around with the boys; at times they also come to her with problems.

The observers believed that the counselors in Concord dealt with individual problems more than did the counselors in the other cottages. Manny left the running of cottage routines largely to his female assistants. Mrs. Pepper was more pervasively involved in informal give-and-take with the youngsters; Mrs. Murphy more frequently participated in games with the youngsters in and around the cottage.

Our quantitative and qualitative data serve to support each other in the comparative analysis of the three cottage systems. Qualitative impressionistic observation seems to evoke global contrasts among the cottages which, in the absence of controls, would probably result in overemphasizing differences. The controlled systematic observation tends to miss contrasts in the tone, flavor, and feel of human interchange.

Our meshing of impressionistic and systematic observation balances the commonalities as well as differences among the three cottages under study. Thus, for example, although Concord is distinguished by a more balanced enactment of functional activities among head counselor and assistant counselors, our quantitative data, in specifying the degree of differences in the component activities, indicates how circumscribed the range of balance is among the three cottages.

In other words, Concord is different from Fairline and Hearthstone but not all that different. The qualitative observations reflect considerable differences in ways of carrying out the functions. Yet, the quantitative material presents cottage differences against a background of system demands that emphasize staff monitoring and individual support, at the expense of group guidance and integration, in all cottages.

This leads us to examine even more systematically, in the following two chapters, specific resident-staff confrontations and the quality of the interaction.

VI. Resident Confrontation and Staff Response

We have previously compared Fairline, Hearthstone, and Concord in two ways: first, the proportionate attention that residents give to adaptation, goal attainment, self-gratification, and integration, and second, the emphasis which staff give to these functions. Since our point of departure in this study is the assumption that staff and boys' behavior in the cottages are related, we shall now compare the functional emphases of counselors and residents.

Even before beginning this comparison we might ask: What is the ideal relationship between staff and boys' functional emphasis? Should the staff present a model of activities and relationships independent of youngsters' current functioning and encourage residents to emulate it? Or should counselors seek to carry out functions as nearly as possible in proportion to the boys' relative attention to each function? Perhaps there should be a compromise whereby the staff emphasis would differ moderately from that of boys, with the intention of gradually inducing the resident group to change its focus.

Or perhaps it is wrong to suggest that counselors' and residents' functional activities should correspond at all. Perhaps the best equilibrium is one in which counselors and residents differ greatly in activities to which they give their attention.

We take the position that there is no fixed pattern of counselor emphasis that is best for all situations, but that each group must be diagnosed and a plan formulated in relation to this diagnosis. At this point, let us simply state some working principles that should be taken into account in developing such a group treatment plan.

1. Autonomy—the resident group should learn to run itself.

2. The ultimate primacy of the consummatory functions—for a resident group to function autonomously, it must not get bogged down in the instrumental activities of custody and individual gratification; it must eventually see instrumental functions as the means to achieve the ultimate gratifications of goal attainment and integration.

3. Time sequence of functions—staff should not move too quickly toward the consummatory functions. There is a natural sequence of group development, as there is in individual child development. In the case of residential cottages, a foundation of adaptation and individual gratification must be achieved first. The success of goal attainment and integration efforts is built on this foundation.

4. Identification—if the group respects a counselor, they may begin an activity to win his approval even though they don't see it as meeting their needs at the time.

5. Internalization—an activity at first carried out to gain adult approval can come to be satisfying in itself as it becomes part of the residents' value structure.

These "principles" of course are often expressed in very homely terms when counselors say that a group "isn't ready for that yet," when they talk about some boys who "should know better," when they indicate that "we've made progress in our cottage," or when they say that youngsters need standards and models to "push" against. In most cases, however, the indicators and standards are not specified. We hope this research will lead to more precise language for relating cottage care to the current developmental level of a resident group.

Returning now to our data, we should remember the conceptual structure of worker-resident "events." The residents' predominant functional activity in each event refers to their behavior just before the counselors address them. Thus, we can consider each counselor's activity as though he chooses, when presented with a particular functional activity by one or more boys, which function he wants to emphasize.

Figure 1.   Boys' and Counselors' Emphasis For Each Cottage and Total Unit.

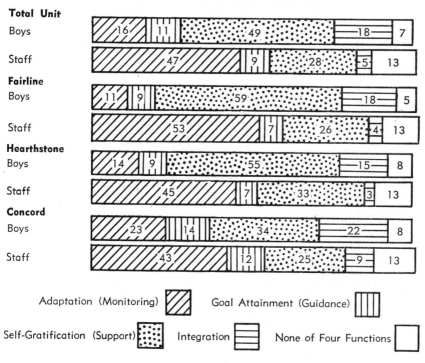

Yet, one must remember that patterns of functional activity carried out by boys in different cottages are themselves determined by past cottage experiences and expectancies. The overall differences among cottages in proportions of functional emphasis by residents no doubt reflects differences in cottage direction that have been communicated to the residents by counselors in previous interactions.

Let us begin by comparing functional activities for boys and staff in the three cottages combined, as shown at the top of Figure 1.

It is clear at first inspection that boys and counselors differ in the function receiving most attention. For boys it is gratifying individual needs, 49 per cent of their total events, and for counselors it is monitoring, 47 per cent of their total. Adaptation—the counterpart of monitoring—does not even rank second in boys' interest. With only 16 per cent of the total, it follows integration, which has 18 per cent. And goal attainment occupies boys' attention least in situations confronting counselors, only 11 per cent of the time.

Although the boys give nearly half their attention to self-gratification, counselors emphasize it in just over one-fourth of the events. The consummatory function of goal attainment is rather similar, about one-tenth for both youngsters and adults, but integration is carried out by boys 18 per cent of the time and receives only 5 per cent of staff attention.

In Fairline the discrepancies between resident and counselor emphasis in the instrumental functions are most marked. Monitoring occupies more than half the attention of Joe Strickland and his staff, yet the boys carry out adaptation activity just 11 per cent of the time before counselor intervention. It is these boys who are most concerned with self-gratification, 59 per cent of their events, but counselors address that function in only 26 per cent of the cases. Boy-versus-staff emphasis in Fairline is quite similar to the total unit pattern for the consummatory functions: not much difference in goal attainment, and considerably more attention to integration by youngsters than counselors.

In Hearthstone, both boys and staff give a little less attention to adaptation than in the unit as a whole, but the difference between them is the same—staff exceed boys' emphasis by 31 per cent. These boys too are very high in attention to their own needs, but their staff provides individual support in one-third of the events —primarily the contribution of Mrs. MacDougall, as we have noted earlier. In Hearthstone, as well as in Fairline, goal attainment receives similar attention from boys and counselors, and here too integration is a considerable interest of the boys, but only a very minor one of the staff.

Concord comes closest in correspondence between boys' and staff attention to adaptation, yet the gap, between 23 per cent for boys and 43 per cent for staff, is still considerable. The difference between resident and staff attention to youngsters' individual needs is only 9 per cent, much less than the other cottages. The correspondence is the result of the fact that Concord youngsters are less concerned with self gratification than the boys in the other cottages, and not that staff attention to individual needs is greater.

As for the consummatory functions, boy-staff differences are similar to the other cottages, but the magnitude of attention to these functions is considerably greater in Concord than in the other cottages. Thus, Concord boys surpass their staff by 2 per cent in goal attainment, just like the boys in Fairline and Hearthstone, but the proportion for Concord residents is 14 per cent, 5 per cent more than each of the other cottages. And Concord boys attend appreciably more to integration than their staff, 22 versus 9 per cent, but both these levels, especially that for staff, are greater than the proportions in Fairline and Hearthstone.

The discrepancies between staff and residents' functional emphasis just described reflect differences in proportions for aggregated events. If we want to know, however, the proportion of events in which boys and counselors' emphases corresponded or differed, their functional activities have to be cross-tabulated.

Table 1. Counselors' Functional Emphasis, by Functions Boys Were Engaged in, for Three Cottages Combined (**percentages**).*

Staff functions	Boys' functions					
	Adapta-tion	Goal attain-ment	Self-gratifi-cation	Integra-tion	None of four functions	Total
Monitoring	81	20	40	50	53	47
Guidance	1	58	2	9	3	9
Support	8	13	45	16	16	28
Integration	3	2	3	18	3	5
None of four functions	8	11	12	9	25	12
Total	101	104	102	102	100	101
(N)	(143)	(95)	(416)	(141)	(68)	(863)

* These cross-tabulations are based upon events of the seven major counselors only. Part-time counselors' events and multiple-coded events for function engaged in by boys are excluded.

Table 1 shows this cross-tabulation. When boys were carrying out the adaptation function, staff addressed themselves to monitoring these activities in 81 per cent of the cases. In 8 per cent, they chose to focus on supporting individual needs and, in another 8 per cent, concerned themselves with activity not directed toward the four functions.

Very seldom did they redirect residents' adaptational activities to group goals or integration. Presented with boys who were carrying out goal activity, nearly three-fifths of the counselors promoted the same function, but another fifth gave primary attention to adaptation.

When boys were engaged in behavior limited to individual gratification, staff sought to gratify it 45 per cent of the time yet gave fully 40 per cent of their attention to monitoring in these events. Even more marked is the discrepancy between adults

Table 2. Counselors' Functional Emphasis in Boys' Adaptation Events, by Cottages **(percentages)**.

Counselors' emphasis	Fairline	Hearthstone	Concord	Total
Monitoring	97	70	80	81
Guidance	0	3	1	1
Support	0	5	12	8
Integration	3	3	3	3
None of four functions	0	19	5	8
Total	100	100	101	101
(N)	(30)	(37)	(76)	(143)

and youngsters in integration. When boys were engaged in informal group activity, only 18 per cent of counselors' events were directed toward this focus and, in half of them, called the boys' attention to the adaptation function. Again, for boys' events when none of the four functions was discernible, staff took a monitoring tack more than half the time.

The staff push toward monitoring rules and regulations seems very clear in this table. It is the only function that shows a high proportion of functional congruence between residents and counselors and it receives a much higher proportion of staff attention than any other in transactions which boys begin by doing other things. Individual support is next in staff attention, both in congruence and in attention when boys' activities are not primarily about self-gratification. When initially carried out by boys, goal attainment meets considerable staff response, but this is not true for integration, which is clearly least supported by staff.

Turning now to cottage comparisons, we shall note similarities or differences in cottage staff emphasis separately for each function carried out by boys. In residents' adaptation events, shown in Table 2, there is a significant difference among cottages, most notably between Fairline cottage, where 97 per cent of the events were carried through by counselors with re-emphasis on the adaptation function, and Hearthstone, where this applies to only 70 per cent of the transactions. In 19 per cent of the Hearthstone cases, boys' adaptation is met by counselors' behavior that is addressed to none of the functional imperatives, appreciably more here than in the other cottages. Thus, although monitoring is high in all three cottages in this respect, the data suggest that the Fairline staff, more than the others, react to residents who are carrying out

Table 3. Counselors' Functional Emphasis in Boys' Goal-Attainment Events, by Cottages (**percentages**).

Counselors' emphasis	Fairline	Hearthstone	Concord	Total
Monitoring	30	31	10	20
Guidance	60	46	63	58
Support	5	12	16	13
Integration	0	8	0	2
None of four functions	5	12	12	11
Total	100	109	101	104
(N)	(20)	(26)	(49)	(95)

tasks and duties with pressure for harder work or more adherence to imposed standards. Hearthstone counselors, in similar circumstances, also do this more than any other function, but their tendency is greater than other staffs to be aloof—not to promote any function.

Table 3, showing boys' goal-attainment events, does not reflect a significant difference among cottages but it does show the trend toward group guidance in Concord, although the proportion is scarcely higher than that in Fairline. It shows as well Concord's lesser emphasis on monitoring.

Cottage differences in Table 4 are similarly not statistically reliable; the number of boys' self-gratification events is larger than goal attainment, but the difference between proportions is not great. Again, Concord counselors tend more to support the boys by gratifying their individual needs and less to redirect them toward meeting institutional requirements.

Table 4. Counselors' Functional Emphasis in Boys' Self-Gratification Events, by Cottages (**percentages**).

Counselors' emphasis	Fairline	Hearthstone	Concord	Total
Monitoring	49	37	32	40
Guidance	1	3	2	2
Support	39	46	50	45
Integration	2	3	5	3
None of four functions	13	12	13	12
Total	104	101	102	102
(N)	(142)	(63)	(111)	(416)

Table 5. Counselors' Functional Emphasis in Boys' Integration Events, by Cottages (**percentages**).

Counselors' emphasis	Fairline	Hearthstone	Concord	Total
Monitoring	61	65	37	50
Guidance	9	5	10	5
Support	18	22	10	9
Integration	12	5	28	18
None of four functions	6	3	15	9
Total	106	100	100	102
(N)	(33)	(40)	(68)	(141)

Boys' integration events, however, reveal highly significant cottage differences. There is a large discrepancy between boys' function and staff emphasis in all cottages, but Hearthstone counselors, who address this function in only 5 per cent of the events, may be said to be almost oblivious of this activity of the boys; Fairline staff respond a little more, with 12 per cent; and Concord counselors, although emphasizing more monitoring than integration, give 28 per cent of their attention to informal relations among boys. Manny Reisner and his assistants, with 37 per cent monitoring, fall far below the staffs of Fairline and Hearthstone in reacting custodially to informal peer-group activity.

To summarize the results of these cross-tabulations, cottage variations in discrepancy between boys' and staff emphasis reveals most clearly that Concord counselors exert less pressure for adherence to rules and regulations in the face of all functions and more awareness of the need to promote other interests that the youngsters express.

We now will turn to a closer examination of the modes and styles that counselors employed in carrying out system functions in the three cottages.

VII. Modes of Enacting
the Functional Spheres

The last two chapters have focused on differences among cottages and among individual counselors in attention to the functional spheres. Although counselor behavior has been viewed with respect to the basic group needs toward which it was directed, our implicit concern has been with the consequences of that behavior.

We shall, therefore, now turn from analysis in functional terms to analysis in terms of the structure of counselor-resident relationships. Up to this point, we have been asking which group requirement the staff behavior sought to fulfil; we now focus on what kind of orientation toward boys is revealed by the counselors' actions.

Before he worked out the functional imperatives in the form which is now familiar to us, Talcott Parsons posited a scheme comprising what he called "pattern variables" for categorizing orientations of one actor toward another. Four pattern variables are posited: affectivity-affective neutrality, universalism-particularism, quality-performance, and specificity-diffuseness.[1] In theory every

1. The original complement contained a fifth, self-collectivity, which was subsequently dropped. See Talcott Parsons, *The Social System* (Glencoe, Ill.:

action of one person *vis-à-vis* another may be located at some point along each pattern variable continuum.

We shall use this pattern variable scheme to amplify the findings of the preceding functional analysis. Since observational items formulated in pattern variable terms can reveal how counselors structure their relations with youngsters, we may then analyze the relationship between pattern variable orientation and functional emphasis. This analysis will be limited to data derived from two of the five pattern variables we used in our observation schedule—specificity-diffuseness and affectivity-affective neutrality.

Two kinds of questions will be asked. First, is there an association between functional emphasis and pattern-variable orientation for all counselors taken together? And second, when functional emphasis is controlled, do differences among individual counselors exist in pattern-variable orientations?

Specificity-Diffuseness

Hawthorne tries to regard each youngster as a whole person and to help him adjust to many facets of life within and outside the institution. The resident-care worker, therefore, is expected to see residents as having a multiplicity of role sets, corresponding to the significant arenas of activity—school, peer group, clinic—in their lives. Yet, from the cottage worker's point of view, it may require all his time and energy to establish one satisfactory role-relation for each of eighteen boys. The larger culture's view of work also tends to support delimiting one's area of responsibility, especially for those counselors with working-class backgrounds and experience in jobs that are neither professional nor entrepreneurial.

We have made use of the pattern variable specificity-diffuseness to distinguish those events in which the counselor deals with matters arising out of boys' positions in relation to his own in the cottage system from those matters pertaining to other roles that boys have within the institution and outside of it. The continuum reflects a range between relations at one end in which one actor's concern with another is narrow, limited to a specific context, and at the other end, relations with a more diffused scope of awareness and interest in the object. In society at large, roles like father, friend, or old-fashioned family doctor suggest diffuse relations, for in each

The Free Press, 1951), pp. 58-67; Talcott Parsons, Robert F. Bales, and Edward Shils, *Working Papers in the Theory of Action* (Glencoe, Ill.: Free Press, 1953), chaps. iii, v.

case the incumbent's interest in another person concerns the totality of that other person. These diffuse relations are opposed to roles like landlord or modern surgical specialist, which are limited to a specific aspect of the reciprocal role incumbent—whether or not the tenant pays his rent on time in the case of the landlord or a patient has an inflamed vermiform appendix in the case of the surgeon.

How child-care counselors relate to children may also be viewed along this continuum: from the very specific housekeeping chores that cottage counselors must make residents perform, to concern with the child's school work, family relations, or future life goals. Positing a general connection between functional emphasis and location on this pattern-variable continuum, we would expect counselors to focus more narrowly on the child's subordinate position *vis-à-vis* counselors when they are addressing the monitoring function. In carrying out other functions the possibility (perhaps necessity) of adopting a larger scope of interest seems apparent.

The findings[2] shown in Table 1 confirm the expectation that monitoring events are more likely to be carried out with specific role emphasis than are the other spheres. Taking all monitoring events, for all cottages, 72 per cent were carried out with specific role focus by counselors, compared to less than 30 per cent for each of the other functions. This is the clearest difference. Among the functions that tend to be carried out at the more diffuse end of the continuum, support is more specific than either guidance or integration. The institution seems to define meeting boys' individual needs as part of the counselor's job too, although with less clarity than custodial tasks. This probably accounts for the fact that the support function is intermediate between adaptation and the other two functions on this pattern variable.

Affectivity-Affective Neutrality

In the child-development literature, it is often emphasized that feelings conveyed by parents in bringing up their children are more important than whether actual behavior is permissive or restrictive, punishing or rewarding. Recent interest in non-verbal communication also seems to stress communication by affect.

Similarly, in the residential cottages, the feelings conveyed by

2. Events with function double-coded or coded as "None of the functional imperatives" were omitted from the analysis by pattern variables.

Table 1. Presence of Cottage Staff-Boy Role Behavior, for All Counselors, by Function (**percentages**).

Staff behavior	Monitoring	Guidance	Support	Integration	Total
Primarily reflecting cottage staff-boy role	72	16	28	12	50
Not primarily reflecting cottage staff-boy role	28	84	72	88	50
Total	100	100	100	100	100
(N)	(472)	(86)	(274)	(51)	(883)

$\chi^2 = 218.57.$
$df = 3.$
$p < .001.$

counselors no doubt have a great deal to do with the kind of impact they have on boys in their charge, as individuals and groups. It is thus profitable to consider how counselors' affectual expressions are related to the emphasis of one or another function.

According to Parsons, the affectivity-affective neutrality dimension focuses attention on whether an actor chooses to pursue interests leading to immediate gratification or to renounce them in favor of instrumental interests. His connection between affectivity and gratification suggests that we ought to measure not only degree of affect but also its direction, because renunciation of gratification may lead to negative as well as neutral affect. This formulation would lead us to predict more positive affect in the consummatory functions of guidance and integration events, less in monitoring and support.

In Table 2 it may be seen that the instrumental function of monitoring is indeed carried out by counselors with less positive feeling tone (only 12 per cent of events in this sphere) than the other functions. At the other extreme, integration is most often enacted with positive feelings (65 per cent). Guidance, however, which is a consummatory function in Parsons' scheme, is carried out with positive affect in just 28 per cent of counselors' events, whereas 39 per cent of the support transactions showed positive counselor feelings.

To explain this discrepancy in the hypothesized association between affect and consummatory functions, let us first attempt to account for the comparatively high proportion of positive support events. Characterizing support as an instrumental function presupposes that it is viewed as a means of satisfying the group function of integration. But the counselors did not see it that way—they viewed satisfying individual needs as an end in itself and, as we have indicated, were not very attuned toward the goal of integration. Among counselors primarily oriented toward the group system, we would expect higher priority for the integration function and lower priority for support.

Table 2. Type of Affect for All Counselors, by Function (**percentages**).

Type of affect	Monitoring	Guidance	Support	Integration	Total
Positive (happy, friendly)	12	28	39	65	25
Neutral (matter-of-fact)	63	65	57	33	60
Negative (angry, anxious, depressed)	26	7	4	2	16
Total	101	100	100	100	101
(N)	(463)	(85)	(270)	(51)	(869)*

$\chi^2 = 155.23$.
$df = 6$.
$p < .001$.

* Does not include events for which affect could not be coded.

It is less easy to explain the low proportion of positive affect shown in guidance. As a consummatory function, we might have expected the proportion of events enacted with positive affect to approach the 65 per cent recorded for integration, but the proportion found, 28 per cent, was much lower. One factor may be that a disproportionate number of guidance events were enacted in Concord cottage by Reisner, a group worker trained to carry out his duties with affective restraint. But we cannot adequately account for the amount of discrepancy in positive affect between guidance and integration.

This problem, given an association between functional choice and modality of coping with the pattern-variable dilemmas for all counselors, leads us back to the question posed earlier. For a given function, are there differences in pattern-variable emphasis among individual counselors, or does functional choice restrict counselors' action modulation so that individual differences are not significant when function is held constant?

If differences among counselors are found, we will need to consider what they mean. Some investigators might wish to pursue the causes of these differences, whether traceable to personality, training, ideology, or whatever. But our interest leads us to look at the other side—the implications these differences have for therapeutic cottage management. We may find staff members whose modalities have implications for functions beyond the one given major stress. For example, a counselor who carries out the monitoring function with relatively more diffuse role orientation toward youngsters than his colleagues may have more significant therapeutic results than one who simply effects orderly adherence to institutional rules. Or take a case in which a counselor seeks to encourage autonomous group goal attainment but characteristically exhibits anger or anxiety in doing so. In such an instance the pattern variable can inhibit the result that the counselor's functional choice is intended to accomplish.

The following comparisons will treat counselors as individuals, by comparing each chief male counselor with his counterparts in the other cottages and, similarly, by comparing each female with her counterparts.

Variation among Counselors in Specificity-Diffuseness

First we shall consider the three male counselors' relative tendencies toward specific or diffuse pattern-variable modalities. For all their events (regardless of function), differences among chief counselors do not quite reach the 5 per cent level of significance. Manny Reisner tended more than the others to handle matters not confined to the staff-resident role pattern. He dealt with other roles in 60 per cent of the cases observed, whereas Mike Littleton focused on such matters in 51 per cent of his events, and Joe Strickland in 44 per cent of his.

When function was controlled for, in Tables 4 and 5 there was no evidence that counselors differ among themselves in choosing to deal with those boys' roles that were specific to the situation. In monitoring events especially, the variation is only 5 per cent (from Littleton's 26 per cent to Strickland's 31 per cent). In support events, the range was greater: Strickland dealt with "specific" roles in 42 per cent of his cases, Littleton in 27 per cent, and Reis-

Table 3. Presence of Cottage Staff-Boy Behavior Among Staff, by Male Counselors (**percentages**).

Staff behavior	Strickland	Littleton	Reisner	Total
Primarily re-flecting cot-tage staff-boy role	56	49	40	48
Not primarily reflecting cottage staff-boy role	44	51	60	52
Total	100	100	100	100
(N)	(124)	(172)	(89)	(385)

$\chi^2 = 5.33$.
$df = 2$.
$p < .10$.

ner in only 19 per cent, but the cases are not numerous, and the chi square indicates a probability of one in four that the observed difference was due to chance. There were not enough guidance or integration events for a statistical comparison.

The overall comparison of women counselors in specificity-diffuseness indicates a range of difference slightly greater than that among males, so that it is significant at the 5-per-cent level. Jamie restricted herself most to child–cottage-staff-member matters;

Table 4. Presence of Cottage Staff-Boy Role Behavior Among Staff, by Male Counselors, in Monitoring (**percentages**).

Staff behavior	Strickland	Littleton	Reisner	Total
Primarily reflect-ing cottage staff-boy role	69	74	72	72
Not primarily re-flecting cottage staff-boy role	31	26	28	28
Total	100	100	100	100
(N)	(71)	(95)	(36)	(202)

$\chi^2 = .45$.
$df = 2$.
$p < .90$.

Table 5. Presence of Cottage Staff-Boy Role Behavior Among Staff, by Male Counselors, in Support (**percentages**).

Staff behavior	Strickland	Littleton	Reisner	Total
Primarily reflecting cottage staff-boy role	42	27	19	28
Not primarily reflecting cottage staff-boy role	58	73	81	72
Total	100	100	100	100
(N)	(19)	(41)	(26)	(86)

$\chi^2 = 2.94.$
$df = 2.$
$p < .25.$

she went outside this arena in only 45 per cent of her events, compared with 54 per cent and 57 per cent for Mrs. MacDougall and Mrs. Pepper. Mrs. Murphy, with 63 per cent, concerned herself most with attention to the boys' life outside their relations with her and other cottage staff.

When we look at monitoring events alone, a significant difference persists—which was not true for a similar comparison among male counselors. The greatest difference among females is the gap between Jamie's great emphasis on resident-staff role set (92 per cent) compared to less than three-fourths for each of her counter-

Table 6. Presence of Cottage Staff-Boy Role Behavior Among Staff, by Female Counselors (**percentages**).

Staff behavior	Rowe	MacDougall	Pepper	Murphy	Total
Primarily reflecting cottage staff-boy role	55	46	43	37	45
Not primarily reflecting cottage staff-boy role	45	54	57	63	55
Total	100	100	100	100	100
(N)	(120)	(20)	(118)	(134)	(492)

$\chi^2 = 8.27.$
$df = 3.$
$p < .05.$

parts in the other cottages. Her attention to this role probably reflects a desire to meet the monitoring expectations of her chief counselor, but also an effort to structure her relations with the boys as much as possible in order to avoid evoking sexual feelings in their encounters. On the other hand, the difference in support events is not great enough for significance at the .05 level. In this case, the greatest difference occurred between all other females and Mrs. Murphy, who once again concerned herself mostly with other roles, dealing with them in 92 per cent of the cases.

Analysis of this variable reveals in an especially striking way

Table 7. Presence of Cottage Staff-Boy Role Behavior Among Staff, by Female Counselors, in Monitoring (**percentages**).

Staff behavior	Rowe	MacDougall	Pepper	Murphy	Total
Primarily reflecting cottage staff-boy role	92	69	74	64	75
Not primarily reflecting cottage staff-boy role	8	31	26	36	25
Total	100	100	100	100	100
(N)	(51)	(36)	(50)	(58)	(195)

$\chi^2 = 12.43$.
$df = 3$.
$p < .01$.

Table 8. Presence of Cottage Staff-Boy Role Behavior Among Staff, by Female Counselors, in Support (**percentages**).

Staff behavior	Rowe	MacDougall	Pepper	Murphy	Total
Primarily reflecting cottage staff-boy role	28	37	25	8	27
Not primarily reflecting cottage staff-boy role	72	63	75	92	73
Total	100	100	100	100	100
(N)	(32)	(54)	(32)	(24)	(142)

$\chi^2 = 7.05$.
$df = 3$.
$p < .10$.

the similar emphasis in resident-care functioning for both male and female counselors in Fairline noted previously. A comparison of all the counselors shows Joe Strickland as having most strongly emphasized the boys' specific role in relating to counselors. This appears to reflect a view on his part that the boys learn proper behavior in the framework of transactions with him, and he seems to have encouraged Jamie, his female assistant, to stress the same code.

Variation among Counselors in Affectivity-Affective Neutrality

Affective responses among male counselors can be seen to differ significantly, even when all those events for which observers made some judgment of affect are taken into account. Mike Littleton was less often neutral than either of the other counselors. He was negative in 26 per cent of his events, slightly exceeding Joe Strickland's 23 per cent, but with 21 per cent of events in the positive category, he had nearly as many as Manny Reisner, who showed positive affect in 28 per cent of his events.

Even before looking at the affect when function is controlled for, we are not inclined to attribute all variation in affect to functional emphasis, because the counselors did not vary in the same way on both items. Strickland was higher than Littleton in monitoring, but it does not follow that his affect was more negative than Littleton's; in fact, it was a little less so. Also, Reisner was notably higher in stressing support than either Strickland or

Table 9. Type of Staff Member's Affect, by Male Counselors **(percentages).**

Type of affect	Strickland	Littleton	Reisner	Total
Positive (friendly, happy)	10	21	28	19
Neutral (matter-of-fact)	67	53	63	60
Negative (angry, anxious, depressed)	23	26	9	21
Total	100	100	100	100
(N)*	(118)	(162)	(86)	(363)

$\chi^2 = 18.67$.
$df = 4$.
$p < .001$.
* Includes only events in which judgment was made.

Littleton, who were about the same, but in positive affect Littleton resembled Reisner more than he did Strickland.

Tables 10 and 11 bear out our expectation that male staff members varied in the kinds of feelings manifested toward boys, even when they carried out comparable functions. For monitoring events alone, Reisner exhibited more positive and less negative affect than the other two head counselors. Littleton's lesser neutral affect was apparent here too, as it was for all events, and the difference is significant at the .01 level. On the other hand, although Littleton appears to have had more positive affect in support events, 41 per cent, than had Reisner or Strickland, who have 21 per cent each, the difference is not statistically significant.

Table 10. Type of Staff Member's Affect, by Male Counselors, in Carrying Out Monitoring (**percentages**).

Type of affect	Strickland	Littleton	Reisner	Total
Positive (friendly, happy)	3	10	22	10
Neutral (matter-of-fact)	67	55	64	60
Negative (angry, anxious, de-pressed)	30	35	14	30
Total	100	100	100	100
(N)*	(69)	(93)	(36)	(198)

$\chi^2 = 14.09$.
$df = 4$.
$p < .01$.
* Does not include events for which affect could not be coded.

The female counselors in all three cottages, like their male counterparts, differed among themselves in the affective tone for all transactions with residents in which they were observed. Jamie was least often positive, compared to the other female counselors. She was preponderantly neutral but also relatively more negative than the others. Mrs. MacDougall, in more than half of her events, conveyed neutral affect. She was positive in just over a third, and negative in 9 per cent. Mrs. Pepper differed from Mrs. MacDougall by having less matter-of-fact feeling tone (49 per cent, less than any other woman) and a little more at each extreme. Mrs. Mur-

Table 11. Type of Staff Member's Affect, by Male Counselors, in Carrying Out Support (**percentages**).

Type of affect	Strickland	Littleton	Reisner	Total
Positive (happy, friendly)	21	41	21	31
Neutral (matter-of-fact), negative (angry, anxious, depressed)	79	59	79	69
Total	100	100	100	100
(N)*	(19)	(41)	(24)	(84)

$\chi^2 = 4.13$.
$df = 2$.
$p < .25$.
* Does not include events for which affect could not be coded.

phy was highest in neutral affect and ranked in the middle, compared to the others, on positive and negative expression.

These differences cannot be explained solely on the basis of functional emphasis, for they persist when function is controlled. When the number of cases justified chi-square analysis, in the cases of monitoring and support events, there was a significant difference of affect observed in each case. For monitoring events, the proportion of positive affect was uniformly lower than for all events, but similar relative positions persisted; Jamie was least often positive, having only 8 per cent of monitoring events in that category.

Her negative affect was much more pronounced—she was judged to be angry or upset in nearly two-fifths (38 per cent) of these events. Mrs. MacDougall was most positive in these events and Mrs. Pepper slightly less so, while Mrs. Murphy was again intermediate and highest in being matter-of-fact. In support events, Jamie was also found to be low in positive feeling tone. However, in this case, Mrs. Murphy was next to Mrs. Pepper, as most positive, and Mrs. MacDougall was in the middle. It is interesting that this pattern, of both females carrying out support with positive feelings, occurred in Concord, where the chief counselor, Reisner, exhibited less positive affect in the support sphere than in other kinds of events. Perhaps this represents a necessary balance in the mode of enacting latency which was worked out, probably

Table 12. Type of Staff Member's Affect, by Female Counselors (**percentages**).

Type of affect	Rowe	MacDougall	Pepper	Murphy	Total
Positive (friend-ly, happy)	18	35	39	24	29
Neutral (matter-of-fact)	62	56	49	64	58
Negative (angry, anxious, de-pressed)	20	9	12	12	13
Total	100	100	100	100	100
(N)*	(115)	(117)	(115)	(128)	(475)

$\chi^2 = 20.31$.
$df = 6$.
$p < .005$.
* Includes only events in which judgment was made.

without the counselors' being fully aware of it. Thus, in that cottage, Reisner took a more detached professional attitude and the women a more overtly "cheering up" one.

In summary, we have noted a tendency among Concord counselors to carry out the functional spheres with an orientation toward youngsters that bespeaks of a more therapeutic management, just as we noted in their functional emphasis. The counselors in that cottage tended generally to take a more diffuse orientation toward

Table 13. Type of Staff Member's Affect, by Female Counselors, in Carrying Out Monitoring (**percentages**).

Type of affect	Rowe	MacDougall	Pepper	Murphy	Total
Positive (friend-ly, happy)	8	26	20	12	16
Neutral (matter-of-fact)	54	60	54	70	60
Negative (angry, anxious, de-pressed)	38	14	26	18	24
Total	100	100	100	100	100
(N)*	(50)	(35)	(50)	(56)	(191)

$\chi^2 = 12.70$.
$df = 6$.
$p < .05$.
* Includes only events in which judgment was made.

Table 14. Type of Staff Member's Affect, by Female Counselors, in Carrying Out Support (**percentages**).

Type of affect	Rowe	MacDougall	Pepper	Murphy	Total
Positive (friendly, happy)	23	41	56	50	42
Neutral (matter-of-fact), negative (angry, anxious, depressed)	77	59	44	50	58
Total	100	100	100	100	100
(N)	(31)	(54)	(32)	(24)	(141)

$\chi^2 = 8.21.$
$df = 3.$
$p < .05.$

residents, that is, to transcend the limited scope of cottage roles defined by the institution.

As for affectivity-affective neutrality, the tendency for Concord staff is not so much visible in terms of generally more positive feeling tone as it is in the choice of function in which positive feelings are expressed. They tended to concentrate their positive affect in consummatory functions, thus using the affective modality to enhance the impact of their already greater focus on these functions. The more traditional pattern in Heathstone, where most of the monitoring was carried out with neutral or negative affect by the male counselor while his female counterpart provided emotional support, was not observably altered by modes of relating. In Fairline, where the professional educator and his assistant might have structured their relations with boys to overcome some of the deficiencies in functional attention, no such patterns were evident; in fact the pattern-variable analysis suggests that these counselors' resolution of the pattern variable dilemmas were even less likely to promote a therapeutic cottage climate than that of the couple in Hearthstone.

If, then, our premises are correct as to which resolutions of the pattern-variable dilemmas are more and which less therapeutic, this analysis of the three cottages yields examples showing ways in which these modalities can enhance or inhibit whatever salutary effects are presumed to derive from appropriate patterns of functional emphasis alone.

VIII. Methods for Studying the Peer Group

In turning our attention from counselor-resident interaction to a description of boys' social behavior within cottages, we shall be concerned with comprehending the range of interpersonal activities carried out by residents—the ways in which boys relate to each other and to staff members—around commonplace issues in daily cottage living.

As in the conceptualization of staff behavior, our orientation toward the peer group also takes its cue from institutional definition. In the case of youngsters, Hawthorne's administration holds it desirable for them to express all but the most destructive facets of their personalities in the cottages and seeks to rehabilitate the child in all areas of social life. Accordingly, our model seeks to include a wide range of possible action patterns composing peer group behavior, constructive as well as destructive, emotional as well as rational, personal as well as public. On the other hand, we want to keep in mind that economy of description is a theory's purpose and to avoid the danger of proliferating concepts in our effort to be comprehensive.

We have chosen the concept of social role as the cornerstone for our theoretical approach to the peer group. The role concept is inclusive, because role theory holds that where any regularities in social behavior exist, they arise from the interaction of group role expectations and incumbents' perceptions and enactment of these expectations. At the same time, social role is an organizing concept, because the knowledge of even a single role occupied by an individual can explain many of his actions in a variety of social contexts.

Emergent Peer-Group Role Structures

Traditionally, sociologists have regarded roles as components of institutionalized social structures, but in recent years the concept has been used to refer to non-institutionalized, but still somehow patterned, expectations of how individuals or categories of people will behave in informal groups. Rushing, for example, has adapted the traditional theory by using the term "normatively oriented behavior" to distinguish conduct based on non-institutionalized role expectations from conduct related to institutionalized roles, which he calls "normatively prescribed behavior."[1]

Our use of role theory in analyzing cottage peer groups reflects this trend, to modify the role concept in applying it to informal structures. For this purpose, we selected the term "emergent role" to emphasize that there is an active process of role-making;[2] it is from this process that the role emerges. We suggest that each residential cottage recapitulates the societal process, by which tasks are differentiated and allocated to individuals in order to maintain the system.[3] As in the evolution of a society, the peer group casts its members in roles that meet the system's requirements. This role allocation is one process by which the functional imperatives—adaptation, goal attainment, pattern maintenance, and integration—are carried out in all social systems, whether husband-wife dyads, isolated primitive tribes, or informal peer groups of boys in residential treatment. However, there can be wide variation in the ways in which each function is carried out; many different kinds of behavior can satisfy a given system prerequisite. For example, goal attainment may come about through physical,

1. William A. Rushing, The Psychiatric Professions: Power, Conflict and Adaptation in a Psychiatric Hospital Staff (Chapel Hill: University of North Carolina Press, 1964), pp. 11-12.

2. Ralph H. Turner, "Role-Taking: Process vs Conformity," in Arnold M. Rose (ed.), Human Behavior and Social Processes: An Interactionist Approach (Boston: Houghton Mifflin, 1961), pp. 20-40.

3. Emile Durkheim, The Division of Labor in Society (Glencoe, Ill.: Free Press, 1947).

intellectual, or emotional activity for different groups. A congregation's members contribute their own labor to build a church, a team of scientists designs a spacecraft, a baseball team's fans cheer them on to win the World Series; in each case, the function is the same although the modes of carrying it out are rather different.[4]

When different modes of behavior are seen as fulfilling the same function, they are called functional alternatives.[5] By considering peer roles as items at the level of functional alternatives, we can see how they implement the needs of the system. For example, such informal cottage roles as "able to arrange for and carry through a ball game with no help from staff" and "can get boys to work together in making things for the cottage" are alternative goal-attainment roles, because each represents a way in which a cottage may choose to work toward a shared goal. They are not, however, alternatives to a role like "smoothes over hard feelings between boys after a fight," because the latter role seems primarily to serve another essential function—the solidification and harmonizing of group members' differences, which we refer to as "integration."[6]

Functional analysis of informal roles yields explanation based on the notion of a system in equilibrium. In this case, it is the balanced articulation of roles in different functional categories so that system needs are maximized, given the limitations and resources of group members and the limitations and resources of the external system. However, what the functional approach does not do is to spell out how the role patterns come about. For that, the genetic mode of explanation is appropriate.[7]

Usually, the question of a role's genesis does not even come up in role analysis of formal structures. The role prescriptions are embodied in the legal order, customary educational practices, and traditional economic arrangements. The patterning of roles is

4. For a discussion of the problems arising when the well-founded concept of functional prerequisites leads to the assumption that certain cultural or social items are indispensable to the fulfilment of each function, see Robert K. Merton, *Social Theory and Social Structure* (rev. ed.); Glencoe, Ill.: Free Press, 1957), pp. 32-34.

5. *Ibid.*, p. 34.

6. We are not suggesting that every role can be thus pigeonholed. Some roles, like institutions, may serve several functions without a primary emphasis. And when the main focus can be discerned, the task is often difficult; frequently the difficulty arises because the most significant function is a latent one. See *ibid.*, pp. 60-64.

7. Ernest Nagel, *The Structure of Science* (New York: Harcourt, Brace & World, 1961), pp. 520-35, 551-76.

taken for granted:[8] the state of regularity they are presumed to have achieved is what sociologists mean by "institutionalization."

However, in dealing with informal groups, the fundamental problem is to identify those processes that result in regularities at the level of observable role behavior. In the absence of institutionalizing mechanisms, it is necessary to ask what the constant determinants are, so that behavior is not subject to the vagaries of situational changes from one minute to the next. It is therefore necessary to explain the term "emergent role" so that it does not do violence to this essential property of the role concept: the existence of some patterning of norms, differentiated by positions in the group, which are independent of the particular individuals occupying the positions.

We might think of emergent roles as shoes that exist before anyone steps in to fill them. For example, there may be a battle among two boys to see who will lead the cottage in delinquent activities. That which they are struggling for—the leadership position—is the role; the struggle itself is evidence that there is something meaningful for which they are competing, even though there is no agreed-upon occupant of the role at the moment.

However, it should also be remembered that, with wearing, new shoes become adjustable to the wearer's feet. Similarly, the group's role expectation undergoes some modification when a new incumbent enacts an old role in his own style. Levinson[9] has pointed to this crucial element in the emergence of roles by showing that even in formal organizations the behavior of a role incumbent is determined not only by organizational prescriptions, but also by the incumbents' personal role definition and style of enactment, and these, Levinson goes on to show, can in turn affect the organizational structure.

The person's role behavior usually has still more impact on the total system in an informal group, where there are no codes of law, theological dogmas, or other institutional means for conveying normative prescriptions. This situation comes about partly by fiat. That is, in the absence of any formally authoritative prescriptions, the incumbent is free to define and enact his role as he wishes, and if he encounters no resistance from conflicting interests, others will

8. Daniel Levinson, "Role, Personality, and Social Structure in the Organizational Setting," *Journal of Abnormal and Social Psychology*, 58 (1959), 170-80.
   9. *Ibid.*

tend to take for granted that his way is *the* way for that role to be enacted.

Furthermore, an incumbent's influence on his own role is not limited to instances in which others are passive. Indeed, most of the recent social science literature on roles deals with more actively reciprocal role relationships, in which each incumbent, through persuasion, bargaining, or coercion, induces others to adopt expectations and behavior toward him in line with his own role definition.

Although incumbent's personality is of special significance in molding the structure of his role in an informal group, the personalities of the other group members also have considerable influence on the emergent role in an informal structure. In effect, as Sarbin has indicated,[10] any given role arises from the interaction between the potential incumbent and significant others in the group. The absence of formal definition heightens the effect of this interaction for informal groups.

When eighteen boys find themselves spending eight or ten hours a day in each others' company, they obviously do not sit down together, make a list of all the jobs that need to be done, consider consciously their group members' abilities and shortcomings, and then make role assignments based on a plan of how the functional imperatives should be carried out so that their social system is in equilibrium. Rather, division of labor and role allocation take place through trial and error, through unconscious as well as conscious processes. The group may in effect "try out" an individual in a role and find out he is not meeting expectations, then throw him out and substitute someone else. Or perhaps two boys' sharing a role or subdividing a task will be more satisfactory than one.[11] Possibly an incumbent will satisfy everyone else except himself and withdraw. Or external forces may militate against the existence of a particular role, or against a particular individual's incumbency in it.

It is clear that group functions, members' expectations, and incumbents' personalities are involved to different degrees in de-

10. Theodore Sarbin, "Role Theory," chap. vi in Gardner Lindzey (ed.), *Handbook of Social Psychology, I* (Cambridge, Mass.: Addison Wesley, 1954), 223-58.

11. In fact, the occupancy of any informal role is seldom an all-or-none fact. Essentially, it is a relative question, of the degree to which one individual perceives himself and is perceived by other group members to occupy the role, compared with the degree to which another individual perceives himself and is perceived by others to be an occupant of the same role.

termining the genesis of informal roles; with tracing the development of different roles considerable variation may occur. In some cases the group's need may be so great that an ego-dystonic role is thrust upon an individual; in other instances, an individual may force others to accept him in a role that meets no one's need but his own.

These differences in the processes by which roles emerge, along with differences in the values members bring to the group and differences in the resources of potential role incumbents, mean that there will be variation among cottages in the roles that emerge. This variation, however, will be constrained by the universal functional requirements we have been discussing all along. A cottage that has members who are recognized as skilled in meeting adaptational tasks, but that also has problems in the integration sphere, will try to recruit or cast new boys in integrative roles rather than adaptational ones. Furthermore, a cottage in which a particular role has met a strong need is likely to try to perpetuate it rather than to find another role that satisfies the same function; thus, the group which has just lost its prize scapegoat may devote proportionately as much of its energy to casting someone else in that role as a professional baseball team would spend of its money to replace a retiring slugger. On the other hand, in most cases the structure is more flexible so that, given a functional requirement, e.g., an integrative role, the personality and value attributes of the group will determine what kind of integrative role will emerge —a friendly and benign role in one group, a destructive and delinquent role in another.

Thus, the structure arising in this kind of informal group depends to a considerable extent on the group membership at a given time. Traditions may be handed down that one cottage has the best baseball team, or that another has more intellectual interests, but unless the requisite skills exist in the present group, the tradition cannot be sustained. Similarly, staff members may stimulate or encourage activities in one interest area rather than another, but their success will be limited by the potential capacities which residents bring to the cottage.

What is most characteristic about informal groups, then, is the degree to which the roles are influenced by attributes of group members. Whereas corporation executives may hold extended discussions and reach a final decision on qualifications necessary for a job without ever considering any particular individuals, the process of role definition in informal groups is invariably personalized. The role categories are expressed in order to describe particular individuals; for example, the group may hold a view that "Joe is the kind of guy who does his share by playing on the cottage ball team," or "This new guy looks like a sickie; we'll have to listen to a lot of crazy ideas from him." Group attitudes and role incumbents' behavior influence each other until a kind of equilibrium comes about, between the regularities in group perceptions and expectations on the one hand, and patterned behavorial tendencies of the boys concerned on the other.

Measurement of Peer Role Structure

We have shown that the role concept, applied to the informal structure of peer-group life in our residential cottages, refers to normative and behavioral patterns that are somewhat, but not completely, independent of the particular boys who reside in a cottage at a given time. We have also shown, in our examples, that the role becomes apparent when it is used as a yardstick, or reference point, for the perception of one or more individual boys.

This formulation leads us to a method for describing the structure of cottage peer groups. If informal structure consists of roles, we need a method for describing the role configuration in each cottage. Since the behavior of emergent roles comes into focus when role categories are applied to particular group members, our procedure for measuring peer-group structure is based on gathering data concerning individuals, even though we are primarily interested in the roles themselves.

Our discussion of roles up to this point has emphasized the social system rather than the cultural system of the peer group, but we should not neglect to pay attention to the peer value system. Like its role structure, the value structure of an informal group could also be called "emergent"; in the absence of the same mechanisms that institutionalize roles in formal structures, informal values too arise out of interaction among group members.

The problem in studying values is that they are usually so abstract that they must be inferred from attitudes toward concrete behavior. In the case of this study, we have already conceived of roles as behavior patterns about which the group holds salient attitudes. Accordingly, we felt it would be useful to study that aspect of the cultural system reflected in each cottage group's evaluation of role behavior.

But before discussing the actual procedures of gathering these kinds of data, we shall indicate how we amassed a pool of role descriptions, selected from among them, and constructed questionnaires from the items selected.

The meaningfulness of role descriptions for Hawthorne boys was first explored by securing from residents about a dozen essays describing their own cottages.[12] The role concept was explained to them in accordance with our personalized view of informal roles, as a child's "particular way of behaving in a variety of situations." The residents were then asked "to write about some of the roles you see in your cottage and how the kids that fit these roles act them out."

We found that the boys were able to think in terms of informal roles, and they gave us some good examples of such roles. In order to tap a wider range of experiences and to give us an opportunity to probe, we conducted tape-recorded group interviews with all Senior Unit boys, half a cottage at a time. The "funnel" approach, frequently used in focused interviewing, was employed. At first we asked open-ended questions about the kinds of behavior different boys exhibited in the cottage and then probed for specific elaboration of peer roles spontaneously mentioned. The distinction between behavior of boys among themselves and those in relation to staff members was explored. We encouraged them to talk about both leadership in general and leadership in particular activities, such as sports and getting house jobs done. We wanted to explore certain roles that are thought to be essential in any cottage social system, so that if expressive leadership was not spontaneously mentioned, for example, the interviewer introduced it by asking who builds morale in the cottage and how it was accomplished. We also asked about boys who were less well-liked, as well as most-liked, in the cottage; about the existence, composition, and activities of cliques; and about boys who were isolated from interaction among other boys in the cottage, and the behavior leading to this isolation.

In our files we had additionally hundreds of pages of source material in process recordings, based on informal participant observation in cottage life by research staff members. These recordings included many descriptions of boys enacting informal roles. From the essays, interviews, and these observation protocols, our basis for deriving peer-group roles seemed sufficiently

12. We are grateful to Mr. Herbert Grossman, who was teaching a summer school civics class at Hawthorne, for having his students write these essays and for making them available to us.

comprehensive to describe both potential and actual group roles in any of the Senior Unit cottages. At this point an item pool of peer group roles was compiled with only minimal selection to avoid obvious repetition, and with only minimal editing to avoid gross unclarity and ambiguity. This compendium of roles included more than two hundred items. We rejected the idea of employing the boys or their counselors at this point to help us select items, because we wanted to keep them uncontaminated for the data-gathering to follow. Accordingly, we enlisted the aid of the two most recent supervisors[13] of the Senior Boys' Unit; between them they had been in charge of the unit for the previous dozen years.

Each supervisor rated every item in the list in regard to how influential, frequent, interesting, or unclear they found the description, on the basis of their experiences with boys in the cottages. "Influential" was defined as having "considerable impact on other boys' behavior"; "frequent," "appears often in the Senior Unit cottages"; "interesting," a role which "you have some clinical, theoretical, or idiosyncratic reason for being curious about," and "unclear," "stated too vaguely or ambiguously."

Simultaneously, we developed an outline for classifying the role items. It contained categories on two levels: content and structure of the role description. The content dimension, interpersonal orientation versus activity orientation, differentiates roles that describe ways of relating to people from roles that describe modes of physical activity engaged in. If the item emphasized the relationship rather than the activity, it was considered an interpersonally oriented role; if the manifest description is of an activity, even though consequences for a relationship may be inferred, we thought of it as activity oriented.

Within content categories, a positive-negative distinction was made: positive in the case of interpersonal roles, if the behavior tended to solidify the relationship; positive in activity roles, if the behavior led to completion of the goal of the physical activity; negative, if the item described behavior having deleterious consequences for a relationship or for an activity goal.

The structural dimension represents an attempt to specify the role set[14] for items with regard to the major status distinction, be-

13. Dr. Jack Adler and Mr. Morton Helfer.
14. Role set is defined as "that complement of role relationships which persons have by virtue of occupying a particular social status," Merton, *Social Theory and Social Structure*, p. 36.

tween staff members and boys, and the incumbent's position in relation to the role set. A distinction was made between direct and indirect roles. In the former the incumbent addresses himself directly to another person or group, if the role is an interpersonal one, or to the physical activity, if the role is activity oriented. Mediating roles are those in which the incumbent's behavior is addressed to a relationship between other individuals or groups. In the case of mediating roles, the content of the interaction between the others to whom the incumbent is relating determines whether the incumbent's role was considered activity or interpersonal orientation. Direct roles were further subdivided according to whether the role reciprocal to the incumbent's was a staff or peer role; for mediating roles there were three possible role sets to which the incumbent may be related; interaction among other boys, among staff, or between other boys and staff. The outline scheme is shown in Figure 1.

Figure 1. Conceptual Outline for Role Categories.

PEER ROLE STRUCTURE

	Direct roles		*Mediating roles*		
	Toward	Toward	Among	Among	Between boys
CONTENT	boys	staff	boys	staff	and staff
Interpersonal orientation					
Positive					
Negative					
Activity orientation					
Positive					
Negative					

In developing this outline, our aim was to categorize roles in basic yet simple terms of structure and content. The distinctions, we hoped, would be useful for indicating the range of roles included in the inventory without the burden of an elaborate theoretical superstructure. Nevertheless, there are connections between this outline and more elaborate theoretical formulations. The content categories, for example, were formulated to reflect a very rough division between roles concerned with doing things and roles concerned with relating to others. Yet this dimension, activity orientation versus interpersonal orientation, appears similar to the external system versus internal system axis of the Parsonian functional imperatives.

Both internal functions, pattern maintenance and integration, are problems of interpersonal relations within the system, in the former case focusing on the connection of individuals to the system entity, and in the latter, on the interconnections of units within the system. On the other hand, adaptation and goal attainment, the external functions, are expressed in behavior having what we call activity orientation; activity directed toward the resources and limitations of the environment was seen as adaptation, and activity in the pursuit of group ends was called goal attainment. The positive-negative distinction in our scheme is, of course, analogous to the distinction between function and dysfunction.

The primary distinction of our structural axis—between direct and mediatory roles—reflects Simmel's comparison between the dyad and triad[15] from a viewpoint strikingly similar to present-day role analysis. Simmel contrasted the direct reciprocity of roles in the dyad with the dependence on a third party's role in the triad relationship. The difference, he showed, is fundamental in the analysis of all social interaction.

For readers familiar with modern social theory there is little explanation necessary for subdividing direct and mediating role structure according to whether other participants in the role set are adults, peers, or both. That adolescents' pattern of relating to peers differ from their relational patterns toward adults is widely acknowledged by investigators who describe a youth subculture, independent of adult culture.[16]

Using this outline in conjunction with the supervisors' judgments, we made the final selection of sixty-eight roles, using as criteria that the final inventory taken as a whole should: (1) cor-

15. Georg Simmel, "The Number of Persons as Determining the Form of the Group," in Edgar F. Borgatta and Henry J. Meyer (eds.), *Sociological Theory: Present-Day Sociology from the Past* (New York: Knopf, 1956), pp. 126-58.

16. Kingsley Davis, "Adolescence and Social Structure," *Annals of the American Academy of Political and Social Science*, 235 (1944), 8-15, and "The Sociology of Parent-Youth Conflict," *American Sociological Review*, 5 (1940), 523-45; Earl Raab and Gertrude Jaeger Selznick, *Major Social Problems* (Evanston, Ill.: Row Peterson, 1959), pp. 388-91; Robin Williams, *American Society* (New York: Knopf, 1952), pp. 70-73. In fact, Bossard and Boll hold that there are three distinct worlds for the adolescent—the family, peers, and non-family adults. James H. S. Bossard and Eleanor Stoker Boll, *The Sociology of Child Development* (3rd ed.; New York: Harper, 1960), pp. 467-69.

respond to roles the boys themselves are aware of and are affected by; (2) include a significant number of boys in each cottage; (3) reflect the theoretical outline by encompassing items for as many of the categories and subcategories as could be represented by observable roles; and (4) contain items which are stated clearly and unambiguously.

The list of roles selected follows, categorized according to the outline.[17]

Role Inventory Categories and Items

I. DIRECT ROLES

A. *Toward boys*

(1) Activity orientation

a. Positive

1. Always helpful to other boys in the cottage
2. Always does his share in house jobs
3. Plays his heart out on cottage teams, but wouldn't be a good captain
4. Has the best ideas for cottage group projects
5. Helps other boys with homework
6. Will give up something he wants to help other boys

b. Negative

7. Refuses to help other boys with house jobs
8. Gets other boys to do his job around the cottage
9. Boy who couldn't be trusted not to steal from another boy's locker if no one was around
10. Unwilling to lend things to other boys
11. Other boys take orders from this boy because they're afraid of him
12. Takes advantage of other boys who try to be nice to him
13. Can get other boys in the cottage to do whatever he wants

17. The reader will note a few departures from the outline scheme. The "aloof" category describes lack of relatedness rather than behavior with "positive" or "negative" affect. Also, direct roles with positive consequences for the incumbent-staff role set have been differentiated as "conforming" and "overconforming." In addition there is a category of "unclassified roles." These special cases reflect our intention to use the outline only as a rough ordering device and not as a rigid criterion for rejecting roles that do not fit into it.

14. Can be influenced by other boys to do things he's not supposed to do

c. Aloof

15. Doesn't care about doing his share of work in the cottage
16. Is hardly ever asked to join other boys in cottage activities

(2) Interpersonal orientation

a. Positive

17. Cheers up boys who are feeling low
18. Other boys like to have this boy in on whatever they're doing

b. Negative

19. Picks on boys weaker than himself, but not on anyone he's not sure he can lick
20. Ranks other boys but can't take it himself
21. Always getting into fights with boys he can't lick
22. Argues with other boys about the least little thing
23. Often picked on by other boys

c. Aloof

24. Is ignored by most boys in the cottage
25. Avoids making friends with other boys
26. Avoids getting involved in conflicts among boys
27. Sticks with his own clique and doesn't pay much attention to other boys in the cottage

B. *Toward Staff*

(1) Activity orientation

a. Positive

i. Overconforming

28. Does house jobs without ever being reminded by staff

ii. Conforming

29. Does just as much as staff tells him to do in the cottage but no more

b. Negative

30. Tries to get special favors for himself from staff
31. Gets around staff without actually breaking rules
32. Tries to bum out of work all the time

(2) Interpersonal orientation

a. Positive

i. Overconforming

33. Never argues with staff
34. More friendly with staff than with other boys in cottage

ii. Conforming

35. Staff members like him more than any other boy

b. Negative

36. Staff members dislike him more than any other boy
37. Argues the most with staff members

II. MEDIATING ROLES

A. *Among boys*

(1) Activity orientation

a. Positive

38. Best all-around leader
39. Often unites the boys in the cottage in whatever they're doing
40. Is good at organizing boys to put their ideas for the cottage into action
41. Able to arrange for and carry through a ball game with no help from staff
42. Can get boys to work together in making things for the cottage
43. Gets everyone to contribute his share for the cottage

b. Negative

44. Turns thumbs down on any new ideas or constructive suggestions from other boys in cottage meetings

45. Tries to sabotage co-operation among boys in the cottage
46. Has to be a leader or he won't participate

(2) Interpersonal orientation

a. Positive

47. Settles arguments before they break out into fights
48. Smooths over hard feelings between boys after a fight
49. Wants everyone to take part in the cottage fun

b. Negative

50. Seems to enjoy it when other boys don't get along
51. Stirs up arguments among boys but stays out of it himself

B. *Among Staff*

(1) Activity orientation

a. Positive

52. Tries to help staff work with each other

b. Negative

53. Tries to play one staff member against the other to get what he wants

C. *Between boys and staff*

(1) Activity orientation

a. Positive

54. Staff members ask this boy to get other boys to do things in the cottage
55. Talks to staff on behalf of other boys who have requests or complaints

b. Negative

56. Causes other boys to be blamed by staff for what he has done

(2) Interpersonal orientation

a. Positive

57. Gets along very well with staff and other boys
58. Keeps other boys from getting in trouble with staff

b. Negative

59. Encourages other boys to get in arguments with staff

III. BEHAVIOR UNCLASSIFIED AS TO POSITION IN ROLE SET

(1) Activity orientation

a. Positive

60. Gets good grades with very little work in school
61. Knows the most about sports
62. Best all-around student in school
63. Best all-around athlete
64. Could beat anyone else in the cottage in a fair fight
65. Doesn't start fights but can take care of himself if anyone gets tough with him

b. Negative

66. Doesn't know how to do anything right

(2) Interpersonal orientation

a. Positive

67. Big joker
68. Very popular with girls at Hawthorne

From the inventory of role descriptions, we constructed two questionnaires. One of them, the "Guess Who" questionnaire, is a modification of sociometric procedures that has been used elsewhere[18] to identify individuals perceived by other members of their groups as exhibiting salient social characteristics. We differ from these other investigators in using the peer nominations to derive group characteristics. The respondents were instructed to "guess

18. Hugh Hartshorne, Mark A. May, and Julius B. Maller, *Studies in the Nature of Character: II. Studies in Service and Self-Control* (New York: MacMillan, 1929); Read D. Tuddenham, "Studies in Reputation: I. Sex and Grade Differences in School Children's Evaluation of Their Peers II The Diagnosis of Social Adjustment," *Psychological Monographs*, 66 (1952), No. 1 (Whole No. 333); Gerald Lesser, "The Relationships Between Various Forms of Aggression and Popularity Among Lower-Class Children," *Journal of Educational Psychology*, 50 (1959), 20-25; Leopold D. Walder, Robert P. Abelson, Leonard D. Eron, Thomas J. Banta, and Jerome H. Laulicht, "Development of a Peer-Rating Measure of Aggression," *Psychological Reports*, 9 (1961), 497-556 (Monograph Supplement 4-V9); Jerry S. Wiggins and C. L. Winder, "The Peer Nomination Inventory: An Empirically Derived Sociometric Measure of Adjustment in Pre-adolescent Boys," *Psychological Reports*, 9 (1961), 643-77 (Monograph Supplement 5-V9).

who" each role description best fitted among boys in their cottage. For each description they were asked to choose at least one boy, but no more than three self-choices were permitted.

The other questionnaire constructed from the role inventory tapped the peer group's value orientation by measuring group attitudes toward the kinds of behavior taken in the abstract as described in the role items. It is called the "Opinion Questionnaire." Using the same role inventory items, in a random order different from that in the "'Guess Who' questionnaire," boys were instructed to indicate whether they have much respect, some respect, some disrespect, or much disrespect for each "kind of behavior" described.[19]

It is these two instruments derived from the role inventory— the "'Guess Who' Questionnaire" and the "Opinion Questionnaire"—which provide the core of data on the peer groups in each senior cottage. To further develop the peer-group picture, three additional instruments were included in the total questionnaire battery— a typical sociometric instrument which we called the "Choice Questionnaire," Levy's Modification of the Allport-Vernon Scale of Values, and Cattell's High School Personality Questionnaire (HSPQ).

The "Choice Questionnaire" was developed primarily to use as a criterion for validating a status indicator derived from the "Guess Who" and "Opinion" questionnaires, but also to indicate relative cohesiveness of cottages and networks of relations among boys, as represented in sociograms. It ascertained whom each boy liked most and least and respected most and least, both within his own cottage and among other boys in the institution. Also, boys indicated their preference among cottage mates for leaders in activities corresponding to the functional imperatives. They were asked to make two choices for each of the questions. Finally, a question on perceived cottage spirit (one indicator of cohesiveness) was asked.

19. The "respect-disrespect" terminology was chosen from a number of alternatives. One possibility was the phrase "personal opinion of the general standing," used by the National Opinion Research Center, "Jobs and Occupations: A Popular Evaluation," *Opinion News*, 9 (Sept. 1, 1947), 3-13. It was rejected because we wanted to get the respondent's own uncontaminated evaluation, not his perception of others' evaluations, implied by general standing. On the other hand, we sought to avoid terms connoting idiosyncratic personal preference, such as "like-dislike." What we were aiming for was a term that would tap internalized social standard and not perceived external standard or non-social personal preference. "Respect-disrespect," we think, connotes this best.

Each of the other two questionnaires—the Levy Value Scale and the Cattell Personality Questionnaire—showed a different facet of the peer group in order to emphasize, by contrast, the kind of cottage descriptions obtained from emergent-role analysis. The Levy Scale is an adaptation (for respondents at the seventh-grade reading level) of the well-known Allport-Vernon Scale of Values. Like the questionnaire from which it is derived, the Levy instrument assesses an individual's relative preference for alternatives stressing social, aesthetic, religious, economic, political, and theoretical values. Describing our cottage populations on these standardized scales provided a frame of reference against which the more specific role evaluations could be interpreted.

Cattell's High School Personality Questionnaire (Form A) measures fourteen independent personality factors: reserved-outgoing, concrete-abstract thinking, affected by feelings-emotionally stable, phlegmatic-excitable, tough-tender minded, vigorous-doubting, self assured-apprehensive. These factors are uncorrelated with each other, making it particularly well suited for research in which group averages are statistically compared on each scale in turn. It indicates what differences in personality attributes obtain among cottages, if any, and it permits us to relate role differentiation within cottages to personality differences among the residents.

In addition to securing information from boys directly by means of these questionnaires and having counselors fill out the boys' role questionnaires for the cottage in which they work, we analyzed the boys' clinical records, in order to find out whether cottages differed in socioeconomic background, psychiatric diagnosis, and so forth.

Procedures for Questionnaire Administration

Because our project was sponsored by the institution whose residents were being studied, we had considerable freedom to arrange conditions for administering questionnaires to suit our research purposes. Still, there were certain restrictions imposed—for example, we were not permitted to remove children from academic classes—so that our procedure was not entirely what we would have chosen if no restrictions had been imposed on us.

All five questionnaires were administered to boys in groups of six to eight during school hours. Sessions were scheduled every Thursday, except that the last session was scheduled for the Tuesday preceding the fifth Thursday to avoid conflicting with school examinations. All boys were given the Levy Scale and evaluation questionnaires in the first session. For the second week, the role-evaluation questionnaire was readministered to half the total group for purposes of measuring test-retest reliability. The following week all boys returned to take the role nomination and sociometric choice questionnaires. The other half, who had taken the role evaluation questionnaire for reliability the second week, repeated the role nomination and sociometric choice questionnaires for reliability the fourth week, and all boys were given the HSPQ at the last session.

The sequence on which questionnaires were presented was determined on the basis of two principles. One is that more abstract questions should precede more specific ones, so that response set evoked by more specific questions would not bias responses to more general ones. Thus, the more general Study of Values precedes the role-evaluation questionnaire, and the role-evaluation qustionnaire (which calls for judgments of role behaviors independent of particular incumbents) preceded the " 'Guess Who' Questionnaire," which explicitly evokes the respondent's association of individuals in his cottage to role descriptions.

The second principle is that rapport with respondents is maximized by presenting the least threatening material first; this principle, too, suggests presenting the more impersonal value and role-evaluation instruments before asking respondents to identify particular role incumbents and personal choices, particularly when some roles are known to be frowned on by authorities in the institution. Since the personality questionnaire, requiring respondents to reflect on their own intimate emotional as well as behavioral traits, was most likely to encounter resistance, it was left for last.

Several aspects of procedure, in addition to the sequence of administering questionnaires, were aimed at encouraging boys to co-operate seriously in filling out the paper-and-pencil instruments. Until we began to administer questionnaires, the research staff was primarily associated in boys' minds with informal observation[20] over a period of months. Research team members had interacted with boys to a limited degree, established casual relationships, and were generally seen as non-threatening and respecting confidences.

Boys were released from non-academic classes—shop, art, etc.— to take the questionnaires. They received passes from the school attendance officers in the same way that notification is given for

20. The intensive systematic observation reported in preceding chapters began ten days before the last questionnaire session.

other routine matters requiring absence from school during the day, such as medical attention and regular appointments with case workers. They reported to a research office, which was arranged like a small classroom, with school desks facing the front. Groups were limited to eight boys or fewer, no more than three at a time from a given cottage. Because there were some boys who did not come when first asked and others who had full academic programs, roughly 10 per cent of testing took place outside of school hours. The time of day, room arrangement, group size, and composition were all planned to carry over the structure associated with school, which balances freedom of expression with limitations on acting out, the kind of atmosphere we felt would also suit our own purposes best.

In the sessions themselves, we arranged for two staff members to be present for about ten minutes at first, until the boys settled down and began work. Assurances of confidentiality were repeated, instructions given, and work began. In the "Guess Who" and "Choice" questionnaire procedures, boys were asked to enumerate other cottage mates using[21] letters instead of names, to minimize resistance. We tried to persuade those boys who were reluctant to take part at times by enlisting the help of school attendance officers and cottage counselors in a few instances, but no punishment was threatened for non-compliance.

By far the larger proportion of boys seemed to take the questionnaire in stride; they took the research seriously and followed instructions carefully. A number of them commented that they found the experience interesting and volunteered to take more questionnaires. Not a few of the boys, however, professed irritation but settled down to the task within a few minutes. In general, we were surprised at the degree of co-operation from the boys.

Included in the questionnaire population were all boys who had been Senior Division residents for three weeks before the first questionnaires were given.[22] There were 52 boys in the group, and we secured complete data on all questionnaires from 49.

In electing to use paper-and-pencil questionnaires as sources of data for groups of emotionally disturbed and delinquent boys, we

21. Robert Falcier suggested this procedure because naming names did evoke resistance in pre-testing a sample of intermediate boys, and it proved to have a remarkable effect in overcoming this block.

22. We selected a time just before the end of the academic year when we knew there would be little turnover in population. In fact, only one boy left in the middle of the questionnaire period and another toward the very end, and several new boys came in who were not included in the study.

weighed the questionnaire method against alternative procedures, notably, interviewing and direct observation. The role-theory orientation directed our attention to boys' perceptions of their cottage mates; particularly for these data, but for the other kinds of data we were interested in as well, we felt questionnaire procedures would be more standardized, less threatening, more economical, and more susceptible to reliability measurement. Fortunately, our rapport with the subjects and the level of their reading ability made paper-and-pencil questionnaires feasible.

We might point out here that for purposes of relating adult-child interaction and peer relations, we were stacking the cards against ourselves by using different procedures for each general variable. On the other hand, whatever connections between the two kinds of systems emerge will be more compelling because we can feel confident they are not due to artifacts of one particular research procedure.

The proportion of questionnaires completed and our observation of boys' behavior during the sessions suggest that these procedures were successful. Quantitative analysis for reliability and validity is included in the Appendix.

IX. The Three Cottage Peer Groups

Peer-Group Description

What a cottage peer group is like, at a given point in time, results from two kinds of factors—the individual children's characteristic attributes before they came to Hawthorne, and the social order of the institution. From the interaction among individuals, and from the interaction between children and adults who represent institutional authority, emerges the social-system configuration we call the cottage peer group. The peer group develops a degree of autonomy as a system, but it continues to be affected by expressions arising from individual personality systems and the larger institutional system. In presenting our description of cottage residents, we propose to distinguish between those qualities that more or less precede institutionalization (and are less changed during residence at Hawthorne) and those qualities that reflect the emergent peer-group system.

We shall begin by describing the Senior Unit population, and subpopulations in cottages, from the standpoint of factors relatively independent of the boys' peer-group membership, before dealing with aspects derived from the peer group itself.

Characteristics of Senior Unit Population on Admission

Our first set of variables, most clearly independent of the peer group, consists of data from that part of the clinical record available when the child was admitted to Hawthorne. This material, based on interviews conducted with parents and children by social workers, on psychological examinations, and on psychiatric interviews, was coded so that quantitative statements could be made about proportions of children, in the unit and in each cottage, in different categories of such variables as: age of child and parents, religion of child and parents, child's race, education and income of parents, child's IQ and psychiatric diagnosis, legal type of child's placement at Hawthorne, and indications of religiosity and family history and composition.

For the unit as a whole, 83 per cent of the 52 boys were between sixteen and eighteen years old. All were white and 86 per cent were considered Jewish, although 8 of the 44 Jewish boys had one Gentile parent. Only 12 per cent had even one parent who attended religious services regularly, however. Fathers' median age was in the forty-six to fifty range, and mothers, forty-one to forty-five. Information on educational attainment was not available for 18 of the fathers and 16 of the mothers, but a high school diploma was the norm for both parents when the information was known. Income level appeared greatly affected by family composition. For natural fathers in the home, when income was known, the median was between $5,000 and $8,000 a year, but 41 per cent of the boys' fathers were not in the household, and in these cases income information was seldom obtained, although it is surely lower than for intact families.

None of the boys was considered neurotic, but 36 per cent were diagnosed as having character or personality trait disorders, 15 per cent psychotic or borderline psychotic pathology, and another 15 per cent situational or adjustment disorders, the last category implying the absence of basic psychological disorder. However, different psychiatrists or psychologists had disagreed in classifying fully 25 per cent of the population and no diagnosis was recorded for another 8 per cent. Of the whole group, 34 per cent were voluntary admissions, 2 per cent were committed by the family court on neglect petitions, and the remaining boys were committed as delinquents or "persons in need of supervision." Psychological testing revealed 38 per cent of boys' IQ's to be in the bright normal (111-120) range, 38 per cent normal (91-110), 10 per cent dull normal (81-90), and 12 per cent superior (over 120).

Since Hawthorne is part of a social agency giving preference to Jewish children as clients, our description must be seen in this frame of reference. It would be inappropriate to compare these characteristics with those from a public institution for socially maladjusted children, or even with a private sectarian institution, because their populations are drawn mainly from the economically less advantaged minorities in the community. The economic level and IQ are probably somewhat lower than would be found among the Jewish population in the larger community. The cultural background of these boys, on the other hand, is dissimilar both to the Jewish population in the larger community and to residents of other institutions.

For only one variable, type of legal placement, was there a significant difference among cottages. Of the residents in Hearthstone, 89 per cent were admitted as delinquents or persons in need of supervision, whereas only 47 per cent of the Fairline boys and 53 per cent of the Concord boys were thus legally designated ($\chi^2 = 7.58$, $p < .05$).

Inspection of the records reveals that a number of the boys in Fairline and Concord, although legally seen as voluntary admissions, had in fact engaged in behavior for which they might have been adjudicated delinquent or in need of supervision but had somehow achieved placement at Hawthorne without legal petition.

By and large, our findings do not indicate significant differences in boys' background at the time of admission to the institution.[1] This does not indicate that the cottages were statistically equivalent. The fact that a given cottage has available space and a certain kind of boy is next in line for admission prevents the institution from maintaining such equivalence even if it tried. What we have demonstrated, however, is that whatever differences may exist are not sufficiently great to be used in explaining differences in the emergent peer group.

1. The administrative policy has changed over the last seven years, from one in which boys were grouped so that cottages were clearly identifiable as "the delinquent cottage" or "the schizophrenic cottage," as Howard W. Polsky indicated in *Cottage Six: The Social System of Delinquent Boys in Residential Treatment* (New York: Russell Sage Foundation, 1962). The present practice is to seek greater diversity within cottages.

Personality Factors, Measured by HSPQ

The psychiatric diagnoses and IQ scores recorded in the clinical records represent two broad aspects of mental functioning which were followed up at the time of administering other questionnaires, with Cattell's High School Personality Questionnaire (1963 revision, Form A). The fourteen factors embodied in it tap relatively enduring personality characteristics; we assume these are not greatly changed during the stay at Hawthorne.

Table 1 shows the mean scores, for cottages and for the total group. Our subjects, on the whole, differed very little from the high school boys' population standard for the HSPQ; the total means shown correspond to sten scores of 5 or 6 (equivalent to the range between the 40th and 60th percentiles) for every factor but one. The Hawthorne mean of 11.00 on Factor E, assertiveness, falls in the seventh sten (60 to 70 percentile range). But on the other thirteen factors, ranging from general factors such as "ego strength" through affective characteristics such as "emotionally calm" to socially defined qualities such as "group-dependence" mean scores for our total group showed no deviation from the average. Comparison of means by analysis of variance revealed no significant differences among cottages. It was apparent from the range of scores that diversity within cottages on Cattell factor variables is the rule, outweighing any distinctions among cottage averages.

Value-Scale Scores

A third kind of variable providing some larger social frame of reference for the peer group description itself is based on the Levy Value Scale. The value orientations tapped—interest in aesthetic pursuits, economic endeavor, religion, etc.—are the kinds of relative preferences on which the institutional experience probably has little impact for most boys; they are more likely traceable to experiences and influence prior to institutionalization.

The mean scores by cottages and for the total unit are shown in Table 2. Since the possible uncorrected[2] score range is the same for each scale, it can be observed by inspection of the uncorrected scores that the boys responded most positively to theoretical, social, and political value items and were least concerned with aesthetic,

2. A correction factor for equating scale means based on scores from a standardizing sample is employed for interpreting individual scores.

Table 1. Cottage and Combined Group Means on Cattell High School Personality Questionnaires.

Factor*	Fairline mean	Hearthstone mean	Concord mean	Total mean	Ratio F	P
A	10.38	10.81	11.59	10.93	.674	n.s.
B	6.75	7.19	7.82	7.27	1.714	n.s.
C	10.55	11.94	10.00	10.82	1.719	n.s.
D	10.25	8.94	10.10	9.76	.645	n.s.
E	11.25	10.00	11.71	11.00	2.120	n.s.
F	11.75	10.31	12.25	11.24	1.192	n.s.
G	11.63	11.94	11.00	11.53	.491	n.s.
H	10.44	11.13	10.65	10.73	.157	n.s.
I	8.25	8.88	9.18	8.76	1.300	n.s.
J	10.31	8.69	8.78	9.24	1.752	n.s.
O	9.31	8.59	11.06	9.71	2.356	n.s.
Q2	10.75	10.06	10.00	10.27	.703	n.s.
Q3	9.63	11.31	11.12	10.69	2.021	n.s.
Q4	9.00	9.00	9.12	9.04	.007	n.s.

* Low-score and high-score descriptions, respectively, of each factor are:

A — *Reserved,* detached, critical, cool (sizothymia) and *Outgoing,* warm-hearted, easy-going, participating (cyclothymia)

B — *Less intelligent,* concrete-thinking (lower scholastic capacity) and *More intelligent,* abstract-thinking, bright (higher scholastic capacity)

C — *Affected by feelings,* emotionally less stable (lower ego strength) and *Emotionally stable,* faces reality, calm (higher ego strength)

D — *Phlegmatic,* deliberate, inactive, stodgy (phlegmatic temperament) and *Excitable,* impatient, demanding, overactive (excitability)

E — *Obedient,* mild, conforming (submissiveness) and *Assertive,* independent, aggressive, stubborn (dominance)

F — *Sober,* prudent, serious, taciturn (desurgency) and *Happy-go-lucky,* heedless, gay, enthusiastic (surgency)

G — *Disregards rules,* undependable (weaker superego strength) and *Conscientious,* persevering, staid, rule-bound (stronger superego strength)

H — *Shy,* restrained, diffident, timid (threctia) and *Venturesome,* socially bold, uninhibited, spontaneous (parmia)

I — *Tough-minded,* self-reliant, realistic, no-nonsense (harria) and *Tender-minded,* dependent, overprotected, sensitive (premsia)

J — *Vigorous,* goes with group, zestful, action-oriented (zeppia) and *Doubting,* obstructive, individualistic, reflective (coasthenia)

O — *Self-assured,* placid, secure, serene (untroubled adequacy) and *Apprehensive,* worrying, depressive, troubled (guilt proneness)

Q2 — *Group dependent,* joiner, follower (group adherence) and *Self-sufficient,* resourceful (self-sufficiency)

Q3 — *Casual,* careless of social rules, untidy, follows urges (low integration) and *Controlled,* socially precise, self-disciplined, compulsive (high self-concept control)

Q4 — *Relaxed,* tranquil, torpid, unfrustrated (low ergic tension) and *Tense,* driven, overwrought, fretful (high ergic tension)

Table 2. Cottage Comparisons on General Values, Measured by Levy's Modification of the Allport Value Scale.

Values	Uncorrected mean value			Uncorrected total	Corrected total	Ratio	
	Fairline	Hearthstone	Concord			F	P
Theoretical	44.63	41.75	46.75	44.11	42.11	1.13	n.s.
Economic	38.86	38.83	38.00	38.47	35.47	.08	n.s.
Aesthetic	36.06	37.06	32.65	35.27	46.27	.88	n.s.
Social	42.69	42.69	45.71	43.70	41.70	1.03	n.s.
Political	42.01	41.11	40.24	41.11	42.11	2.94	n.s.
Religious	36.02	38.61	37.29	37.36	32.36	.82	n.s.

religious, and economic orientations. When the correction factor is introduced, it becomes possible to speak about our subjects in relation to the male population in general. In this comparison, they were well above average on the aesthetic scale and a little above on social, political, and theoretical values, whereas economic and religious scores were notably lower than the scale norm.

Analysis of variance was performed to determine whether cottages differed among themselves in these general values. As indicated in the table, none of the F ratios was large enough to indicate significance at the 5-per-cent level of confidence. In sum, then, the data on orientations toward the broad values measured by the Levy Scale reveal no differential value baselines that might affect cottage differences in role evaluation.

Role Evaluation

The reader will recall our earlier formulation, in which evaluation of emergent peer-group roles was said to operationalize the culture of the peer group. The boys' evaluations of each role, in our evaluation questionnaire, were scored on a five-point scale. One point is equal to "much disrespect"; 2 points, "some disrespect"; 3 points, no response; 4 points, "some respect"; and 5 points, "much respect." Thus, norms above 4.50 indicate an average response in the "much respect" range, and those below 1.50, "much disrespect." The 3.50 to 4.50 range reflects mean evaluation of "some respect," scores between 1.50 and 2.50 indicate "some disrespect," and the 2.50 to 3.50 range signifies mixed evaluation, indifference, or indecision.

To begin with, we should like to know how the total group

Table 3. Mean Role Evaluation by Cottages.

	Fairline mean	Hearthstone mean	Concord mean	Total mean	F
I. Direct roles					
A. Toward boys					
(1) Activity orientation					
a. Positive					
1. Always helpful to other boys in the cottage	4.69	4.17	4.53	4.45	3.76*
2. Always does his share in house jobs	4.31	4.00	4.29	4.20	2.35
3. Plays his heart out on cottage teams, but wouldn't be a good captain	3.94	4.22	4.29	4.16	.59
4. Has the best ideas for cottage group projects	3.94	3.89	4.00	3.94	.06
5. Helps other boys with homework	4.31	3.89	4.35	4.18	1.78
6. Will give up something he wants to help other boys	4.69	4.44	4.88	4.67	2.58
b. Negative					
7. Refuses to help other boys with house jobs	2.69	2.61	2.47	2.59	.32
8. Gets other boys to do his job around the cottage	1.38	1.89	1.29	1.53	3.81
9. Boy who couldn't be trusted not to steal from another boy's locker if no one was around	1.63	1.89	1.29	1.61	1.46
10. Unwilling to lend things to other boys	2.59	2.78	2.24	2.54	1.14
11. Other boys take orders from this boy because they're afraid of him	1.25	1.89	1.53	1.57	1.03
12. Takes advantage of other boys who try to be nice to him	1.44	1.67	1.24	1.45	1.12
13. Can get other boys in the cottage to do whatever he wants	2.94	2.72	3.03	2.90	.31

Table 3. Mean Role Evaluation by Cottages.

	Fairline mean	Hearthstone mean	Concord mean	Total mean	F
14. Can be influenced by other boys to do things he's not supposed to do	1.81	1.82	1.65	1.73	.16
c. Aloof					
15. Doesn't care about doing his share of work in the cottage	1.75	1.99	1.71	1.80	.27
16. Is hardly ever asked to join other boys in the cottage activities	3.06	3.06	2.65	2.92	.81
(2) Interpersonal orientation					
a. Positive					
17. Cheers up boys who are feeling low	4.81	4.33	4.65	4.59	1.86
18. Other boys like to have this boy in on whatever they're doing	4.06	4.03	4.53	4.21	1.69
b. Negative					
19. Picks on boys weaker than himself, but not on anyone he's not sure he can lick	1.44	1.44	1.24	1.37	.41
20. Ranks other boys but can't take it himself	1.13	1.50	1.12	1.26	4.10*
21. Always getting into fights with boys he can't beat	2.06	2.50	2.06	2.22	.74
22. Argues with other boys about the least little thing	1.56	2.03	1.47	1.70	1.86
23. Often picked on by other boys	2.31	2.78	2.35	2.49	.72
c. Aloof					
24. Is ignored by most boys in the cottage	2.81	3.17	2.65	2.88	.91
25. Avoids making friends with other boys	2.19	2.33	2.29	2.27	.08
26. Avoids getting involved in conflicts among boys	4.44	4.17	3.94	4.18	1.07

Table 3. Mean Role Evaluation by Cottages.

	Fairline mean	Hearthstone mean	Concord mean	Total mean	F
27. Sticks with his own clique and doesn't pay much attention to other boys in the cottage	1.81	2.78	2.01	2.24	4.14*
B. Towards staff					
(1) Activity orientation					
a. Positive					
i. Overconforming					
28. Does house jobs without ever being reminded by staff	4.19	4.00	4.24	4.14	.60
ii. Conforming					
29. Does just as much as staff tells him to do in the cottage but no more	3.44	3.50	3.41	3.45	.04
b. Negative					
30. Tries to get special favors for himself from staff	2.25	2.61	1.65	2.18	4.80*
31. Gets around staff without actually breaking rules	3.31	3.28	2.53	3.04	.06
32. Tries to bum out of work all the time	1.44	1.83	1.29	1.53	3.70*
(2) Interpersonal orientation					
a. Positive					
i. Overconforming					
33. Never argues with staff	3.75	4.28	3.47	3.84	2.18
34. More friendly with staff than with other boys in the cottage	2.19	2.78	2.59	2.53	.99

Table 3. Mean Role Evaluation by Cottages.

	Fairline mean	Hearthstone mean	Concord mean	Total mean	F
ii. Conforming					
35. Staff members like him more than any other boy	3.13	3.39	3.82	3.45	1.82
b. Negative					
36. Staff members dislike him more than any other boy	2.56	2.50	2.18	2.41	.85
37. Argues the most with staff members	2.38	1.82	1.76	1.94	1.74
II. Mediating Roles					
A. Among boys					
(1) Activity orientation					
a. Positive					
38. Best all-around leader	4.19	3.94	4.65	4.26	2.86
39. Often unites the boys in the cottage in whatever they're doing	4.63	4.28	4.71	4.53	3.96*
40. Is good at organizing boys to put their ideas for the cottage in action	4.31	4.44	4.65	4.47	.96
41. Able to arrange for and carry through a ball game with no help from staff	4.25	4.33	4.18	4.26	.24
42. Can get boys to work together in making things for the cottage	4.50	4.11	4.35	4.31	1.47
43. Gets everyone to contribute his share for the cottage	4.44	4.17	4.53	4.35	6.92**
b. Negative					
44. Turns thumbs down on any new ideas or constructive suggestions from other boys in cottage meetings	1.50	1.47	1.35	1.44	.14

Table 3. Mean Role Evaluation by Cottages.

	Fairline mean	Hearthstone mean	Concord mean	Total mean	F
45. Tries to sabotage co-operation among boys in the cottage	1.44	1.64	1.18	1.42	8.54**
46. Has to be a leader or he won't participate	2.13	1.89	1.35	1.78	2.49
(2) Interpersonal orientation					
a. Positive					
47. Settles arguments before they break out into fights	4.47	4.22	4.71	4.46	1.67
48. Smooths over hard feelings between boys after a fight	3.94	4.22	4.24	4.14	.03
49. Wants everyone to take part in the cottage fun	4.63	4.39	4.53	4.51	2.62
b. Negative					
50. Seems to enjoy it when other boys don't get along	1.50	1.67	1.29	1.49	1.68
51. Stirs up arguments among other boys but stays out of it himself	1.19	1.86	1.18	1.42	9.91**
B. Among staff					
(1) Activity orientation					
a. Positive					
52. Tries to help staff work with each other	3.69	4.33	4.24	4.10	1.76
b. Negative					
53. Tries to play one staff member against the other to get what he wants	1.69	2.06	1.24	1.67	2.66

Table 3. Mean Role Evaluation by Cottages.

	Fairline mean	Hearthstone mean	Concord mean	Total mean	F
C. Between boys and staff					
(1) Activity orientation					
a. Positive					
54. Staff members ask this boy to get other boys to do things in the cottage	3.69	3.61	4.12	3.80	1.35
55. Talks to staff on behalf of other boys who have requests or complaints	3.94	3.94	4.12	4.00	.81
b. Negative					
56. Causes other boys to be blamed by staff for what he has done	1.13	1.82	1.24	1.37	2.03
(2) Interpersonal orientation					
a. Positive					
57. Gets along very well with staff and other boys	4.56	4.33	4.82	4.57	2.63
58. Keeps other boys from getting in trouble with staff	4.13	4.22	4.56	4.30	3.20*
b. Negative					
59. Encourages other boys to get in arguments with staff	1.13	1.82	1.12	1.33	7.72**
III. Behavior unclassified as to position in role set					
(1) Activity orientation					
a. Positive					
60. Gets good grades with very little work in school	3.13	3.00	3.71	3.27	1.73
61. Knows the most about sports	3.81	3.89	4.00	3.90	.22

Table 3. Mean Role Evaluation by Cottages.

	Fairline mean	Hearthstone mean	Concord mean	Total mean	F
62. Best all-around student in school	4.06	4.22	4.53	4.27	1.66
63. Best all-around athlete	4.06	4.00	4.47	4.18	1.90
64. Could beat anyone else in the cottage in a fair fight	3.50	3.83	3.76	3.71	.63
65. Doesn't start fights but can take care of himself if anyone gets tough with him	4.38	4.39	4.59	4.45	.38
b. Negative					
66. Doesn't know how to do anything right	2.56	2.78	2.76	2.71	.24
(2) Interpersonal orientation					
a. Positive					
67. Big joker	2.31	2.83	2.70	2.63	.68
68. Very popular with girls at Hawthorne	3.88	3.94	4.24	4.02	1.51

* $p < .05$
** $p < .01$

responded to the items. Of the total mean scores on the 68 roles in Table 3, we find that 5 were in the range of "much respect," 26 were given "some respect," 12 in the intermediate range, 16 were evaluated with "some disrespect," and 9 evoked "much disrespect."

The most highly valued role, "Will give up something he wants to help other boys," had a mean evaluation of 4.67. Other roles in the range above 4.50 are "Cheers up boys who are feeling low," "Often united the boys in the cottage in whatever they're doing," "Wants everyone to take part in the cottage fun," "Gets along very well with staff and other boys."

The role "Ranks other boys but can't take it himself" is most disvalued with a score of 1.26. Other "much disrespected" roles are "Takes advantage of other boys who try to be nice to him," "Picks on boys weaker than himself but not on anyone he's not sure he can lick," "Turns thumbs down on any new ideas or constructive suggestions from other boys in cottage meetings," "Tries to sabotage co-operation among boys in the cottage," "Seems to enjoy it when other boys don't get along," "Stirs up arguments among boys but stays out of it himself," "Causes other boys to be blamed by staff for what he has done," and "Encourages other boys to get in arguments with staff." The high evaluation of roles contributing to group solidarity and the strong disapproval of behavior descriptions destructive to interpersonal relations provide convincing evidence that the well-being of the peer group is itself a salient value for Hawthorne residents.

These mean evaluations for all boys in the Senior Unit represent a composite of evaluations which may, however, be significantly different among cottages. Although, of course, the larger societal and institutional structure influences cottage norms, our concept of cottage cultures suggests that differences in staff management patterns may result in differences among cottages in the evaluation ascribed to a given mode of peer-group enactment. Analysis of variance can be used to compare mean evaluation scores for each role among cottages; a significant ratio would mean, for a role item, that the observed difference denotes a real difference in respect or disrespect for that behavior. There are four roles for which differences among cottage means were highly significant ($p < .01$): "Gets everyone to contribute his share for the cottage," "Tries to sabotage co-operation among boys in the cottage," "Stirs up arguments among boys but stays out of it himself," and "Encourages other boys to get in arguments with staff." The last three have total mean ratings of 1.42, 1.43, and 1.33 respectively. They are among the nine roles in which the unit's average judgment was that of "much disrespect."

For each of these three roles, cottage differences consisted of strongly negative evaluation, in the "much disrespect" range, by both Fairline and Concord as compared to less strong disapproval, in the "some disrespect" range, by Hearthstone boys. The direction of these differences suggests that something about Fairline and Concord results in stronger disapproval of disruptive roles than in Hearthstone. The other side of the coin is seen for the positive role with a highly significant difference among cottage mean evaluations. The rating of "Gets everyone to contribute his share for the cottage" is 4.44 in Fairline and 4.53 in Concord, but only 4.17 in Hearthstone. In this case, Hearthstone is distinguished by less strong approval of a positive role, rather than less strong disapproval of a negative one.

The same pattern is manifest for the eight roles that showed differences among cottages significant at the .05 level of confidence. Three of them were roles strongly disvalued by Fairline and Concord and less strongly disvalued in Hearthstone, and another two were strongly valued in Fairline and Concord and less strongly valued in Hearthstone. The generalization, that Hearthstone residents have less strong feelings about what is good or bad in cottage behavior than either Fairline or Concord residents, holds true for the total inventory of 68 roles, including those in which differences are not statistically significant. Of the 31 roles whose total mean evaluation is in the range of "some respect" or "much respect," Hearthstone was closest to the indifference point in 17 instances. Furthermore, Concord boys exceeded those in Fairline in strength of respect; their means were higher on 23 positive roles and Fairline means exceeded those of Concord on the other 8 positive items.

As for roles that were generally disrespected, i.e., for which the mean average evaluations were below 2.50, Concord's strength of values is even more apparent. Concord's mean disrespect for these negative roles was greatest in 19 cases out of 25, one was evaluated the same, and Fairline exceeded Concord in disrespect for the other 5 roles. Here Hearthstone was the most chary of strong disapproval; they were closest to the indifference point for 20 of the 25 roles.

The cottage differences we were able to find in these role evaluations should be interpreted in the perspective of what we did not find. We had expected that value differences would be patterned along such parameters as the categories used in our role-inventory classification. It turned out, however, that the major differences occurred in how strongly role items on the whole were evaluated rather than which ones were greatly respected or disrespected in particular cottages. The tendencies for Fairline and Concord to be further from the indifference point than Hearthstone, and for Concord to show somewhat stronger opinions than Fairline, were reflected in high scores for roles contributing to group goals or solidarity, as well as low scores for disruptive item descriptions. We might say that cottages are distinguished by the degree to which each has a kind of collective superego strength—a level of value commitment with respect to group-oriented behavior which is not specific to particular functions or role sets. And it is this finding which we shall seek to explain in Chapter X, by relating it to differences in counselor management patterns.

Emergent Peer Role Structure

Turning now to the cottage role structures themselves, our basic data will be not an average of individual judgments, as was the case for role variations, but a measure of agreement among boys' perceptions. Since the extent of such agreement may be taken to define the presence of emergent roles, as shown in Chapter VIII, split-half correlations of nominations received on role items can serve not only to indicate reliability of the questionnaire instrument but also to compare roles, within and between cottages, as to how well-articulated they are in the peer-group structures. Corrected by the Spearman-Brown formula, the correlation coefficients indicate, for each cottage peer group, the degree of consensus on the incumbency of each role.

Quantitative comparison among staff-management patterns, in Chapter VI, was introduced by noting and discussing cottage differences item by item and then elaborating these differences by describing and comparing cottage configurations. Following the same general procedure, we shall note statistically significant differences between cottages in role-nomination correlation coefficients, taken by item categories. Comparison of role configurations will follow, based on identifying the role items that have correlation coefficients exceeding an arbitrary level in a cottage and comparing their contents with those of roles equally well defined, by the same criterion, in the other cottages.

The correlation coefficients for each cottage on each role are

Table 4. Corrected Split-Half Reliability Correlations for Role Nominations Received by Cottages.

	Fairline r_1	Hearthstone r_2	Concord r_3	z_{12}	z_{13}	z_{23}
I. Direct roles						
A. Toward boys						
(1) Activity orientation						
a. Positive						
1. Always helpful to other boys in the cottage	.79	.34	.80	2.53*	.06	2.59**
2. Always does his share in house jobs	.87	.00	−.01	3.60**	3.57**	.04
3. Plays his heart out on cottage teams, but wouldn't be a good captain	.48	.74	.59	1.17	.41	.76
4. Has the best ideas for cottage group projects	.89	.92	.88	.47	.09	.56
5. Helps other boys with homework	.86	.55	−.11	1.79	3.61**	1.94
6. Will give up something he wants to help other boys	.46	−.25	.98	2.02*	4.50**	6.67**
b. Negative						
7. Refuses to help other boys with house jobs	.73	.74	.76	.02	.17	.19
8. Gets other boys to do his job around the cottage	.91	.26	.77	3.49**	1.41	2.05*
9. Boy who couldn't be trusted not to steal from another boy's locker if no one was around	.84	1.00	.86	.00	.00	.00
10. Unwilling to lend things to other boys	.90	.65	.53	1.90	2.37*	.51
11. Other boys take orders from this boy because they're afraid of him	.96	.92	.98	1.19	.49	1.69
12. Takes advantage of other boys who try to be nice to him	.85	.90	.76	.58	.72	1.67
13. Can get other boys in the cottage to do whatever he wants	.75	.95	.51	2.41*	1.11	3.54**

Table 4. Corrected Split-Half Reliability Correlations for Role Nominations Received by Cottages.

	Fairline r_1	Hearthstone r_2	Concord r_3	z_{12}	z_{13}	z_{23}
14. Can be influenced by other boys to do things he's not supposed to do	.39	.96	.49	3.96**	.34	3.61**
c. Aloof						
15. Doesn't care about doing his share of work in the cottage	.66	.24	.93	1.47	2.28*	3.79**
16. Is hardly ever asked to join other boys in the cottage activities	.65	.82	.92	1.03	2.23*	1.23
(2) Interpersonal orientation						
a. Positive						
17. Cheers up boys who are feeling low	.72	.58	.85	.67	.87	1.55
18. Other boys like to have this boy in on whatever they're doing	.83	.79	.94	.33	1.46	1.80
b. Negative						
19. Picks on boys weaker than himself, but not on anyone he's not sure he can lick	.80	.90	.84	.96	.36	.60
20. Ranks other boys but can't take it himself	.60	.46	.94	.52	2.72**	3.28**
21. Always getting into fights with boys he can't beat	.96	.95	.97	.45	.25	.70
22. Argues with other boys about the least little thing	.87	.84	.81	.34	.58	.25
23. Often picked on by other boys	.80	.89	.51	.93	1.38	2.33*
c. Aloof						
24. Is ignored by most boys in the cottage	.66	.66	.90	.00	1.80	1.83
25. Avoids making friends with other boys	.72	.94	.91	2.14*	1.69	.43
26. Avoids getting involved in conflicts among boys	.72	.57	.94	.71	2.16*	2.90**

Table 4. Corrected Split-Half Reliability Correlations for Role Nominations Received by Cottages.

	Fairline r_1	Hearthstone r_2	Concord r_3	z_{12}	z_{13}	z_{28}
27. Sticks with his own clique and doesn't pay much attention to other boys in the cottage	.82	.12	.68	2.81**	.87	1.92
B. Toward staff						
(1) Activity orientation						
a. Positive						
i. Overconforming						
28. Does house jobs without ever being reminded by staff	.27	.02	.30	.65	.13	.78
ii. Conforming						
29. Does just as much as staff tells him to do in the cottage but no more	.57	.45	.90	.35	2.26*	2.64**
b. Negative						
30. Tries to get special favors for himself from staff	.70	.52	.94	.79	2.35*	3.18**
31. Gets around staff without actually breaking rules	.90	.74	.66	1.39	1.79	.44
32. Tries to bum out of work all the time	.69	.35	.67	1.31	.10	1.21
(2) Interpersonal orientation						
a. Positive						
i. Overconforming						
33. Never argues with staff	.85	.66	.54	1.22	1.72	.53
34. More friendly with staff than with other boys in the cottage	.40	−.07	.72	1.33	1.27	2.63**

Table 4. Corrected Split-Half Reliability Correlations for Role Nominations Received by Cottages.

	Fairline r_1	Hearthstone r_2	Concord r_3	z_{12}	z_{13}	z_{23}
ii. Conforming						
35. Staff members like him more than any other boy	.87	.66	.95	1.42	.25	2.72**
b. Negative						
36. Staff members dislike him more than any other boy	.90	.88	.88	.32	.25	.07
37. Argues the most with staff members	.92	.70	.82	2.00*	1.14	.85
II. Mediating roles						
A. Among boys						
(1) Activity orientation						
a. Positive						
38. Best all-around leader	.98	.77	.97	3.61**	1.06	2.54*
39. Often unites the boys in the cottage in whatever they're doing	.98	.84	.91	3.11**	2.21*	.86
40. Is good at organizing boys to put their ideas for the cottage into action	.95	.97	.85	.56	1.51	2.09*
41. Able to arrange for and carry through a ball game with no help from staff	.89	.81	.96	.79	1.55	2.37*
42. Can get boys to work together in making things for the cottage	.92	.80	.77	1.19	1.43	.26
43. Gets everyone to contribute his share for the cottage	.94	.81	.97	1.74	.96	2.72**
b. Negative						
44. Turns thumbs down on any new ideas or constructive suggestions from other boys in cottage meetings	.62	.56	.61	.26	.05	.21

Table 4. Corrected Split-Half Reliability Correlations for Role Nominations Received by Cottages.

	Fairline r_1	Hearthstone r_2	Concord r_3	z_{12}	z_{13}	z_{23}
45. Tries to sabotage co-operation among boys in the cottage	.92	.94	.70	.61	3.93**	4.61**
46. Has to be a leader or he won't participate	.34	.73	−.13	1.55	1.29	2.86**
(2) Interpersonal orientation						
a. Positive						
47. Settles arguments before they break out into fights	.85	.53	.85	1.80	.02	1.78
48. Smooths over hard feelings between boys after a fight	.67	.42	.97	.95	3.55**	4.56**
49. Wants everyone to take part in the cottage fun	.65	.84	.84	1.19	1.11	.05
b. Negative						
50. Seems to enjoy it when other boys don't get along	.89	.77	.81	1.14	.45	.68
51. Stirs up arguments among boys but stays out of it himself	.77	.88	.68	.99	.52	1.52
B. Among staff						
(1) Activity orientation						
a. Positive						
52. Tries to help staff work with each other	.00	.48	.91	1.41	4.00**	2.65**
b. Negative						
53. Tries to play one staff member against the other to get what he wants	.62	.89	.87	1.85	1.65	.17

Table 4. Corrected Split-Half Reliability Correlations for Role Nominations Received by Cottages.

	Fairline r_1	Hearthstone r_2	Concord r_3	z_{12}	z_{13}	z_{23}
C. Between boys and staff						
(1) Activity orientation						
a. Positive						
54. Staff members ask this boy to get other boys to do things in the cottage	.97	.75	.87	2.95**	1.95	.96
55. Talks to staff on behalf of other boys who have requests or complaints	.80	.89	.95	.87	2.02*	1.19
b. Negative						
56. Causes other boys to be blamed by staff for what he has done	.98	.23	.86	5.24**	2.39*	2.81**
(2) Interpersonal orientation						
a. Positive						
57. Gets along very well with staff and other boys	.45	.80	.95	1.66	3.50**	1.90
58. Keeps other boys from getting in trouble with staff	.56	.92	.78	2.57*	1.07	1.48
b. Negative						
59. Encourages other boys to get in arguments with staff	.89	.62	.72	1.86	1.36	.48
III. Behavior unclassified as to position in role set						
(1) Activity orientation						
a. Positive						
60. Gets good grades with very little work in school	−.05	.67	.72	2.31*	2.56*	.29
61. Knows the most about sports	.91	.95	.95	.88	.70	.16

Table 4. Corrected Split-Half Reliability Correlations for Role Nominations Received by Cottages.

	Fairline r_1	Hearthstone r_2	Concord r_3	z_{12}	z_{13}	z_{23}
62. Best all-around student in school	.56	.86	.83	1.78	1.49	.27
63. Best all-around athlete	.96	.73	.91	2.65**	1.09	1.54
64. Could beat anyone else in the cottage in a fair fight	.94	.97	.99	.89	3.73**	2.90**
65. Doesn't start fights but can take care of himself if anyone gets tough with him	.91	.76	.96	1.37	1.17	2.56*
b. Negative						
66. Doesn't know how to do anything right	.91	.99	.91	3.96**	.03	3.99**
(2) Interpersonal orientation						
a. Positive						
67. Big joker	.94	.88	.85	.97	1.22	.27
68. Very popular with girls at Hawthorne	.97	.64	.86	3.79**	2.36*	1.29

* $p < .05$
** $p < .01$

given in Table 4, followed by values of *z*, which indicate the significance of differences between correlation coefficients for each possible pair of cottages.[3]

Among positive, activity-oriented, direct roles toward boys, there was at least one significant difference between *r*'s on four of the six items. The general item "Always helpful to other boys in the cottage" was significantly better recognized in Fairline and Concord than in Hearthstone. Fairline's *r* (.87) is reliably greater than those for Hearthstone and Concord on an activity reflecting compliance with adult demands, "Always does his share in house jobs," but it was Concord which was higher than the others on the altruistic role, "Will give up something he wants to help other boys." From roles in this category, it appears that Fairline and Concord have the most clear-cut positive roles, with Fairline more structured around a specific housekeeping role.

The housekeeping goal of Fairline was observable in negative role structure as well; item 8, "Gets other boys to do his job around the cottage," has an *r* of .91 in Fairline, significantly higher than Hearthstone but not significantly above that in Concord. The major differences in this negative category, though, were roles suggesting a delinquent structure, for which Hearthstone has reliably higher *r*'s than the other two cottages: "Can get other boys in the cottage to do whatever he wants," and "Can be influenced by other boys to do things he's not supposed to do." We also found an observed positive role in Concord to have a counterpart in the aloof category; just as positive sharing roles were more reliably perceived in Concord, so are the incumbents of non-sharing roles. When there was consensus on who did participate most in an activity, abstention from such activity was apparently also conspicuous.

Neither of the positive direct roles toward boys which are interpersonally oriented showed cottage differences, but among negative roles in this group, Concord, with an *r* of .94, is highest on the complex description "Ranks other boys but can't take it himself" and significantly lower than Hearthstone in perceiving objects of aggression in the role "Often picked on by other boys." Several roles in this category, items 19, 21, and 22, deal with physical and

3. The *r*'s, with Spearman-Brown correction, were converted to *z* scores. From differences between *z* scores, for pairs of cottages, *z* values were calculated. The .01 level of confidence is reached when $z > 2.575$ and is indicated in the table by **; the .05 level, when $z > 1.96$, is indicated by *. All differences discussed in the text are those for which $p < .05$.

verbal aggression and are fairly high, $r > .80$, in all cottages, with no significant differences among them. Two roles describing aloofness from interpersonal peer relations show significant differences. For "Avoids making friends with other boys," Hearthstone is significantly higher than Fairline, with Concord intermediate. The detached role in Concord which has a higher correlation, .94, than the other two cottages, "Avoids getting involved in conflicts among boys," does not suggest isolation in the usual sense, although it implies reluctance to participate in negative acting out.

Peer-group roles directed toward staff members were on the whole more clearly differentiated in both Fairline and Concord than in Hearthstone. Item 29, describing boys who just come up to the level of adult expectation, is more reliably perceived in Concord than in the other cottages, as is the negative item 30, "Tries to get special favors for himself from staff." Concord also has higher r's than Hearthstone on "More friendly with staff than with other boys in the cottage," and "Staff members like him more than any other boy." Only on the negative role "Argues the most with staff members" was Fairline significantly highest in this category. Apparently, individual relationships with staff, positive or negative, are most marked in Concord, least in Hearthstone.

The broad category of mediating roles among boys, describing greater complexity of structure rather than dyadic interaction, highlights further the contrast between Hearthstone and Concord, the latter high on positive and the former high on negative roles, with Fairline showing itself significantly higher than Hearthstone on activity roles. For example, Fairline, with an r of .98, was higher than Hearthstone on "Best all-around leader," and Concord's r on this role, .97, is also reliably different from the coefficient of .77 attained by Hearthstone. All of the positive-activity oriented roles are quite reliably perceived in all cottages, but the coefficient in Fairline was so high as to be significantly different from both other cottages on "Often unites the boys in the cottage in whatever they're doing." The magnitude of Concord's coefficient is higher than that of Hearthstone for "Gets everyone to contribute their share for the cottage." However, in the case of item 40, "Is good at organizing boys to put their ideas for the cottage into action," Hearthstone's coefficient significantly exceeded that of Concord.

As for corresponding negative roles descriptive of activities among boys, Hearthstone has the largest coefficients; the items are "Tries to sabotage co-operation among boys" and "Has to be a leader or he won't participate." Again in the interpersonal arena, the single role exhibiting significant cottage differences, "Smooths over hard feelings between boys after a fight," had a lower r for Hearthstone than for the other groups of boys.

There were a total of eight mediating peer roles in which staff members were a part of the role set: in only one case was the r significantly higher for Hearthstone; it exceeds Fairline on item 58, "Keeps other boys from getting in trouble with staff," a role suggesting aloofness from rather than integration with the adult figures. A positive role, "Tries to help staff work with each other," was clearly highest in Concord, and that cottage is higher than Hearthstone on "Gets along very well with staff and other boys." Exploiting cottage mates with the weapon of adult authority is seen in the role "Causes other boys to be blamed by staff for what he has done." It is highest in Fairline and lowest in Hearthstone, differences between each pair of cottages being significant.

As for more general behavior descriptions which do not specify the relevant role set, there seemed no general trend in cottage differences. Fairline and Concord recognize their best athletes more reliably and the role "Doesn't know how to do anything right" less reliably than Hearthstone. The boy who was most popular with girls was best identified in Fairline, and the resident who "Could beat anyone else in the cottage in a fair fight" was perceived most reliably in Concord.

Altogether, of the total of 204 comparisons (68 x 3), a total of 63 significant differences emerges, 18 between Fairline and Hearthstone, 20 between Fairline and Concord, and 25 between Hearthstone and Concord. Concord appears to have more roles emphasizing peer-group members' interpersonal loyalties, goal-sharing, and awareness of responsibility for each other, whereas solidarity in Fairline was focused in some activities, especially meeting staff expectations.

In Hearthstone, role structure appears more centered on anti-social behavior, where such structure exists, but the emergent roles are generally less consensually validated than in the other cottages. As for peer roles in relation to cottage staff members, the relative absence of any such roles was marked in Hearthstone. Roles of this type that occurred in Fairline were restricted to adaptational tasks, whereas Concord boys were related to staff in wider, more general roles than in the other cottages (although the content of these items were negative as well as positive).

The foregoing discussion highlights those emergent roles for which we can say, with a specified degree of confidence based on

Table 5. Roles With Corrected r's Above .90, Ranked in Descending Order by Cottages.

Roles	Corrected r
Fairline	
38. Best all-around leader	.98
39. Often unites the boys in the cottage in whatever they're doing	.98
56. Causes other boys to be blamed by staff for what he has done	.98
54. Staff members ask this boy to get other boys in the cottage to do things	.97
68. Very popular with girls at Hawthorne	.97
11. Will give up something he wants to help other boys	.96
21. Always getting into fights with boys he can't beat	.96
63. Best all-around athlete	.96
40. Is good at organizing boys to put their ideas for the cottage into action	.95
43. Gets everyone to contribute his share for the cottage	.94
64. Could beat anyone else in the cottage in a fair fight	.94
67. Big joker	.94
37. Argues the most with staff members	.92
42. Can get the boys to work together in making things for the cottage	.92
45. Tries to sabotage co-operation among boys in the cottage	.92
8. Gets other boys to do his job around the cottage	.91
61. Knows most about sports	.91
65. Doesn't start fights but can take care of himself if anyone gets tough with him	.91
66. Doesn't know how to do anything right	.99
10. Unwilling to lend things to other boys	.90
31. Gets around staff without actually breaking the rules	.90
36. Staff members dislike him more than any other boy	.90
Hearthstone	
9. Boy who couldn't be trusted not to steal from another boy's locker if no one was around	1.00
66. Doesn't know how to do anything right	.99
40. Is good at organizing boys to put their ideas for the cottage into action	.97
64. Could beat anyone else in the cottage in a fair fight	.97
14. Can be influenced by other boys to do things he's not supposed to do	.96
13. Can get other boys in the cottage to do whatever he wants	.95

Table 5. (Continued)

Roles	Corrected r
61. Knows the most about sports	.95
21. Always getting into fights with boys he can't beat	.95
25. Avoids making friends with other boys	.94
45. Tries to sabotage co-operation among boys in the cottage	.94
4. Has the best ideas for cottage projects	.92
11. Other boys take orders from this boy because they are afraid of him	.92
58. Keeps other boys from getting into trouble with staff	.92
12. Takes advantage of other boys who try to be nice to him	.90

Concord

64. Could beat anyone else in the cottage in a fair fight	.99
6. Will give up something he wants to help other boys	.98
11. Other boys take orders from this boy because they are afraid of him	.98
21. Always getting into fights with boys he can't beat	.97
38. Best all-around leader	.97
43. Gets everyone to contribute his share for the cottage	.97
48. Smooths over hard feelings between boys after a fight	.97
41. Able to arrange for and carry through a ball game with no help from the staff	.96
65. Doesn't start fights but can take care of himself if anyone gets tough with him	.96
55. Talks to staff on behalf of other boys who have complaints or requests	.95
35. Staff members like him more than any other boy	.95
57. Gets along very well with staff and other boys	.95
61. Knows the most about sports	.95
18. Other boys like to have this boy in on whatever they are doing	.94
20. Ranks other boys but can't take it himself	.94
26. Avoids getting in conflicts with other boys	.94
30. Tries to get special favors for himself from staff	.94
15. Doesn't care about doing his share of work in the cottage	.93
16. Is hardly ever asked to join other boys in cottage activities	.92
21. Avoids making friends with boys	.91
25. Always getting into fights with boys he can't beat	.91
52. Tries to help staff work with each other	.91
63. Best all-around athlete	.91
66. Doesn't know how to do anything right	.91

statistical procedures, that they differed among the cottages in the amount of agreement residents demonstrated in perceiving incumbents of the roles. Next, we view the pattern constituted by those roles which, by having relatively high correlation on the " 'Guess Who' Questionnaire," are taken to be the most salient in each cottage's structure. For this purpose, we have arbitrarily chosen .90 as the cut-off point and listed, in descending order for each cottage, the roles with corrected *r*'s no lower than that point (Table 5).

The listings in Table 5 bear out the previous observation, that Hearthstone roles tended to be less well structured than those in the other two cottages. Whereas Fairline has 22 roles with a corrected correlation coefficient of .90 or above and Concord has 24 such roles, Hearthstone has only 14.

Fairline appeared to have a number of roles with high reliability correlations that reflect consensus on leadership, mostly activity-oriented leadership, as previously indicated. The highest *r* in this cottage, .98, was for "Best all-around leader" followed by "Often unites the boys in the cottage in whatever they're doing," with an *r* of .98. Other Fairline roles for which there was agreement in this area include "Staff members ask this boy to get other boys to do things in the cottage," "Is good at organizing boys to put their ideas for the cottage into action," "Gets everyone to contribute his share for the cottage," "Can get boys to work together in making things for the cottage."

On the other hand, there were also in Fairline a number of roles disruptive of peer-group relations, not as many and with lower *r*'s: "Tries to sabotage co-operation among boys in the cottage" ($r = .92$) and "Gets other boys to do his job around the cottage" ($r = .91$).

In this cottage, roles concerning fighting were clearly recognized. "Always getting into fights with boys he can't beat," "Could beat anyone else in the cottage in a fair fight," and "Doesn't start fights but can take care of himself if anyone gets tough with him" were all in the list of well-defined roles in Fairline.

We also note in this list roles reflecting peer organization in relation to staff members, most of which are negative. "Causes other boys to be blamed by staff for what he has done" had the third-highest *r* (.98) of the 68 roles in this cottage. Also included among the well-defined roles are "Staff members ask this boy to get other boys to do things in the cottage," "Argues the most with staff members," "Staff members dislike him more than any other boy," and "gets around staff without actually breaking rules." "Best all-around athlete," "Knows the most about sports," and "Big joker" were among the general capacities reflecting roles in Fairline as well as "Doesn't know how to do anything right."

The list of roles for Hearthstone showed, even more clearly than statistical comparison of cottage differences by roles, the negative character of the existing structure in that cottage. The two highest roles in that cottage were "Boy who couldn't be trusted not to steal from another boy's locker if no one was around" ($r = 1.00$) and "Doesn't know how to do anything right" ($r = .99$). We found the reciprocal power relationship clearly reflected in Hearthstone roles —"Can be influenced by other boys to do things he's not supposed to do" and "Can get other boys in the cottage to do whatever he wants them to do" ($r = .96$ and .95 respectively). Other disintegrative roles in this cottage include "Tries to sabotage co-operation among boys in the cottage," "Avoids making friends with other boys," "Other boys take orders from this boy because they're afraid of him," and "Takes advantage of other boys who try to be nice to him." With the preponderance of these negative roles, there were only two positive leadership roles to offset it: "Is good at organizing boys to put their ideas for the cottage into action" and "Has the best ideas for cottage group projects."

Striking, too, in this list was the absence among well-defined Hearthstone roles of any clear-cut characteristic positions for boys in relation to staff members. The only role in this list with an r of .90 or above was "Keeps other boys from getting in trouble with staff"; as pointed out before, this scarcely suggests warmth between boys and adult counselors. Thus, in this cottage it appeared that delinquency and disruptive peer-group behavior took part not in a well-organized way in opposition to staff members but in a vacuum; if Hearthstone staff exerted any real influence on the resident group in their charge, it was not reflected in these data.

In regard to Concord, one is confronted by the simultaneous appearance among the best-perceived roles of both socially desirable and undesirable elements in the peer-group organization. "Could beat anyone else in the cottage in a fair fight" had the highest degree of agreement ($r = .99$), and the two roles with the next highest r's, .98, are "Will give up something he wants to help other boys" and "Other boys take orders from this boy because they're afraid of him." Other well-defined roles in the cottage were "Best all-around leader" and "Able to arrange for and carry through a ball game with no help from staff," "Gets everyone to contribute his share for the cottage," "Smooths over hard feeling between boys after a fight," and "Ranks other boys but can't take it himself." Except for the role involving the ability to arrange for a ball game, most of these leadership roles in Concord are more purely interpersonal, indicating preference for having the role incumbent in on whatever the group was doing, whereas in Fairline the leadership roles were predominantly instrumentally oriented, whether the activities are in the adaptational or goal-attainment spheres.

In Concord, as in Fairline and in contrast to Hearthstone, there were a number of well-defined peer roles involving staff—"Talks to staff in behalf of other boys who have requests or complaints," "Staff members like him more than any other boy," "Gets along very well with staff and other boys," and "Tries to help staff work with each other." What sets this peer-group structure in relation to staff apart from that in Fairline is the predominantly positive character it had. Only "Tries to get special favors for himself from staff" in this list can be considered a negative role in relation to staff.

These configurations amplify the statistical differences so that we might characterize Fairline as a cottage in which there were positive peer-group roles, and negative roles within the role set of residents' transaction with staff. In Hearthstone there was a great deal of negative and some positive role structure among peers, but structured peer roles in relation to staff were virtually absent. In Concord both positive and negative peer roles existed side-by-side among the best structured roles, along with group roles involving staff, which were almost exclusively positive. If we assume that both positive and negative roles are likely to be generated within any cottage system, we find that in all three of our cottages there was some peer-role organization with both socially desirable and undesirable behavior. However, whereas there was negative behavior expressed toward staff in Fairline, there were no negative staff-oriented roles reliably perceived by the Hearthstone group, and in Concord the orientation toward staff members was primarily positive.

Role Incumbency and Personality Factors

In addition to identifying the emergent role structures of the senior cottages, we wanted to explore the relationship between these social-system variables and personality factors, to ascertain what attributes of personality, if any, are characteristic of individuals who occupy particular roles in a cottage. Since the social system of a cottage is an important variable affecting such relationships, the occupants of a given role in one cottage may have personality characteristics different from the occupants of that role in another cottage.

Our procedure for this analysis was to correlate the number of choices boys received for roles on the " 'Guess Who' Questionnaire" with scores on the Cattell High School Personality questionnaire, by cottages. To have correlated each role with each factor for each cottage would have entailed 2,856 correlations (68 x 14 factors x 3 cottages), a task that would have required more of our resources than we could allocate to it. Instead, we selected one and, in some cases, two personality factors which seemed to reflect a trait related to each role item. We ended up with 78 hypothesized correlations, with each role and each personality factor included in one of the 78 selected correlations.

Each of the 78 hypotheses was tested by correlating the role choice and questionnaire scores separately for each of the three cottages, yielding 234 correlation coefficients. Those r's that were significant ($p < .05$) are shown in Table 6.

In Fairline, only one of the 78 correlations reached statistical significance at the 1-per-cent level of confidence, and another three at the 5-per-cent level; this is just the number of correlations out of 78 that might appear significant by chance, so we cannot be very confident there is any real association between role and personality traits in Fairline.

However, in Hearthstone seven r's were significant at the 5-per-cent level and two more at the 1-per-cent level; and in Concord 11 r's were significant at the 5-per-cent level and another one at the 1-per-cent level. This is more than would be expected by chance for both cottages, so that there is a likelihood that some factor other than chance underlies the findings.

We shall examine the items found to have significant correlations to see if, on the basis of the role patterns just noted, the associations can be explained.

Cattell's Personality Factor A (cyclothymia), labeled as "outgoing, warmhearted, easy-going, participating," was responsible for seven of the significant correlations: two in Fairline and Hearthstone and three in Concord. However, the role items with which it correlates were quite different in the different cottages.

In Fairline, this kind of boy tended to "get along well" both with his peers and staff; he was also popular with girls. A boy

Table 6. Significant Correlations Between Cattell Personality Factors and Number of Role Choices Received, by Cottages.

Cottage	Role		Personality factor	r
	A	outgoing	57. Gets along very well with staff and other boys	.60**
	A	outgoing	68. Very popular with girls at Hawthorne	.43*
Fairline				
	D	excitable	53. Tries to play one staff member against the other to get what he wants	.53*
	O	apprehensive	16. Is hardly ever asked to join other boys in activities	.55*
	A	outgoing	29. Does just as much as staff tells him to do in the cottage but no more	.63**
	A	outgoing	9. Boy who couldn't be trusted not to steal from another boy's locker if no one was around	.66**
	B	intelligent	2. Always does his share in house jobs	.50*
	B	intelligent	48. Smooths over hard feelings between boys after a fight	.46*
Hearthstone	B	intelligent	43. Gets everyone to contribute his share for the cottage	.43*
	C	emotionally stable	8. Gets other boys to do his jobs around the cottage	.54*
	F	happy-go-lucky	23. Often picked on by other boys	.56*
	F	happy-go-lucky	41. Able to arrange for and carry through a ball game with no help from staff	.46*
	F	happy-go-lucky	38. Best all-around leader	.54*
Concord	A	outgoing	49. Wants everyone to take part in the cottage fun	.45*
	A	outgoing	29. Does just as much as staff tells him to do in the cottage but no more	−.55*

Table 6. (Continued)

Cottage	Role	Personality factor	*r*
	A outgoing	52. Tries to help staff work with each other	.44*
	B intelligent	2. Always does his share in house jobs	—.43*
	C emotionally stable	67. Big joker	—.52*
Concord			
	C emotionally stable	20. Ranks other boys but can't take it himself	—.43*
	C emotionally stable	59. Encourages other boys to get in arguments with staff	—.44*
	D excitable	3. Plays his heart out on cottage teams but wouldn't be a good captain	.59**
	F happy-go-lucky	39. Often unites the boys in whatever they are doing	—.44*
	G conscientious	7. Refuses to help other boys with house jobs	—.49*
	O apprehensive	39. Often unites the boys in the cottage in whatever they are doing	—.44*
	O apprehensive	50. Seems to enjoy it when other boys don't get along with each other	.50*

* $p < .05$.
** $p < .01$.

who scored high on this point in Concord is likely to be concerned with encouraging both staff and boys to get along well, and he did not stop with doing just what is required of him in the cottage —this correlation was negative. In Hearthstone, on the other hand, outgoing, participating boys were the ones who, when it comes to meeting staff expectations, did just enough and no more; they also tended to be boys who couldn't be trusted not to steal from others.

The characteristics attributed to Factor A indicate the kind of person who would enter most wholeheartedly into the life of the peer group. Recalling our previous comparisons of the peer groups, the roles into which these boys fit were those that are relatively clear-cut. In Fairline, where peer roles tended to be positive, we found the outgoing person carrying out positive peer roles. Hearthstone's negative peer-group roles were most prominent, and here we found that the boys with socially expressive personalities occupy roles that were not institutionally approved. And Concord, which had consensually validated roles directed toward peer-group and staff integration, turned out to have a correlation between such behavior and the outgoing, participating personality factor.

In Hearthstone, there was a positive association between Factor B, intelligence, and the roles "Always does his share in house jobs," "Smooths over hard feelings between boys after a fight," and "Gets everyone to contribute his share for the cottage." It is interesting that, in this cottage, with its predominantly delinquent atmosphere and general lack of clear-cut positive roles, intelligence is correlated with constructive role behaviors. We may suggest one possible explanation: that brighter residents were more likely to perceive both the lack of staff attention to integration and the system's need for such behavior and addressed their own efforts toward fulfilling this need. This explanation takes on added weight when compared with the finding in Concord that intelligence is correlated with doing one's share in house jobs. The integrative aspect of "doing one's share" will be less important in a cottage like Concord, where the staff pays more attention to the integrative function, so that the intelligent boy could use his ability to avoid responsibility with the confidence that staff would prevent his behavior from having greatly deleterious consequences for the system.

Factor C, emotional stability, is negatively correlated with four roles, one in Hearthstone and three in Concord. They were generally destructive—ranking and taking advantage of other boys in house jobs, and promoting staff-resident dissention. Being a "Big joker" also correlated with Factor C in Concord; this role may have either positive or negative connotations. In both these cottages we found what we would probably find in any group, that emotional stability was inversely proportional to destructive role incumbency.

Factor D is defined as "demanding" as well as excitable. A demanding person would, not surprisingly, turn out to "Try to play one staff member against the other to get what he wants" as was found in Fairline, which had problems in staff relations, as pointed out earlier. Concord, in contrast, seemed to provide more positive opportunities for the energetic boy; he can translate his excitement into athletic endeavor, playing his heart out for a cottage team.

Factor F, happy-go-lucky or enthusiastic, is like Factor B (intelligence) in that it is associated with positive behavior in Hearthstone and negative behavior in Concord. It may be that enthusiasm is a helpful personality characteristic, along with intelligence, for supplying the integrative function left void by staff in Hearthstone, but we are at a loss to explain why it is related negatively to the integrative function in Concord.

Factor G, conscientiousness, appears in significant relationship to a role only once in these data. It is negatively correlated with refusal to help other boys in house jobs in Concord. Where loyalty to the peer group was most emphasized, as in Concord, boys whose personalities predispose them to conscientiousness tended to express their superego strength in relation to this norm of loyalty.

Factor O, apprehensiveness, was at the opposite end of the scale from untroubled adequacy. The absence of apprehensiveness appeared conducive to leadership in Concord, since the trait negatively correlated with "Often unites the boys in the cottage in whatever they're doing," and its presence suggests a divisive influence, as shown in the positive correlation with "Seems to enjoy it when other boys don't get along with each other." In Fairline, however, it was correlated with isolation, "Is hardly ever asked to join other boys in activities," and did not suggest more apparent pleasure derived from others' interpersonal problems, as was the case in Concord.

Summary

In this chapter we called attention to differences, and the absence of differences, among cottages seen from the residents' point of view, and more especially from the point of view of the boys' groups as boundaried systems. A part of this chapter has indicated some variables that can be ruled out in explaining cottage differences. It has also been suggested that there may be some causal relations between staff-management patterns and peer-group configurations in the three cottages. These connections will be the substance of Chapter X.

X. Cottage Management and the Peer Culture

Two levels of cottage life have been described in preceding chapters: group functions emphasized by counselors in dealing with boys, and the informal role configurations of each cottage peer group. We assume that the way in which counselors run a residential cottage has an effect on the children who live in it. Of course, our frame of reference has much to do with how the effect is conceptualized. The staff too has ideas of how their behavior affects children. Since these conceptions constitute partial explanations of the impact of child care on peer groups, we shall briefly characterize them before presenting our own social-system analysis.

The least sophisticated counselors see their duties as administering institutional rules and regulations firmly and meeting benignly the legitimate material and emotional needs of the children. They work in this way not only because they are expected to but also because they believe that such management has a therapeutic effect. The youngsters' problems in the community, in their view, stem from a lack of parental discipline and affection; providing these needs is thought to enable the children to overcome their problems. The disciplinary role is considered primarily the function of the adult male in the cottage, and the nurturant role, the function of the female. Benign custody, it is expected, will over-come the distress and hostility that has emerged in response to earlier deprivations, thus enabling the child to respond with con-formity and appreciation. By and large, this viewpoint was rep-resented by Mike Littleton and Mrs. MacDougall in Hearthstone cottage.

A somewhat more sophisticated view of the child-care role is concerned with the transaction between counselors and children as total systems. Joe Strickland, in Fairline cottage, tended to espouse this orientation. From this perspective, the totality of a counsel-or's functioning—how he presents himself as a human being, all his interests and activities—is seen to affect the children in his presence. This philosophy also encompasses a larger view of the child. It holds that cottage management should be related to the child's total personality. If cottage counselors can exert a positive influence on residents' basic perceptions, values, and aspirations, the boys will be able to fashion more constructive modes of relating to their social environment.

This position emphasizes the moral component of personality connoted by the old-fashioned expression "building character" and implies the process depth psychologists call "identification." Without the trappings of psychoanalytic theory, its basic assump-tion is that socialization occurs through an automatic process in which the child takes on wholesale the basic attributes that he sees valued by and embodied in persons who are important to him. The head male counselor, by virtue of the institutional power vested in him, is thought to be an especially significant person in each boy's life. Thus, the child's adoption of more positive social be-havior is a function of the adult image projected by that counselor.

A third way of thinking about counselors' effects on children is subscribed to by the psychiatric social workers, the psychiatrists, and the supervisors of child-care workers. Taking the medical model as its starting point, this view considers the institution's major thrust to lie in the provision of individual psychotherapy tailored for each child to remedy the kind of pathology indicated by his psychiatric diagnosis. It assigns an adjunctive role to the child-care staff, for it suggests that each child's therapist can best prescribe how counselors should structure that child's cottage experience so that it will support and facilitate his psychotherapy. Like the brands of "milieu therapy" employed at Bettelheim's Ortho-genic School and at the Menninger Clinic, it seeks to fashion a patient's social experience according to the desiderata of a psychiatric treatment plan.

In the analysis that follows, we consider the functional pattern of staff management in each cottage together with its peer-group organization as a social system. This approach contrasts with the individualistic orientation of the three perspectives mentioned above. Manny Reisner, the chief counselor in Concord cottage, was oriented to the social system in his cottage because of his group-work training, but he did not consciously formulate his plans in terms of the functional imperatives. Moreover, the administrator who supervised him operated primarily from an individual casework perspective, so that none of the three cottages fully applied our analytical approach in practice. Yet, recognizing the effect of functional emphasis on the peer group suggests useful procedures for cottage management, which we shall attempt to spell out following our analysis of the cottage systems.

Viewed as a system, cottage life is an arrangement of resident and staff roles that form a distinctive unity. We probed the patterning of these roles by concentrating upon organizational tendencies toward internal stability and adaptation to the institution as well as indigenous goal attainment. Our theoretical framework concentrated upon four basic system processes:

1. The demands made upon the cottage by the institution and mediated chiefly by the worker in a monitoring role (adaptation).

2. The goals that cottage members evolve "independently" of the institution to which they must adapt, aided by the worker as guide (goal attainment).

3. The informal life within the cottage with the worker as friend and integrator (integration).

4. The specialized support given to cottage members who have difficulty maintaining themselves in the system (latency or pattern maintenance and tension management).

The above functional patterns are enacted by individuals, yet the patterns of their activity can be formulated independently of the personalities of cottage members. In the total institution, individual personalities are severely circumscribed by their roles. They confront each other in the cottage as worker and resident with complementary obligations and rights.

Our employment of the functional imperatives as the paradigm for describing the relations between workers and residents rests on the assumption that the observer can discern and verify activities that have objective consequences for the whole cottage system.

An event (a sequence of interactive behavior between worker and residents) is seen from the point of view of the actor in the situation as well as from the perspective of the observer, who views the consequences of the interaction for the cottage system. Unless the observer has a somewhat wider compass than the individuals in the midst of action, it would not be possible to codify cottage activity. The "wider knowledge" of the observer only means that he has a comprehensive scheme available to him for demarcating and categorizing important events in the cottage.

We assume worker and resident generally select appropriate means for the attainment of desired ends, although the ultimate consequences are often not calculated by the actors in the system. We observe cottage members responding to each other with a vague and incomplete conception of the results of their interaction for the system. To say that cottage members are acting rationally in a situation does not necessarily mean that they have insight or control over the consequences of their activity for the total situation.[1] As observers we find the meaning of the interaction by categorizing it within a theoretical framework that comprehends social behavior as consequential for ongoing cottage life.

The use of this functional model enables us to assess patterns of social interaction in three cottages on a comparative basis. Functionalism raises the question of balance among the imperatives in relationship to the pathology of the system but does not settle beforehand what kind of balance is optimum for health or illness, for equilibrium or disequilibrium. Each cottage culture has its costs; we have tried to estimate the outcome of the varying management modes, first, by impressions of how the cottage as a whole functions and, second, by appraisal of the impact upon the residents. The resultant functional balance ultimately can be judged by the values of the institution and professionals in the field, but an immediate alternative for assessing the different balances that emerge in the three cottages is to conceptualize the cultural totality of each cottage. In other words, how did the ways in which the workers manage the residents add up to the unitary pattern that emerged in each cottage?

Our choice of names for the cottages reveals our estimate of the total configuration of each cottage. The search for a "configurative" title for each cottage was not easy and took us a great deal of time. We were attempting to represent a whole that was

1. S. F. Nadel, *The Foundations of Social Anthropology* (Glencoe, Ill.: The Free Press 1951), p. 271.

more than the sum of the functional parts. We were looking for a unitary quality not found in the elements considered singly or grouped together in a mechanical way. To be sure, this unity is derived from our understanding of the way in which the cottage was functionally interrelated, but we were looking for some embracing description of the cottage organization as a whole.

This unitary character emerged from our comparative analysis of patterns of cottage management and the proportional enactment of the functional imperatives. In other words, we analyzed first in great detail specific interactive processes between workers and residents before we built up the "whole." Each cottage appeared to us consequently to be organized on different principles.

When we speak about a cottage configuration, we do not mean that all its modes of action are integrated into a firm and coherent manner but that a characteristic pattern of staff management emerges. Each cottage selects and utilizes only a few of the potential courses of action open to it. It emphasizes one or another of the functional spheres and de-emphasizes the others. The spheres that are selected become themes for elaboration and are cumulatively built up while others are relatively underutilized. A more-or-less consistent pattern of interaction then appeared to prevail in each cottage.

Ultimately, this configuration is based on the way in which the instrumental and expressive dimensions of cottage life are integrated. The expressive orientation in a culture rests on the emotional-informal relationships (the "mood") within the cottage. The instrumental dimension is based on the way in which the cottage organizes to meet the requirements of the institution and promote its own goals (its "efficiency").

The "problems" of maintaining internal cottage cohesiveness and coping with the institution must somehow be balanced. The cottage worker is the internal regulator of the cottage to the institution; he can facilitate or frustrate the development of constructive autonomous cottage goals. These youngsters could not be maintained in the larger community. The main internal "opposition" lies in unresolved individual needs of the residents that were diagnosed as inadequate for coping with the open community.

In the cottage we called "Fairline," the head counselor with the support of his assistants emphasized conformity with high standards of cottage maintenance. Since this was the main line and generally carried out in an impartial manner, we called the cottage "Fairline." Of the three cottages, we found that Fairline staff members devoted the greatest amount of attention to monitoring, spending more than half of all their events so engaged. Another quarter of their events reflected attention to boys' individual needs, which is similar to Concord and lower than Hearthstone. Like Hearthstone, only 7 per cent of Fairline counselor activity was directed toward group goal guidance, and only 4 per cent to integration.

Joe Strickland set the pattern of monitoring in Fairline, which is closely followed by Jamie, his assistant. Strickland emphasized the custodial function more than any other counselor, and among female counselors, Jamie was high in attention to this function. To boys' individual needs, Strickland devoted just under one-fourth of his events, and Jamie somewhat more. In this sphere they were not very different from the counselors in the other cottages. In sharp contrast to Concord, they resembled the child-care workers in Hearthstone by paying relatively little attention to group guidance and integration.

Not only in choice of function but also in modes of carrying out a chosen function, the adult pair in Fairline showed characteristic differences from their colleagues in the other senior cottages. Especially in monitoring, they used controlling modes more often and were less likely to express warm feelings toward the boys. Furthermore, Jamie was notable for the frequency with which the content of her interaction with boys was restricted to the specific obligations of the subordinate-resident and superordinate-counselor configuration.

How did this kind of cottage management affect the peer group in Fairline? Fairline boys, it will be remembered, had worked out a pattern of informal leadership among themselves. Even though these staff members placed little stress on group goals, such roles as "Is good at organizing boys to put their own ideas for the cottage into action" and "Can get boys to work together in making things for the cottage" were well recognized. How can we account for it?

One clue was suggested by Strickland's constant complaints that he did not have adequate personnel to enforce custodial tasks properly, much less to provide guidance in group activities. Jamie, too, expressed a desire to organize group projects with the boys, but she was unable to free herself from enforcing conformity to Strickland's norms and so could find no time to give to such projects. Yet they both did present the possibilities of more extensive group activities to the boys, although they were not often observed to be actively engaged in promoting them. Our general observation of Fairline boys indicated their awareness of these possibilities. They seem to have been able, with this minimal stimulation from counselors, to develop group activities and corresponding roles within the peer group. However, staff inattention to peer-group activity resulted as well in clear-cut roles that disrupt the group, for example, "Tries to sabotage co-operation among boys in the cottage." A staff more actively involved in group goal attainment should be in a position to redirect negative role incumbents toward more constructive participation.

The most direct connection between counselors' emphasis in Fairline and roles in the peer group has to do with boys' roles opposed to staff authority. Fairline residents knew that the standards in their cottage were not enforced in other cottages, and this set the stage for organized resistance. Their tendencies to oppose and circumvent the requirements come out in a number of reliably perceived roles: "Gets other boys to do his job around the cottage," "Gets around staff without actually breaking rules," "Argues the most with staff members," and "Causes other boys to be blamed by staff for what he has done." This last role description, more reliably perceived in Fairline than in the other two cottages, suggests the ambivalence of group opposition to staff; it is not solitary resistance to expectations which were felt to be unrealistic, but a challenge to authority that threatened the relations of boys to each other was well as relations between boys and staff.

Hearthstone cottage presents quite a different picture, although on the surface there were similarities to Fairline. Both were similar in the proportion of counselor attention to goal attainment and integration, although they differ in monitoring and individual support. The head counselor in each paid relatively more attention to monitoring than did Manny Reisner in Concord, but Strickland did so more than Littleton. Littleton was content to have the boys in his charge conform minimally to the rules, whereas Strickland went further in imposing higher standards. Because both Strickland and Littleton are Negroes and their charges white, the likelihood of boys' identification with them may have been less than that of Concord boys with Reisner. Strickland consciously sought to present himself as a model of moral conduct, masculine strength, and educational achievement for the boys to emulate; Littleton, on the other hand, was occasionally prone to encourage mildly delinquent conversation and play.

The females in these two cottages differed more widely. Jamie endeavored to support and emulate Strickland, what we might call a supplementary role *vis-à-vis* his functioning. By contrast Mrs. MacDougall left most of the monitoring to Littleton and addressed herself to individual needs—a division of roles that could be termed complementary.

The less stringent standards in Hearthstone and Littleton's major concern in this area left Mrs. MacDougall freer to be concerned with individual needs. She carried out this function to a much greater extent than any other counselor in the unit, in fully 47 per cent of her events. By giving attention to group goals in 10 per cent of the events, she somewhat offset Mike Littleton's low proportion of 5 per cent in this sphere. Hearthstone and Fairline counselors were similar to each other in devoting less attention to integration than the Concord counselors.

Overall, in modes of relating to children, Hearthstone's pattern is closer to Concord than to Fairline. Both Hearthstone and Concord were lower on control and higher on positive affect than Fairline: in proportion of events embodying the superordinate counselor-subordinate resident role set, Hearthstone was intermediate, Fairline high, and Concord low.

The functional complementarity between Littleton and Mrs. MacDougall, noted above, does not carry over to working mode when function was controlled for; they were not very different from each other in affect, control, or role emphasis in carrying out a given function. However, in the monitoring sphere, Mrs. MacDougall shows more positive affect and controls less than did Littleton. In the other cottages, the female counselors carried out this function with less positive affect than did their male counterparts. We chose "Hearthstone" because routines were administered dictatorially, connoting "stone." Yet considerable individual support was warmly given by Mrs. MacDougall, the "Hearth" in Hearthstone.

The peer-group structure in Hearthstone is as interesting for the roles it lacked as for those it contained. Whereas Concord had six roles of reliability greater than .90, which indicates modes of encouraging integration and constructive activities among cottage mates, and Fairline had five such roles, Hearthstone had only two: "Is good at organizing boys to put their ideas for the cottage into action" and "Has the best ideas for cottage projects." On the other hand, most of the reliable roles in Hearthstone, like "Can get other boys in the cottage to do whatever he wants," "Can be influenced by other boys to do things he's not supposed to do," and

"Other boys take orders from this boy because they're afraid of him," indicate a delinquent power structure. Also notably absent were any roles, positive or negative toward staff, suggesting that we are not here confronted with the kind of solid organization against authority that is characteristic of prison inmates. This lack of solidarity among peers is confirmed by roles like "Tries to sabotage co-operation among boys in the cottage."

This general picture of the peer group in Hearthstone can be traced to their counselors' management orientation. The chief counselor, Mike Littleton, was at times observed to take part in kidding with the boys, but his relation to the group was generally marginal. He offered them very little guidance in group activities, and whatever contribution he may have made is not reflected in any peer-role patterns directed toward positive group goals. Neither did Mrs. MacDougall's contribution to the cottage, as chief nurturer to individual boys, enhance the potential for constructive group activity. Hearthstone cottage lacked any meaningful intervention directed toward goal attainment and integration, because these counselors saw their tasks exclusively in the realms of custody and nurturing. The result was a cottage in which boys organized themselves very little along constructive lines. The peer hierarchy appears to have been based on physical coercion. There was dissension among boys, and many remained aloof from their peers and from adults. Thus, the indigenous peer-group activity recapitulates, within the institutional setting, antisocial values and pathological processes that caused society to reject these children in the first place.

In Concord cottage, the proportion of attention allocated by its counselors to the four functional spheres reflects a tone established by the head counselor, Manny Reisner, who received his training in group work. The informal expressive interaction between counselors and residents was freer and lighter; everyone had more fun. We were so impressed with this contrasting spirit to Fairline and Hearthstone that we finally agreed on the name "Concord." Here the staff paid more attention to goal attainment and integration than did their counterparts in the other two cottages. They were scarcely lower than Fairline counselors in attention to individual-supportive events and only a little less than the Hearthstone staff in custodial emphasis. But the excess attention which Fairline expended on monitoring and that Hearthstone devoted to satisfying individual needs was channeled by Concord counselors into goal guidance and integration. Each counselor took nearly equal responsibility in stressing custodial requirements. Reisner and Mrs. Pepper tended to meet individual needs more than did Mrs. Murphy; in this, Concord's division of labor reverses the pattern in the other two cottages, where the male counselor spent less time on boys' individual needs and more on meeting requirements of the external situation than his female assistants. Reisner assumed the principal responsibility for goal guidance, and Mrs. Murphy supports this emphasis, but Mrs. Pepper devoted no more attention to peer-group goals than Littleton, who was less oriented toward peer guidance than any of the other counselors. Unlike goal attainment, however, integration is not a specialized function in this cottage; each Concord counselor paid about the same proportion of attention to this sphere.

Not only did Concord counselors, as a group and individually, place no undue stress on monitoring (in contrast to the other cottages), but when dealing with custodial issues they managed to maintain a comparatively warm manner and to avoid asserting the power inherent in their superordinate status. Among head counselors, Reisner was least controlling and warmest in affect in monitoring. Mrs. Pepper and Mrs. Murphy were intermediate between Jamie and Mrs. MacDougall in proportion of custodial transactions carried out with positive affect, although events in this sphere were primarily transacted with neutral feeling tone by all female counselors. More than did any other female counselor in these events, Mrs. Murphy avoided exercising manifest control, and Mrs. Pepper showed less control than did Jamie and more than did Mrs. MacDougall.

In carrying out individual-supportive events, there are few significant differences among the male and female counselors. The women in Concord, however, did show a tendency to carry out this function with positive affect. Each of them showed positive feeling tone in 50 per cent or more of latency events; the proportion for Mrs. MacDougall was under one-half, and, for Jamie, less than one-quarter.

The staff configuration in Concord did not by any means result in an ideal peer group. As in the other cottages, there existed roles among Concord boys indicating relationships frowned on by the institution. Such delinquent patterns show themselves in roles like "Other boys take orders from this boy because they are afraid of him" and "Always getting into fights with boys he can't beat." They are more than offset by roles reflecting positive modes of interaction: "Gets everyone to contribute his share for the cottage" and "Will give up something to help other boys." Fairline, too, had these roles, but Concord's peer group, presumably in response to their counselors' consistent attention to integration, had positive relationship-centered roles as well. They reflect a norm that boys assume responsibility for each other, such as, "Smooths over hard feelings between boys after a fight" and "Other boys like to have this boy in on whatever they're doing."

Also not found in the other two cottages was another kind of consensually validated role in Concord. Represented by such items as "Tries to help staff work with each other," "Talks to staff on behalf of other boys who have requests or complaints," and "Gets along pretty well with staff and other boys," the Concord peer group alone maintained notably good relations with staff. This closer relatedness to staff members apparently had pitfalls, shown by perceptions of partiality in the role structure: "Tries to get special favors for himself from staff" and "Staff members like him more than any other boy." Yet these staff-resident relations were on a different level from the antagonisms and subterfuge between boys and staff in Fairline and from the distance between boys and staff in Hearthstone.

It is not possible to attribute better staff-resident and interpeer relationships in Concord, compared with Fairline and Hearthstone, to staff differences in emphasizing any particular function, because it is the configuration that produces this effect. By restraining themselves from too much emphasis on conforming to institutional requirements, Concord staff members made the youngsters receptive to their overtures in other spheres. Still, it is doubtful that the peer-staff and peer-peer roles found in Concord would have emerged if the staff had confined its attention to individual needs and not gone on to promote the consummatory functions, integration, and peer goal attainment. Attention to these functions is what makes the group aware of itself as a group, thus making possible a network through which staff members can enable youngsters to gain satisfaction in autonomous peer interaction and activities.

In sum, it appears that the prerequisite for constructive group activity is to make residents aware of its possibilities and advantages. Concord counselors addressed this function directly. Through their own participation, they encouraged the incorporation of such roles in the boys' group structure. In Fairline, the counselors indicated these possibilities to the boys but did not act upon them. While their counselors were devoting themselves overwhelmingly to custody and individual needs, Fairline boys seem to have worked out the mechanisms for meeting group-centered needs on their own. But Hearthstone counselors' lack of awareness of the possibility of group activities resulted in a virtual absence of constructive peer roles among boys in that cottage.

The uniformly stronger emphasis on integration in Concord, compared to the other two cottages, appears to have had a direct effect on the peer organization: Concord had more positive inter-peer relational roles than did Fairline or Hearthstone. On the negative side, none of the variations in counselor management patterns in the three cottages effectively inhibited the formation of negative roles in boys' peer relations. Negative peer roles predominated in Hearthstone; they existed in Fairline and Concord as well but in these cottages were counterbalanced by more positive roles.

The other major impact of Concord's staff direction on residents vested in the peer-group roles oriented toward adults. Such roles were virtually absent in Hearthstone and opposed to staff authority in Fairline, whereas in Concord they were consonant with staff efforts to help children negotiate constructively the institutional environment.

In addition to helping boys develop individual and peer-group autonomy, an important aim of rehabilitation is assisting children to supplant pathological modes of relating to adults with healthier ones. Youngsters in Concord regarded their counselors as non-threatening, so that they neither avoided them as in Hearthstone nor resisted them as in Fairline but were able to accept the adults' efforts on their behalf. An inability to trust any adults or to accept any guidance from parents and teachers is what led, for the most part, to the removal of these boys from the community. It is not unreasonable to hope that, on returning to society, Concord's more positive modes of group participation will help boys who lived there to accept educational and occupational direction more readily.

Based upon the data that we have gathered, we can make several interpretations about the worker's role in the cottage and institution. The unanticipated consequence of the custodial emphasis is the imposition of minimally acceptable standards upon the residents in the cottages. The minimum standards of performance tend to become a common pattern for most residents and thus become maximum standards for them. Minimum performance by workers and residents leads to a discrepancy in the organizational goals held by the administration and the way of life that is generated in the cottages. Pressures are then placed upon supervisors to check more closely upon the cottage workers. This increases the visibility of the actual relationships between workers and residents in the cottages, leads to increasing tensions, and disturbs the equilibrium of the system.

We have postulated that the cottage system requires two kinds of leadership to operate efficiently. One leader, the instrumental, is important in the task-oriented sphere of the cottage. Here the leader can emphasize custodial tasks or stimulate and guide the residents in formulating and executing autonomous goals. In the internal sphere the worker as expressive leader takes one of two directions. Either he can emphasize the nurturing and supportive role of enabling individual residents to cope with cottage life and/or he can direct his attention to the informal group life of the cottage.

Functional theory suggests that cottages will be more effective in task achievement and membership satisfaction when they have competent workers in both the instrumental (monitor and guide) and expressive (supporter and integrator) spheres and where these kinds of leadership are mutually supportive. Concord staff's greater facility in managing routines less and with less conflict, while simultaneously promoting cottage goals, supports this thesis.

The functional model also suggests the kinds of disequilibria or pathologies that will emerge if leadership roles are underemphasized or if mutual support is absent. Task efficiency will be low when the instrumental leader is deficient or incompetent and satisfaction will be low when the expressive leader is inadequate or absent. Both efficiency and satisfaction will be reduced when the two leaders are in conflict.

Within this hypothetical frame we will reinterpret our findings in the three cottages as follows:

In Fairline, the emphasis upon custodialism led to a cottage situation in which the residents were coerced into maintaining high standards, especially in routines; the lack of leadership in the internal sphere resulted in considerable cumulative resident dissatisfaction. In Hearthstone, a better balance emerged between the custodial emphasis and individual support; however, the head counselor's standards were not high and his custodial leadership was poorly administered, resulting in the dirtiest Senior Unit cottage. Concord, compared to the other cottages, exhibited the most balance among the functional spheres in worker leadership and appeared the smoothest functioning in resolving conflicts and fulfilling cottage routines. The youngsters were described as the most spirited and autonomous.

The cottage is not a natural group in a tenuous social network. Workers do not interact as individuals or in multiple statuses with residents, but as the representatives of the institution. The counselor articulates the cottage with the institutional organization. In the total institution this leadership is ultimately based on power, that is, force to compel residents to perform tasks whatever their desires may be. But workers also have to develop a modus vivendi with the residents.

The relationship of the counselor and the resident is difficult to conceptualize. From one perspective, they belong to different solidary systems. The counselor is the custodian of the boys. The resident is at Hawthorne to be protected and to be treated. Inevitably, however, in the compact living cottage situation, resident and staff come to regard themselves as belonging to the same solidary system. This is the dilemma of the counselor's marginal role in the total institution. His foremost institutional responsibility is to supervise the daily routines. This is reflected in our overall average figures, where in over 50 per cent of his transactions the counselor assumes various aspects of the custodial role. The next largest number of transactions falls into pattern maintenance and tension management. The massive dependency of the youngsters and the accent upon individual therapy in the institution extends into the cottages, where the counselor also spends a considerable amount of time (about one-fourth) responding to individual problems, albeit in quite a different manner than the psychotherapist.

Significantly, the counselor is least occupied with areas where he has the most autonomy and the least direction by the administration! He spends relatively little time enabling youngsters to attain indigenous goals and is least involved in informal integrative activity.

Influencing residents' motivational and normative orientations rests ultimately upon the ability of the counselor to provide leadership to the cottage in all four spheres. Residents' "acceptance" of the organizationally provided leader depends to some degree on what the counselor himself chooses to emphasize within the cottage. A counselor can emphasize order, the fulfilment of routine activities in a way that requires relatively little commitment from the residents. In fact, what we discovered in the Senior Unit is that counselors put their main emphasis upon the custodial role and secondary emphasis on providing support for individual residents. Counselors spent least time and were apparently less effective in enabling youngsters to formulate and execute their own goals and in promoting the informal life of the cottage.

The cottage worker's organizational power does not automatically assure the residents' loyalty to the cottage or the institution's values, goals, or rules. An exclusive emphasis upon custody seems to be most conducive to the development of indigenous peer groups based upon antisocial values and roles. Fairline residents showed the most disregard for socially approved values.

The cottage care worker's role is largely shaped by the goals and structure of the institution. The emphasis by the institution for custodial leadership affects the kind of social life that will emerge in the cottage. When the instrumental leadership is chiefly custodial, the cottage is more likely to generate tensions, especially if expressive leadership is not afforded by other counselors in the cottage or if it is weak and ineffective. If the institution wishes to inaugurate rehabilitation (a therapeutic milieu) rather than custody in the cottage, it must develop workers that can give to the cottage other kinds of leadership.

Workers who emphasize custodial controls ultimately depend upon low commitment by the residents for satisfactory levels of adaptation. The residents in the first place are antagonistic to the institution and tend to reject it. The custodial-oriented counselor expects this resistance and relies on his superior power to contain it. Strickland commanded compliance of his charges in Fairline, but the enactment of relatively high standards was not internalized any more in these boys than their compeers in other cottages.

Until quite recently the standard practice of child-care supervisors was the exercise of sound judgment. These *ad hoc* decisions did not contribute much to the theory of child care in residential centers. Whatever principles did emerge were never given explicit codification.

The institution itself had not developed a set of goals or guidelines of what it ideally wanted the cottages to be and what their contribution to the rehabilitation of their residents should be. During the period of observation we saw little direct supervision of workers by the Senior Unit or institutional administration. In general, our feeling was that the cottage-care workers were given broad scope and responsibility for running the cottages. Supervision seemed to center upon individuals or groups of residents who did not conform to the regulations of the cottage or institution. This is more true of Fairline and Hearthstone than of Concord. In the latter cottage, Reisner, the head counselor, was supervised on a continuous basis. However, our belief is that the nature of that supervision revolved around discussions of individual youngsters in the cottage.

Thus, few guidelines were developed for management of the cottage in areas other than the custodial. Administrative officials had evolved over the years a considerable body of "practice wisdom" by which they ran the institution and supervised the cottages. For example, the administration believes that each of the cottages should have at least one woman worker. Often the administration is forced to select counselors from a very limited pool of applicants. This institution has had chronic difficulty in attracting competent non-professional cottage care workers.

In a word, none of the workers in the cottages was given a blue-print by the institution of how to manage the cottage. Rather, the actual management of the cottages was a result of the social and educational background of the workers, general supervision of custodial care, and resident pressures.

Now we come to the problem of how to fashion workable procedures for cottage management based on this system orientation and analysis. To begin with, practitioners accustomed to thinking of cottages as aggregates of individuals must become attuned to the operation of the social system. They must enlarge their focus from the person to the group. They must learn to see individuals' problems as relationship difficulties that can be worked through in the interpersonal arena, and to view personal traits in the light of how they contribute to or detract from group life. The child-care task then is aimed at constructing a well-functioning cottage group —that is, in terms of the Parsonian functional imperatives, one that will increasingly take responsibility for adapting to the limitations and resources of its environment, working toward goals shared by the group, meeting the needs of individual members, and maintaining *esprit de corps* within the group.

The social-system approach to child care uses a different theory from the psychiatric approach, but the process of translating the theory into practice is similar to the psychiatrist's method of employing personality theory. In each case, the practitioner uses the theory as a framework for description, evaluation, and planning. First, each theory provides terms for describing the state of the system, personal or social, at a given point in time. Second, the theory presents a model of a properly functioning system against which the system described can be evaluated. And third, the theory suggests strategies of helping the system move from its present state toward a more stable equilibrium.

As an example, let us begin with a typical description in social-system terms. Suppose that we start with the description of a cottage where performance of custodial tasks is the recurring point of conflict between boys and staff. Here, boys are accustomed to asking a counselor for something and having him meet the request but without encouraging them to take some initiative in meeting their own needs. The boys are described as bored: there is no feeling of group solidarity, many conflicts among individuals are observed, and boys tend to keep to themselves.

Evaluation might determine that the custodial emphasis of staff does not exceed a level appropriate to meeting institutional demands but that it seems ineffective because of the modes used to enforce it. Perhaps staff respond to individual needs too greatly and thus leave deficiencies in the areas of integration and goal attainment.

Planning can consist of deciding to employ different modes—perhaps less punishment of misbehavior and more reward of positive achievement—in the custodial sphere. Division of staff labor is also part of strategizing. With a staff of three it may be determined to distribute the latency function more widely, for example, to a head male counselor who was primarily responsible for custodial demands in the past. A female counselor whose responsibility had been previously nurturant could take on more custodial duties, and special group projects might be conceived as the special province of a third, younger counselor. Each might concentrate on his own way of promoting integration—one by spending time in informal bull sessions, another by conducting regularly scheduled group discussions.

A characteristic problem practitioners confront when attempting to help a group meet its own needs better is the potential dependency of the group on the practitioner. This dependency can keep group members from developing skills in maintaining their own group. Thus, part of the child-care worker's task is to diagnose the group's capacity to carry out the functions autonomously and to plan accordingly. This strategy implies a timetable, although of course it is one to be periodically reconsidered rather than rigidly adhered to. Ultimately, however, it is the worker's responsibility to maximize peer-group autonomy. For example, he may decide for the present to place less emphasis upon custody and more on individual need and integration and to defer a thrust toward peer-group goal attainment until a certain level of autonomy in the first three spheres has been attained.

In advancing a concept of resident care which includes description, evaluation, and planning for a cottage social system, we are indicating an ideal. It does not, of course, come about all at once. But in time and with proper training, we suggest, a team of cottage workers can learn to develop rather comprehensive plans for a cottage and periodically reassess and reformulate them within this social-system theory of child care.

XI. The Future of Child Care in Residential Treatment

No one familiar with the rapidly growing field of residential treatment can fail to note the increasing self-consciousness of all personnel with the total ongoing life of their rehabilitation communities. It is no longer assumed that therapy is the special province of a professional therapist treating an individual client. It is now recognized that the ways in which staff and residents become engaged with one another results in a social system that has important influence upon the residents' therapeutic outcome.

In their pioneering work with children, Bettelheim and Sylvester, still conceiving of the therapeutic milieu as an environment prescribed for individuals on the basis of a psychiatric diagnosis, recognized the treatment possibilities of manipulating patients' total life experiences in a closed setting.[1] A few years later Maxwell Jones called attention to the importance of relationships among staff and patients in adult wards and throughout the hospital.[2]

1. Bruno Bettelheim and Emmy Sylvester, "A Therapeutic Milieu," *American Journal of Orthopsychiatry*, 28 (1948), 191-206.
2. Maxwell S. Jones, *et al.*, *The Therapeutic Community* (New York: Basic Books, 1953); Maxwell S. Jones, *Social Psychiatry* (London: Tavistock Publications, 1952).

Stanton and Schwartz stressed essentially the same theme,[3] which was followed by a survey of trends of therapeutic residential care.[4] It soon became fashionable to classify institutions as custodial or therapeutic on the basis of administrative practices and staff attitudes. A therapeutic milieu, according to Schwartz and Schwartz,[5] is characterized by three orientations: democratic social structure, kind and understanding staff interaction and relations with patients, and efforts aimed at helping patients to achieve insight into their illnesses and to develop more satisfying interpersonal relations.

A number of research studies dealing with therapeutic components in mental hospital care[6] indicate it is very much a status symbol to have an experimental "therapeutic community" program in the institution. Many institutions trying to maintain reputations or build prestige pay "lip service" to establishing milieu therapy.

The focus of this study may be highlighted by pointing out two overall shortcomings we found in previous studies.

First, custodialism has been practically equated with sin. "Custodial" staff members are seen as the "bad guys"—as waging a "holy crusade." Of course, the overtones of "custodialism" are usually more subtle, but even when the lower-echelon staff members are exonerated of moral culpability, the blame is displaced onto administrators, who are then regarded as dominated by a desire for the status quo and a balanced budget.

The problem is that this pejorative view of custody tends to obscure the positive function of such behavior. Even if one assumes that simply replacing "custodial" practices with more "therapeutic" procedures will have a beneficial effect, it would be helpful in effecting this replacement to be aware of the system needs that gave rise to the "custodial" practices. And it may turn out that

3. Alfred H. Stanton and Morris S. Schwartz, *The Mental Hospital* (New York: Basic Books, 1954).

4. Milton R. Greenblatt, Richard York, and Esther L. Brown, *From Custodial to Therapeutic Care in Mental Hospitals* (New York: Russell Sage Foundation, 1955).

5. Morris S. Schwartz and Charlotte G. Schwartz, *Social Approaches to Mental Patient Care* (New York: Columbia University Press, 1964), pp. 164-65.

6. Jay Jackson, "Toward the Comparative Study of Mental Hospitals: Characteristics of the Treatment Environment," in Albert F. Wessen (ed.), *The Psychiatric Hospital as a Social System* (Springfield, Ill.: Charles C. Thomas, 1964), pp. 35-146; Doris C. Gilbert and Daniel J. Levinson, "Ideology, Personality and Institutional Policy in the Mental Hospital," *Journal of Abnormal and Social Psychology*, 53 (1956), 263-71; Daniel J. Levinson and Eugene B. Gallagher, *Patienthood in the Mental Hospital* (Boston: Houghton Mifflin Company, 1964).

some kinds of "custodial" practices enhance rather than hinder the rehabilitation of inmates. The intent in our study was not, of course, to exalt custodialism but to observe and analyze custodial behavior in the light of the functional imperative it represents. We thus see our treatment of the function of adaptation (monitoring) as a needed corrective to the view of custody presented in other studies.

The second problem in the way the custody-therapy continuum has been conceptualized is the failure to specify the meaning of therapy in social-system terms.

We have no quarrel with investigators who may be interested in following up the effects of group treatment on individual rehabilitation,[7] but this does not substitute for an analysis of the group on its own terms. To espouse the importance of the social system as a therapeutic tool dictates that one describe therapeutic system-functioning at that level. We thought it important in this study to specify the characteristics of resident care and its impact on peer-group roles in three cottages. Our focus upon social-system differences—particularly, the differential emphasis of the functional imperatives—obliged us to describe resident care consistently as a system-oriented process.

Our findings suggest that this approach may prove useful as a practical orientation for prescribing resident care work and for training workers to carry out with systematic deliberation their duties and responsibilities.

Considerable research and observation in residential treatment centers to date point to the opposite conclusion. Manipulation, force, deception, and a chronic state of tension alternating with apathy often pervades the living situation in which both workers and residents feel that they are "doing time."

The split in treatment in total institutions where the professional therapist administers therapy and the resident-care worker conducts a "holding operation" has led to stultifying conflicts between counselors and residents.

The monopoly of control exercised by counselors in the cottages is always precarious. Since they cannot oversee all the youngsters every moment of the time, the deployment of repressive sanctions often serves as a model of agression with which the resident can identify. The value system that emerges in the cottage is very much related to the way in which cottage workers manage the

7. H. A. Weeks, *Youthful Offenders at Highfields* (Ann Arbor: University of Michigan Press, 1958).

cottage. The basic pattern of resident-counselor interaction pre-cipitates a system of opposing values and interests.

The following analogy to the teacher may help set the per-spective for our discussion of the present position and future direction of the non-professional resident care worker in residential institutions. Suppose for a moment the school teacher's main task is custodial: keeping children in order and out of trouble. Suppose also that the task of teaching the children was handed over to another person, a master-teacher, who taught the child or children for one hour during the day. Finally, imagine integration meetings in which the master-teacher advises the custodial-teacher how to best control the child in the most educational manner. To leave no doubt in the reader's mind, we are equating the resident care worker with the custodial-teacher and the psychiatrist or social worker with the master-teacher.

The resident-care worker in residential treatment often becomes a custodial specialist. Our discussion will be better understood if we distinguish at the outset between the specialization of tasks and the specialization of people.[8] "Task specialization" refers to work specificity—making activities more specific so that they fit in with the overall objectives of the institution. "Personal specialization," on the other hand, refers to the development of resident-care workers who can rehabilitate youngsters in the total living-in cottage situation.

The resident-care worker as a youth-culture specialist would tend toward a professional status. He would develop as his role becomes more meaningfully relevant to the rehabilitation of young-sters in the cottage setting. If what he does becomes more highly valued by others he can gain a partial monopoly in resident-care work. Other personnel become dependent upon him and learn to accommodate to his job. His fate is much more controlled by him-self and peers in concert than by the resident care-custodian. Resi-dential institutions have not met the personal and social needs of the resident-care worker nor fully employed their potential in the cottage. The role has become static, filled by inadequately trained people who have little control over their own work. Professional and non-professional staff developed little "team" solidarity—turnover is large.

The resident-care worker as a task specialist (in many settings a custodian) moves in the direction of an ever more specific and

8. Victor A. Thompson, *Modern Organization* (New York: Alfred A. Knopf, 1961), chap. iii, pp. 25-58.

narrowing round of repetitive routines. He becomes specialized at controlling youngsters. This unidimensional responsibility results in little development in work skills. He becomes expendable and others can be rapidly trained to perform his role.

The idea of custodial specialist is fostered by many institutions because he is easier to control, does not threaten the treatment monopoly of psychiatrist and social worker, and, in the short run, is less expensive to train and maintain.

Narrowing the resident-care job to overseeing routines virtually prohibits his innovative impact on developing his work to fit the needs of the youngsters. Most important of all, he has little prestige among the professionals and very little voice in the institution. His contribution is not only belittled or ignored, but is often considered detrimental to the youngsters' growth and development.

The emphasis upon individual therapy at Hawthorne has resulted in the non-professional controlling large groups of youngsters the "other twenty-three hours." This one-sided perspective worked against developing the therapeutic potential in the cottages, the youngsters' daily living situation.

Task specialization and personal specialization are antithetical. The more the child-care worker becomes a custodian, the less he develops as a residential-care specialist. Only when the cottage-care worker assumes more responsibility for residential treatment will he become less of a custodian. The movement of resident-care workers toward youth specialization rather than more sophisticated custody depends ultimately upon the development of a new concept of resident-care work and the redefinition of the worker's role.

Resident-care workers must deal with all aspects of individual and group life of their charges as a social, developmental, and organic process; imposing upon the resident care worker the primary task of custody is an organizational process. The worker requires a social function commensurate with the complex total living situation that confronts him. He performs socially valued functions that untrained and unskilled people cannot do adequately. This new comprehensive resident-care function must be compatible with his capacities, residents' needs, and organizational objectives. As standards improve, salaries will have to be raised considerably. As the job becomes multi-functional, the new speciality of youth specialist will take a longer time to master than the older custodial orientation. A sophisticated training program will also be necessary.

The necessity of a well-planned training orientation stems from two sources. First, an impassable division emerged between professional and non-professional personnel. As the professional became increasingly sophisticated, the gap between him and the non-professional was increased. This coincided with the desire on the part of administrators (who are usually professionals) and professional therapists to avoid dependency upon the lower-status non-professional resident-care workers. These workers were kept docile by holding the threat of displacement over them through lower wages and little power. Hence, a training program was never developed and conceptualization of their role did not advance to the point where they could begin to assume a therapeutic child-care specialty.

In order to inaugurate a well-planned training program, the residential institution must first develop a sound theory of the function of the resident-care worker. As a segregated organization, the institution is beginning to learn that it needs commitment rather than obedience of its residents. The "friend" (integrator) and "teacher" (guidance) roles are important because the institutional setting serves as a powerful constraining force against change of residents. The dense interactions of residents with one another lead them to reject the institution's values and its personnel. Anti-institutional leaders and cliques constantly spring up among residents in the cottages. These counter-forces in the institution and resident group can only be negotiated by skilled cottage-care workers who can balance their roles as institutional representatives to the residents with a role as the residents' representative to the institution.

This balance is extraordinarily complex and difficult because the cottage-care worker oversees the youngsters' fulfillment of routines and yet must enable them to work toward their own goals. He is supposed to be an informal group leader and at the same time give special support to the most inadequate youngsters in the cottage.

Perhaps this can be best done by developing a model of what the counselors want to attain in the cottage during different phases of its development by sensitive differential attention to the functional spheres. If the cottage is to move toward institutional goals, the residents must be committed to socially constructive values and roles. To do this, cottage workers will have to develop skills to influence the cottage in informal ways as well as enabling residents to formulate and execute autonomous goals. All this must be done while simultaneously cottage routines are overseen and special support is imparted to the more unstable youngsters in the cottage.

It is our conviction that the next stage of institutional development is the promotion of a perspective of residential treatment in which the resident groups are offered an opportunity to plan and execute goals stemming from their own interests and needs. In several total institution settings, this program is already being advanced. Two outstanding examples are Jones's[9] therapeutic milieu and the program of sociotherapy initiated by Paul Daniel Sivadon in France.[10] The latter is especially perceptive about the need to promote autonomous goals by resident groups.

Sivadon asserts that one of the main problems of residents in institutions is the great amount of time that lies heavily on their hands. Furthermore, there are the ever-present gripes and complaints that the residents have about the restrictions on their freedom and their ability to plan and attain goals. The basic need to overcome passivity within the controlled authoritarian environment is met by provoking the residents into confronting their complaints with positive and constructive group activity. Sivadon has asserted, in fact, that the most important function of the resident counselor is to incite the residents to work out their gripes in positive programs of group action. If institutional life is boring for the residents, they should be helped to voice their complaints but also encouraged to take the next step in planning a program that can overcome their ennui. This has the advantage of using group process not only for developing programs but also for enabling the residents to work more effectively with each other. Through these activities the residents learn from their own errors and, instead of projecting their impotency onto the institution and into enervating intra-institutional conflict, they are forced to look more at their own individual and joint functioning, to locate their inadequacies, and to develop strategies for overcoming them.

We visualize the resident-care worker's new role as linking the youth's needs with a dynamic reciprocal impact upon the institution. This means that his function is not merely to make the cottage adapt to institutional regulations but to create, with the

9. Jones, *The Therapeutic Community*.
10. Paul D. Sivadon, "Techniques of Sociotherapy," *Psychiatry*, 20 (1957), 205-10.

youth, goals that they can attain within the authoritarian setting. It also means that the worker must have more significant influence with the administration to carry on, within and outside the cottage, a variety of goals that are increasingly planned and executed by residents for themselves.

XII. Epilogue: Report of an Action Program for Fostering Resident Autonomy in an Institutional Setting[1]

Resident Autonomy: The Goal of Institutional Treatment

In a research-demonstration project subsequent to this study, we attempted to feed back selected aspects of our theoretical approach and findings to a group of child-care workers. We thought, perhaps naively, that a comprehensive view of child-care work would give cottage workers an opportunity to discuss what they wanted to achieve as well as their current activity. Initially, the weekly meetings consisted of unstructured wide-ranging discussions of their work in each of the functional spheres.

One result of this action program was to clarify for us and highlight a point of view about institutional treatment. The point of departure of our orientation to residential treatment is contained in a World Health Organization report, which states that in order to create a "therapeutic atmosphere" patients must be

1. This chapter is based in part on a paper read at annual meeting, American Sociological Association, Aug. 28-31, 1967, San Francisco.

regarded as "capable of responsibility and initiative and provided with planned purposeful activity."[2]

Residential treatment seeks to change its clients so that they can cope more effectively with their environment during and after their stay in the institution. It is thereby distinguished from custodial care, where inmates are forced or allow themselves to be taken care of. When inmates stand in a dependent relationship to authority, as in custodial institutions, routine management tasks can be carried out most conveniently; for example, menus, time schedules, and work assignments can be handled by administrative fiat if no need for residents to direct their own affairs is recognized.

Residential treatment, however, assumes that clients are to be encouraged to exercise and maximize their autonomy in the institution so that they may learn to cope better with the world outside. Thus, one of the central problems in residential treatment is to maintain the press toward resident autonomy in the face of powerful countervailing forces for institutional conformity.

There are special problems, moreover, in encouraging autonomy among residents who have been placed in institutions because of antisocial behavior. Such inmates tend to mistrust opportunities for independent action when offered and refuse them; or if they accept them, they exploit the opportunities to repeat past delinquent patterns. To help such clients exercise autonomy in a socially adaptive way involves much more than simply handing over to them more power to control their lives in the institution. It involves sustained relations and intervention by personnel trained in special techniques for introducing residents to new goals and processes of autonomous functioning. This training was a central focus of the research-demonstration project.

Great differences existed in the attitudes and performance of the workers in the custodial sphere. Two of the four workers, young counselors in their early twenties, who were also part-time college students, proved to be more permissive than the other two, a middle-aged female worker (a secretary in the school) and an older Negro male worker in his thirties, also a college graduate. Their differences persisted over several months of weekly meetings, although all the workers did become more aware of differing orientations toward custodial problems.

2. "World Health Organization Report" (1953), p. 17, par. 4.1.1., quoted in Morris Schwartz and Charlotte Green Schwartz, *Social Approaches to Mental Patient Care* (New York: Columbia University Press, 1964).

The research team that conducted this study emphasized in the meetings with the workers the possibilities for creating a more therapeutic milieu by enabling the youngsters to formulate and implement goals through more efficient organization. Although the workers recognized the therapeutic potential in enabling youngsters to carry out indigenous goals, there was, actually, very little persistent activity initiated by the workers in goal attainment.

We became impressed by the realization that in addition to recognizing the importance of autonomous peer goals in the cottage, the workers themselves would have to be skilled at formulating goals and plans with these inadequate youngsters. We then realized that the research team would also have to be much more explicit about the steps and components in the process of goal formulation and implementation.

Often the cottage living units are very restricted in developing their own goals because the counselors are unable to negotiate effectively with the institution. Moreover, the residents have to be stimulated by the workers to develop their own goals and then the worker has to help the youngsters negotiate with each other and the larger system to implement them.[3] The totalistic character of residential institutions leaves little "space" open for counselors and residents to exercise initiative and autonomy in formulating and implementing indigenous goals.

Our previous research indicates that counselors generally emphasize the custodial role. This emphasis upon carrying out rules and regulations can detract from fashioning a therapeutic milieu in the cottage. When counselors define their role essentially as maintaining order and overseeing routines, little "local initiative" is expended in enabling the residents to make other spheres of cottage life a more gratifying experience. If youngsters could be stimulated and taught how to develop and implement their own goals, we believe that the custodial sphere would diminish in importance. The counselor's central role should be to enable the residents to assume more self-direction over their life situation. Custodialism becomes less an issue if there are significant activities in the cottage organized by the youngsters for which they are taking responsibility.

We broadened and converged upon the concept of goal-oriented activity as the chief vehicle for promoting resident group autonomy

3. Paul Daniel Sivadon, "Techniques of Sociotherapy," *Psychiatry*, 20 (1957), 205-10.

ın the cottage living situation. We gradually realized that it would be possible for youngsters to be engaged much more in a self-directed group process in all of the functional spheres of cottage life, provided they could become more skilled and responsible for formulating and implementing group goals that could become their own. This we envisaged as the heart of our treatment approach.

The Peer Group As a Vehicle for Autonomous Goal Activity

The main thrust of our present work is to redefine the role of cottage workers. Specifically, we are interested in how they can carry out their responsibilities through resident group activity and shared goals. Group confrontation, we feel, provides a testing ground for common needs and interests, goal formulation, and strategies for reaching goals. For one thing, many of the kinds of problems that residents will be confronted with on discharge from the institution will arise in a group context and call for group solutions. For another, these adolescents tend to be suspicious of adult authority and are prone to express themselves in antisocial activity. The peer group helps to mobilize and sustain their anti-authority posture.

The skill that counselors have to develop, therefore, is mobilizing the strengths of the group toward constructive goals and processes rather than delinquency and yet not being trapped into a repressive authority role.

As a theoretical problem of attitude change, our goal may be seen in terms of Herbert Kelman's theory.[4] Change, in our view, should not rest with external conformity, or compliance, in Kelman's terms. Nor should it be ultimately based on identification with the superordinate. Our concept of autonomy assumes another psychological basis for the residents' performance—internalization. That is, residents may also perform according to the values of the adults in the institution because the adults' values and goals coincide or are complementary with the residents' own value system. The thrust of our project is premised on this social-psychological basis. We are concerned with how residents can internalize new values and ways of behaving that are part and parcel of their own developing philosophy and value system.

4. Herbert C. Kelman, "Compliance, Identification, and Internationalization: Three Processes of Attitude Change," *Journal of Conflict Resolution*, 2 (1958), 51-60.

Phases and Components of Autonomous Group Functioning

In thinking about the central problem of how counselors can encourage youngsters to take more initiative over their lives in the cottage and institution, we become concerned with specifying the methods that can be used by counselors and residents in approaching and articulating a problem, interest, or need and devising plans to cope effectively with an issue. We sought to distinguish the components of the group process that culminates in goal attainment. As we did so, it occurred to us that this component analysis could serve as a device for workers to approach the key problem of fostering resident autonomy in the process of goal-oriented activities. A scheme was devised from the literature and our experimentation in the cottage on group goal processes, ranging from the initial problem encountered to evaluation of the outcome. Below is a description of each of these subprocesses relevant to carrying out group goal-oriented activities.

In order for a group to work on a problem or issue, communication channels have to be established and members convened so that they can talk to one another. This is what we mean by *convening the members.*

We think the following sources of group action can be reworked by the group into a goal perspective. "Needs" refers to individual or group psychological pressures—the internal condition of the group members. "Interests" refers to more objective concerns, for example, leisure-time activities that cottage members are attracted to. "Problems" refers to difficulties and frustrations in the living situation.

Needs, interests, and problems when shared by a group result in a kind of *group diagnosis*, so that the issue is further clarified and defined in the minds of the initiating members and the rest of the group.

The third step entails converting the need, interest or problem into a *shared concrete realizable goal.*

This is followed by *developing a plan and formulating strategies* for reaching the goal. A next logical step is defining and *allocating roles and tasks among the group members* to carry out the plan to attain the group goal. Some kind of differentiation of tasks and roles occurs.

Essentially, we view goal attainment as a boundary exchange process. In order for the cottages to formulate and carry out goals of its own, they have to negotiate with the institution to *procure necessary resources* for implementation that only it can provide. Furthermore, if the cottage is to become more autonomous, it will have to secure permission from the institution to broaden the scope of its responsibilities. This too is a matter of *negotiation with the institution.* Hence, we make the distinction between securing resources and negotiating with the external authority structure to increase the latitude for autonomous goal-functioning.

The phrase "carrying out goal activities" means actual *implementation of the goal.* We can distinguish this phase, actual implementation, from the preparatory activities of setting goals and planning strategies.

The next phase or component, *evaluation*, consists of workers' and residents' talking about and assessing what they have done. Evaluation may be used also to discuss how the next activity can be more efficiently or effectively implemented.

The components discussed above emphasize the instrumental activities in consummating group goals. We are well aware that working at goals sparks all kinds of feelings and attitudes. Thus, we also directed our attention to the *integration* sphere—the informal, expressive dimension of group activity that we divided into three components: solidarity among the members, degree of commitment to the task and goal, and affect expressed during an activity.

We believe our process model of goal attainment sensitized the workers to the following issues: it is a comprehensive view of the process; it implies (although it is not fully clarified at this stage of our research) a sequence of steps in goal attainment; it obligates the worker to bear in mind both the residents' and his own contribution to the entire process; it places a boundary around each activity so that it can be analyzed in itself as well as in relationship to subsequent activities that can lead to the attainment of a goal; it implies varying emphases of the component steps in the development of a goal-oriented activity and between different kinds of activities; it helps locate specifically in the process where difficulties arise.

The Cottage Worker's Tasks in Fostering Peer-Group Autonomy

Our research evaluation of autonomous resident goal attainment postulates three main dimensions[5] that can be visualized in their

5. For an analysis of these three action dimensions—depth, progression, and breadth—in the development of individual autonomy, see Andras Angyal,

interrelationships as follows (the mnemonic phrase, *C DIGS ARNIE I* comprises the components in goal attainment):

Figure 1. Three Dimensions of Autonomous Goal Attainment.

Dimensions — The Components of Goal formulation and Implementation

Depth:	C	DI	G	S	A	R	N	I	E	I
	O	A	O	T	L	E	E	M	V	N
Degree of	N	G	A	R	L	S	G	P	A	T
autonomy	V	N	L	A	O	O	O	L	L	E
exercised by	E	O		T	C	U	T	E	U	G
peers	N	S	F	E		R	I	M	A	R
	I	I	O	G	.	C	A	E	T	A
	N	S	R	Y		E	T	N	I	T
	G		M		O	S	I	T	O	I
			U		F		O	A	N	O
			L				N	T		N
			A		R			I		
			T		O			O		
			I		L			N		
			O		E					
			N		S					

Progression: Degree of extension of an activity (consummation)

Breadth: Degree of cumulative goal attainment and autonomy with diverse cottage activities

The system principle of cottage life that underlies our theoretical orientation is the double dynamic pattern in group life formed by two major trends: The trend toward specification, formulation, and attainment of group goals, and the involvement of the residents in the process to enhance their individual and group autonomy. These trends divide and subdivide and branch out from very general into more specific attitudes and skills toward shared group goals. These tendencies interact with the opportunities and contraventions presented by the institutional environment.

The domain in which the goal-attainment sphere of cottage life processes are distributed and arranged has three dimensions. The dimension of progression implies a teleological or means-ends organization, each phase being the end for the preceding and the means for the following phase. In studying these sequences, the practitioner (and researcher, for that matter) has a certain choice

"Personality as an Organized Whole," in Angyal, *Neurosis and Treatment: A Holistic Theory* (New York: Wiley, 1965), pp. 48-51.

in the size of the parts and phases that are to be considered. But the internal articulation of the process is determined by the nature of the goal, the timing and pace in order to attain it, its complexity, etc.

The dimension of depth is designed to help us focus specifically on the quality and extent of initiation and participation in the goal activity by the resident. We call it "depth" because it is a trend that leads from potentiality to actuality and is formed by individual members in their increasingly individualized elaboration of group skills which come to the surface and are expressed by manifest behavior that becomes accessible to direct observation. The arrangement of this vertical or depth structure is a concretization or partial manifestation of responsibility and decision-making, obligation assumption, and feeling of solidarity, etc., that residents are willing to express toward one another, the staff, and the institution in becoming integral parts of institutional life.

In addition to differentiating activities on a means-ends and consummation continuum and "depth-to-surface" quality of participation by the residents, the dimension of breadth in the cumulative development of the culture of cottage life is concerned with the build-up of more complex processes and activities upon simpler editions. Perhaps the key principle underlying this dimension is the residents' increased skill in co-ordinating their various abilities and interests to attain more complex group goals and evolve cottage solidarity.

These dimensions represent principal aspects of the cumulative development of a cottage culture based upon the ways in which the cottage organizes itself to meet individual and group problems, interests, and needs. Long-range personal and group goals are organized by many diverse activities into a hierarchy of superordinate and subordinate goals and consist of the co-ordination of cumulative multiple efforts along the progression, depth, and breadth dimensions.

The Cottage Worker's Dilemma

The child-care worker, confronting these major foci of our orientation—autonomy and goal attainment—inevitably comes face to face with a dilemma. Shall he emphasize progression along the phases that culminate in attainment of complex goals, "production," in the language of the marketplace? Or, shall he emphasize

Figure 2. The Cottage Worker's Grid.

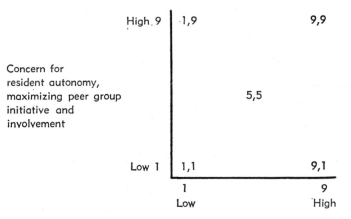

the resident group's autonomy in the process? The dilemma may be schematized as shown in Figure 2.[6]

Theoretically, six major types of worker's orientations can be postulated as well as numerous mixed types. Orientations also vary according to developmental phase, pressures exerted upon the cottage, residents' and staff's skills and personalities, etc. 1,1 is characterized by low concerns in both areas—the transitory, uninvolved worker who is in the cottage, not really part of it, and wants either a sinecure or cannot wait to leave; 9,1 gets things done, often primarily in the custodial sphere, by imposing his authority; 1,9 characterizes the overly permissive, non-directive counselor who believes in "order out of chaos"; 5,5 goes halfway in both concerns; and, 9,9 manifests skill in both planning for complex goals and strategies and thinking through imaginatively how to motivate and inspire the residents in the process.

Frequently we have noted "pendulum swings" from 1,9 to 9,9 approaches, alternate periods of crises and calm. Workers often manifest not only a major orientation but a "back-up style" for varying situations.

We have also noted that a 9,9 orientation can be better approximated when the worker has thought through an initiation plan as well as continuity projections of the goal components as the group is mobilized to implement a peer-group activity.

6. This formulation is indebted to Robert R. Blake and Jane S. Mouton, *The Managerial Grid* (Houston, Texas: Gulf Publishing, 1964).

We still have much to learn about the relationship of these two concerns and the varying orientations that result from their integration or lack of it. Limited application of the above theoretical orientation has also revealed an intermediate stage of group conflict related to the varying interests, skills, motivation, and personality strengths of cottage members. We have been able to identify "positive," "neutral," and "resistant" (or "negative") factions in the course of a series of goal activities and have begun to think through strategies for converting stultifying conflict into a positive force for increasing peer-group autonomy through cumulative goal-attainments.

Experience to Date and the Future

We have been experimenting for about a year with this model of resident autonomy in an Intermediate cottage at Hawthorne Cedar Knolls School. The boys are between fourteen and sixteen years of age. One of our first decisions was to expand the staff in the cottage from three to five counselors: four young men in their mid-twenties with B.A.'s or several years of college and a young woman with a B.A. degree. The counselors reported regularly several times during the week to the two researchers (the authors of this book). In addition, the counselors filled out a schedule[7] which in a gross way indicated the relative initiative and involvement of staff and counselors in the components of the group-autonomy model over the course of several projects to which each counselor was primarily attached.

A number of activities were organized with varying degrees of resident involvement: participation in a bowling league, a guitar and singing group (that got as far as a recording studio), remodeling parts of the cottage, social activities, tournaments, and various other athletic and recreational programs.

Three substantial obstacles were never overcome: difficulties in the custodial sphere—getting the boys to conform to standard institutional rules and regulations, generation of sustained motivation for the youngsters to persist in an indigenous activity, and lack of resources. We also felt that the counselors were unsuccessful in creating a significantly trustful climate in the cottage. We now believe that much more intensive pre-service and in-service training programs were necessary to train the counselors in group methods and institutional confrontation.

7. See Figure 3 for sample rating scale.

Figure 3. Sample Rating Scale for Each Component in Goal Attainment.*

a. Overt Behavior

b. Relative Attention

9	8	7	6	5	4	3	2	1
Practically the only process		Major but not only process		Notable but not major process		Occasional attention to this process		Almost none of this process

c. Boys versus Staff Impetus

9	8	7	6	5	4	3	2	1
Boys' impetus alone; no staff help		Mostly boys' impetus; little staff direction		Staff and boys equal in impetus		Mostly staff's impetus; boys follow directions		Staff impetus alone; boys take little part

d. Success or Failure

9	8	7	6	5	4	3	2	1
Nearly complete success		Mostly successful		Partial success; partial failure		Mostly failed		Nearly complete failure

e. Problems

* See Figure 1 for list of components.

The other major deficiency of the program was lack of basic involvement, co-operation, and commitment to the demonstration program by the administration. We mistakenly believed that it would be possible to experiment in one cottage and demonstrate our methods to the administration. Actually, we became unduly isolated from the institution. There was a constant lack of re-sources, conflicting supervision, and distortion of difficulties in the custodial sphere. The institution was not able to create meaningful opportunities that could be exploited by counselors' and residents' collective efforts.

It is our feeling that the introduction of an action program for fostering resident autonomy in an institutional setting demands much more extensive commitment by the administration. It may be possible to introduce change of some kinds in a fragmented man-ner, but the program that we envisioned required much more commitment by the entire institution. Such involvement could only be won by engaging all staff across hierarchical lines in co-operatively exploring how to design an institution that can afford opportunities for creative group efforts by residents and counselors in the basic living units.

Such thoroughgoing discussions on the basic purposes and meth-odology for restructuring the cottage living unit to foster autonomy could perhaps be initiated by methods pioneered by the National Training Laboratory.[8] The philosophy and practical techniques developed by the National Training Labs, in creating a trustful climate and specific procedures for feed-back and promotion of helping relationships between individuals and groups among all strata in the institution, could possibly open up new avenues of institutional living. Top-echelon staff especially have to be drawn into redesigning their social system to maximally expand the op-portunities for autonomy among personnel at all levels as well as the residents. The combination of NTL sensitivity training pro-grams and our process model of building autonomy through group goal attainment could very well usher in a new era in milieu therapy.

The cottage is an important battleground for mediating the self-oriented impulses of the residents and the requirements of a com-munity. Control of residential behavior by superordinates operates here as within every social system. However, the core of cottage life need not lie predominantly in the sphere of custodial controls.

8. See Leland P. Bradford, Jack R. Gibb, and Kenneth D. Benne, *T-Group Theory and Laboratory Method* (New York: Wiley & Sons, Inc., 1964).

We must ask what is accomplished as a result of the custodial emphasis and the way in which custody is carried out. We must ask what is relevant not only for institutional stability but also what is serviceable in the living situation to the goal of treatment of the residents. Both counselors and residents have a strong vested interest in maintaining the custodial system, for it powerfully shapes the behavior of both groups. Workers' control of the residents involves substantial elements of their activity in the institution.

It is our belief that administrators have kidded themselves into believing that they can effectively transmit a new set of values, goals, and behavior to their resident population through custodial domination in their living situation. Furthermore, we do not believe that rehabilitation goals are substantially furthered by compartmentalizing custodial controls in the cottage and treatment in individual sessions with "commuter" therapists.

We recognize among these residents considerable conflict and apathy or indifference between self and cottage community. What we are interested in is how the staff can structure cottage life so that indifference and frustration can be worked through in social action. Hence, we are concerned with two key aspects of the resident's life—one centered on the self as a purposive individual and, the other, the degree of concordance with the goal-striving and style of living of cottage and institution (his "community").

In the perspective of our functional approach, we believe that the resident-care staff inadequately provided institutionalized means for the residents, individually and collectively, to internalize constructive societal values because of an overemphasis upon custody and individual counseling.

It is our contention that life in the cottage can become a therapeutic community if the child-care worker's role can be reconstructed so that he can guide a process in which youngsters can become more independent and autonomous in *their* community. We believe that this can come about only through knowledge of the residents' aspirations and enabling them to formulate concrete plans and specific strategies for individual and group goal attainment. We think the key to this process lies in knowledge and skill of goal formulation and social organization by guiding residents to assume more autonomy and responsibility in a community action program.

This radical redefinition of the resident-care worker's function with youth has many implications for the institution. A dynamic community-action program with the residents will call forth new demands upon the institution in the following areas: a focused revitalized training program for cottage-care workers; expanded resources and facilities in carrying out meaningful cottage and community programs; modification of internal institutional routines and procedures; and, if the skills of the residents can be sufficiently upgraded, much more participation by the residents in shaping the social, cultural, and administrative life of the institution.

Our major point is that a new role definition of child care ultimately hinges upon a new institutionalized relationship with the residents. Our emphasis is upon a community-action program in which residents are enabled to organize themselves more efficiently and independently to carry out group activities that are also intimately related to individual goals and that are acceptable by the institution.

It is our hope that a successful community-action program can help resolve essential conflicts between the residents' self-interests and community interests. We believe that older adolescent residents can attain the requisite skills and a more appropriate self-image to function as members of a community. At the same time, their energies could be harnessed to improve the quality of cottage and institutional life.

To significantly upgrade the child-care worker's job, three interrelated tasks are necessary: (1) A new concept of child-care work that transcends the custodial emphasis but does not deny its crucial importance; (2) a training program in which workers can develop practical group and community skills and a deeper theoretical understanding of working with residents so as to constantly increase their decision-making and autonomy; and (3) recruitment of more competent workers who can be trained to assume these new tasks in child care.

With personal specialization, the child-care worker's relationships with professional therapists, supervisors, and administrators would have to change. Authority would still be necessarily centralized, but more autonomy and decentralization could emerge for the cottage worker as a result of a more comprehensive resident-care function. This could occur only when the segmental, narrow organizational definition of custody is replaced by an orientation that accepts the rehabilitative efforts of group living and that entails much more skill and training than is now afforded cottage workers.

In summary: we feel that the crucial issue in residential treatment is enabling residents to become more autonomous and self-directive in their total living situation. Our approach addresses itself specifically to the processes of encouraging and developing resident autonomy through group goal attainment. We believe that this orientation has important implications for work with residents in other kinds of treatment settings. We want to unlock the process whereby groups of patients in an institution can be provided with the opportunities and taught the skills to become more responsible and autonomous and to assume more direction over their lives so that they can be better prepared to function with others in the outside community.

Appendixes

Appendix A. Cottage Event Observation Schedule

I Identifying Data

1-3	1. Observation period ....
4	2. Event no. ....
5-9	3. Date of observation ....
10-11	4. Staff member observed ....
12-13	5. Other staff on duty ....

6. Cottage group observed (check one)

14	.... 1.	Fairline
	.... 2.	Hearthstone
	.... 3.	Concord

7. Staff member focused on: (check one)

15	.... 1. Male professional
	.... 2. Female professional
	.... 3. Male non-professional
	.... 4. Female non-professional

8. Description of event

9. Duration of event   (check one)

.... 1. Less than ten seconds
.... 2. Ten seconds, less than thirty seconds
16   .... 3. Thirty seconds, less than one minute
.... 4. One minute, less than two minutes
.... 5. Two minutes, less than five minutes
.... 6. Five to ten minutes, natural end.
.... 7. Ten minutes, artificially ended.

10. Location of event   (check one)

.... 1. boy's room
17   .... 2. staff member's room or office
.... 3. public location inside cottage
.... 4. outside cottage in cottage area
.... 5. dining hall
.... 6. elsewhere; specify ....

11. Day of week   (check one)
18   .... 1. Monday   .... 5. Friday
.... 2. Tuesday   .... 6. Saturday
.... 3. Wednesday   .... 7. Sunday
.... 4. Thursday

12. Hour of day   (check one)
19   .... 1. 7- 8 A.M.
.... 2. 8- 9 A.M.
.... 3. 3- 4 P.M.
.... 4. 4- 5 P.M.
.... 5. 5- 6 P.M.
.... 6. 6- 7 P.M.
.... 7. 7- 8 P.M.
.... 8. 8- 9 P.M.
.... 9. 9-10 P.M.

II Situation Confronting Staff Member

13. Number of boys in staff member's "field"   (check one)
20   .... 1. 1   ....3. 3   ....5. 6- 8   ....7. more than 12
.... 2. 2   ....4. 4 or 5 ....6. 9-12   ....8. none.

14. Number of boys **actively confronting** staff member   (check one)
21   .... 1. 1   .... 5. 6-8
.... 2. 2   .... 6. 9-12
.... 3. 3   .... 7. More than 12
.... 4. 4 or 5   .... 8. None

15. Which of the following kinds of peer-group functions were the boys attempting to carry out in the situation?
22   .... 1. meeting institutional, staff requirements
.... 2. organizing for and carrying out peer-group or sub-group goals
.... 3. satisfying their own individual needs

.... 4. promoting harmonious relations among themselves
.... 5. none of the above
.... 0. d.k.

16. Degree of interaction among boys

23   .... 1. no interaction or interstimulation of one boy with another.
.... 2. co-acting aggregate
.... 3. interacting aggregate
.... 0. d.k.

17. What was the immediate object of boys' behavior

24   .... 1. other boy or boys
.... 2. staff member or members
.... 3. other person or persons
.... 4. physical environment
.... 0. d.k.

18. To which role system was the content of boys' behavior primarily released?

25   .... 1. (personality)
.... 2. cottage peer group or subgroup
.... 3. peer relationship outside cottage
.... 4. cottage staff
.... 5. school
.... 6. non-cottage recreation and athletics program
.... 7. therapy
.... 8. higher administrative staff
.... 9. boy-girl relations
.... 0. d.k.
.... X. not applicable (no social role related to content of boys' behavior.)

26   .... 1. family
.... 2. other;   specify ....

III   Staff Behavior

19. In general, how many boys at a time did the staff member address?

27   .... 1. one boy at a time
.... 2. two boys at a time
.... 3. three boys at a time
.... 4. four or five boys at a time
.... 5. six to eight boys at a time
.... 6. nine to twelve boys at a time
.... 7. more than twelve boys at a time
.... 8. no boys addressed by staff member

20. To which kind of function did the staff member address himself in dealing with the boys?

28   .... 1. meeting institutional, staff requirements
.... 2. organizing for and carrying out cottage group or subgroup goals

.... 3. satisfying individual boys' needs
.... 4. promoting harmonious relations among boys
.... 5. none of the above
.... 0. d.k.

21. What method of control did the staff member use in attempting to bring about adherence to staff norms?

29 .... 1. concrete reward or promise of reward
.... 2. symbolic reward
.... 3. neither reward nor punishment
.... 4. symbolic punishment
.... 5. concrete punishment or threat of punishment
.... 0. d.k.
.... X. not applicable (staff did not try to bring about adherence to staff norms)

22. In responding to boys' request did the staff member

30 .... 1. grant the request or requests fully?
.... 2. deny the request or requests completely?
.... 3. grant the request or requests in part, or grant a substitute for the original request?
.... 4. defer or delay a response or a decision on the request?
.... 5. refer the child to someone else with the request?
.... 6. ignore the requests?
.... 0. d.k.
.... X. not applicable (no requests)

23. Which of the following feeling tones was displayed by the staff member?

31 .... 1. matter-of-fact
.... 2. friendly, affectionate
.... 3. angry, irritable
.... 4. anxious or fearful
.... 5. sad, depressed
.... 6. happy, euphoric
.... 7. other; specify ....
.... 8. d.k.

24. How strongly was the feeling tone displayed?

32 .... 1. mild feeling
.... 2. moderate feeling
.... 3. strong feeling
.... 0. d.k.
.... X. not applicable

25. To which boys' role system was the content of the staff member's dealing with boys related?

33 .... 1. (personality)
.... 2. cottage peer group or subgroup
.... 3. peer relationship outside cottage

.... 4. cottage staff
.... 5. school
.... 6. non-cottage recreation and athletics program
.... 7. therapy
.... 8. higher administrative staff
.... 9. boy-girl relations
.... 0. d.k.
.... X. not applicable (no boys' role system related to content of staff member's behavior)

34 .... 1. family
.... 2. other; specify ....

26. What degree and mode of authority did the staff member take in relating to boys?

35 .... 1. dictatorial
.... 2. supervisory
.... 3. equal to boys
.... 4. subservient to boys
.... 0. d.k.
.... X. not applicable (staff member did not relate to boys)

27. How did the staff member evaluate boys' behavior?

36 .... 1. appropriate to the behavior?
.... 2. showing favoritism toward boy or boys in the event
.... 3. discriminating against boy or boys in the event
.... 0. d.k.
.... X. not applicable (no evaluation of behavior)

28. What was the basis of the standards mentioned by the staff member for his actions, decisions, or evaluation? Was it based on the desires, needs, capacities, power of

37 .... 1. staff member himself
.... 2. other staff members particularly mentioned
.... 3. boy or boys directly dealt with
.... 4. other boy or boys particularly mentioned
.... 5. "staff" as an entity, or the institution
.... 6. boys in the cottage, or unit, or institution, as an entity
.... 7. in terms of physical resources
.... 8. in terms of larger societal or abstract moral standards
.... 0. d.k.
.... X. not applicable (no basis of standards mentioned)

29. (Code this item for first event in observation period only.) Did
38 the staff member spend the greatest proportion of time during the observation period
.... 1. in interaction with boys?
.... 2. in interaction with other cottage staff?
.... 3. in interaction with other persons?

.... 4. not in interpersonal interaction?

.... 0. d.k.

39   30. Observer's name ....

31. Time elapsed between end of observation period and recording of event

40   .... 1. less than 1 hour

.... 2. 1 hour, less than 2 hours

.... 3. 2 hours, less than 4 hours

.... 4. 4 hours, less than 8 hours

.... 5. 8 hours, less than 16 hours

.... 6. 16 hours, less than 24 hours

.... 7. 24 hours, or more

Appendix B. Observation Procedures

Procedure for Systematic Cottage Observation and Coding

A. *Sampling Observation* / We want to try to sample observation periods in such a way that the events we collect will reflect an accurate sampling of the impact of staff behavior on cottage residents. We will work from the unit or cottage supervisor's schedule of time during which each staff member is on duty. Some staff members are typically on duty in the evening whereas others are more often on duty during the morning; and there are certain staff members who work much more on weekends than others. Thus, we will inevitably have some staff members more likely to confront certain issues than others, for example, parents' visits on Sundays. We accept this fact of cottage life and ignore the hypothetical question of whether any staff member would behave differently if his schedule were different.

For a given staff member, our observation schedule will aim to represent the behavior of the staff member during the time for which he is responsible for child care. As for aggregating staff members to reflect the total staff impression on the cottage, we will get at this by scheduling an equal number of observation periods for each full-time staff member and half as many observations for a staff member in a cottage in which he worked half-time.

B. *Events* / An event consists of a social situation in which a staff member perceives or might be expected to perceive boys in the cottage for which he is responsible, and of his behavior toward them. The observer will go into the cottage at a prescribed time and seek out the staff member whom he is assigned to observe at that time. If that staff member is not on duty, his substitute will be selected if known. If this is not possible to determine, the observer will try to observe the staff member he has least recently observed in the past. Future observation schedules will not be changed. If the staff member is interacting with a boy or boys around an issue which the observer never comes to understand because he was not there when it started, he will not regard it as an event. If later, in the context of the discussion, the observer is able to reconstruct the situation which gave rise to the interaction he is observing, it may be recorded as an event.

If the staff member is not in a room with boys visibly interacting with them, the observer will wait until the staff member comes into contact with the boys, at which point the event will start. If the staff member is within a room or otherwise in close proximity to boys, or if there is some stimulus to which it would be considered appropriate for the staff member to respond and he does not, these circumstances should be treated as an event. "Appropriate circumstances" are instances of boys actively confronting the staff member, situations in which staff norms are being violated, or other circumstances when boys are clearly in need of attention, or help, even though there is no direct request.

The point of demarcation between one event and another will be indicated by a change in boys with whom the staff member is interacting, or by a change in function in the situation (item 15). If he is talking or being talked to by one boy and another boy joins them and takes an active part in the proceedings, the interaction should be treated as a new event at the point at which the second boy joined the dyad. If two boys are talking to a staff member and a third boy joins them it will not be treated as a new event. But if two boys are talking to a staff member and two more join, it will be treated as the beginning of another event when the two other boys join. The criterion is that the majority (meaning half or more) composition of the beginning group changes, or that the function changes. Also, for purposes of maintaining a sample which includes several events for each observation, after 10 minutes have elapsed after the beginning of an event, either during which a staff member has not interacted with boys or he has been interacting with the same boys, proceedings that follow will be treated as the beginning of a new event.

Every observation period should contain at least three events, if possible, but be no longer than 30 minutes. If the observer has been observing during a time when the staff member has been interacting with many boys, so that the observer feels he has all the events he can remember after 15 minutes, he may leave after 15 minutes. But an observation period should never be less than 15 minutes and should be less than 30 minutes only if the observer feels he can record six events for the period. If the staff member is not accessible for part of the observation period, the observer should try to remain until he has obtained the requisite number of events or observed the staff member for 30 minutes, even if not consecutively.

The code number of the observation period (each observation period will have its own code numbers assigned to it when observations are scheduled) should be recorded in the upper right-hand corner. The first event coded for the observation period should be given number 1, the second number 2, etc. No observation period should have more than nine events.

Item 3—the date of observation should be noted. Item 4—the observer should record the name of the staff member observed as given on the observation schedule. The names of other staff members known to be on duty even if not seen should be written in item 5.

Item 6—the cottage for which the staff member is responsible should be checked.

For purposes of item 7, a professional is defined as an individual who has received a graduate or undergraduate degree in a field of applied behavioral science.

Description of the event in item 8 should sketch circumstances that came to the staff member's attention and his response to the circumstances up to the point where he shifted his attention or his attention was diverted to another interpersonal situation.

Item 10—the predominant location of the event is the location in which the most significant proceedings of the event transpired.

Item 12—the hour of the day during which most of the event took place should be checked. Observation periods will not be scheduled before 7:00 A.M. or after 10:00 P.M.

Item 13—the number of boys in the staff member's "field" during the event refers to the number of boys who, during the larger part of the event, were physically close enough to the staff member, or were making sufficient noise, so that their behavior might reasonably be expected to impinge on the conscious awareness of the staff member. We are using the word "field" in the Lewinian sense, except that we try to operationalize it objectively.

Thus, we use the words "might reasonably be expected" to indicate that the observer should make his judgment of whether the other boys were loud enough or close enough so that "the average person," fictional though he may be, serves as the criterion of "reasonable expectation." This approach does differ from the Lewinian approach, in which, we take it, we would wait and see what the actor did before deciding what stimuli were impinging on him. We want to avoid this because we want to define the situation independently of the response of the staff member.

In item 14, we distinguish "active confrontation" from "field." An active confrontation is considered making or participating in a conscious move—probably but not necessarily verbal—to bring some matter to the staff member's attention.

For purposes of items 15 through 18, "boys in the situation" refers to those in the "active confrontation" (item 14) if there is such a confrontation. If there is no such confrontation, "boys in the field" (item 12) are taken as the "boys in the situation." For our purposes, the first alternative in item 15 will be taken to reflect the function of adaptation in the Parsonian scheme, taking the peer group as the system focused on, and expectations of staff members in the cottage or higher administrative staff as the external system with which the peer group comes to terms. The second alternative—working for or consummating group or subgroup goals—refers to activity pointed toward some state of affairs which is conceived as a shared aim of the total cottage group or smaller group of boys within the cottage. The third alternative—satisfying individuals' needs—refers to the satisfaction of individual personality needs and to motivations that may in fact be shared but not held forth as a collective goal as such. The fourth alternative—promoting harmonious relations among boys—reflects behavior whose function is deriving satisfaction from interpersonal association as such, in contrast with the second alternative, which represents more purely task-oriented working together.

At this point of coding, the first item in which behavior is categorized, it should be pointed out that in all behavioral categorization the observer should make an effort to select the one category that best describes the behavior in the event. However, in cases where the observer finds it impossible to make a choice, more than one category in the behavioral items may be coded.

Provision is also made in the behavioral items for a "don't know" (d.k.) check, for instances where the observer finds it impossible to make a judgment; it should never be one of multiple codes. Also, it should be distinguished from "not applicable" where the latter is an alternative. "Not applicable" should be reserved for instances where the kind of behavior relevant to the item is judged to have been absent in the event, whereas "don't know" refers to a circumstance in which the observer cannot make the relevant categorization.

In general, the "none of the above" category should be used when there does appear some functional behavior, but which is not related to the maintenance of the peer-group or individual personality systems, and the "don't know" category when the function is not apparent.

In coding item 15, the apparent function should be coded on the basis of evidence of satisfaction derived or likely to be derived as a consequence of the behavior. (See special instructions.)

In item 16, the first alternative, "no interaction or interstimulation" refers to behavior in which a boy or boys in the situation are each engaged in an activity on their own, i.e., where there are not other boys doing the same thing. A "co-acting aggregate" refers to boys who are doing the same kinds of things—several boys doing homework in each other's presence where they are aware, or might be expected to be aware, that there are other boys carrying on the same activity but where they are not really interacting in the same sense that one boy's response is not closely tied to an immediately preceding bit of behavior of another boy. This situation might be seen in a study hall where several boys are doing homework, or in an instance where several boys are cleaning up the cottage. Thus, this category refers to cases in which it appears that the boys serve as stimuli to each other in an indirect sense. Seeing other boys working on house jobs or doing homework undoubtedly does influence a boy to carry out his house job or do his homework but the way in which he does his house job or the homework he is doing may not be closely connected to the way in which the other boy is carrying out his behavior. A third alternative, "interacting aggregate," refers to interaction in the direct sense of give-and-take where one boy does a given task, say a co-operative house job, as a direct response to somebody else's task, i.e., two boys working together in a room where one boy is moving the furniture out of the way for another boy to polish the floor, the boy moving the furniture is doing it especially in order that the other boy may polish, and the other boy who polishes does so in a particular place just because the other boy has moved the furniture. A prototype of in interaction is an ordinary give-and-take conversation, in which there is some connection between what one person says and what somebody else said previously.

Item 17—"the immediate object of boys' behavior in the situation"—refers to the object to which the boy is addressing himself in the immediate situation, without considering his ultimate goal. In many cases this would be the object he is using as a means to an end. For example, he may be telling another boy what he thinks of a staff member. In that case, it would be the other boy who would be the immediate goal object.

In contrast with item 17, item 18 is an attempt to get at some assessment of the role-system reference related to issues dealt with by boys in the situation: whether they are primarily trying to work out conflicts within themselves (category 1), whether they are acting out relations within the cottage peer group (category 2), etc. Question 18 can be understood as an application of Robert Merton's concept of "status set," although we use the generic term "role." That is, every boy had different statuses and roles in relation to the institution and the outside world: one in relation to the peer group, another one in relation to cottage staff members, one as a student, one as a participant or non-participant in athletics, one in relation to his family, etc. In the sense that all behavior is goal-directed and, assuming that there is some significant social component in behavior we observe in the cottage, we are asking what is the primary system reference within which the boys are taking the roles which are apparent in the situation. Coding judgment should be based directly on content, not on inferences as to underlying processes, etc.

If a boy is talking about his personal feelings, category 1 is appropriate; if he is relating to the peer group in a manner appropriate to and not going outside that relationship, category 2 should be coded. If the boys are relating to a staff member and dealing with a matter not primarily outside their role relationship, category 4 should be coded. In general, then, if the content is related to the role relationship being enacted, that should be the basis for coding, but if the content is related to another role relationship, that relationship should be coded.

Before going to the third section on staff behavior, we should point out that all of section II, describing the situation, should be coded independently of staff response to that behavior. The observer, as an objective human being, should make the assessment from the point of view of the physical position of the staff member, but he should not allow observations or inferences about the staff member's psychological state to influence the description of the situation.

Item 19 refers to the staff member's selectivity in relation to item 13. Given the boys in the field, did the staff member try to include all boys or even bring more boys into the field, did he deal with the boys who were present in the field, or did he select from that group a smaller number of boys to deal with?

Similarly, item 20 should be seen in relation to item 15. Given the functional situation, toward what functions did the staff member address himself? If the staff member did not respond in terms of functions impinging on the peer group, but rather in terms of his own personal or some other requirements, alternative 5 should be coded, but if the observer is unable to determine the function, alternative 6 is appropriate.

Item 21, method of control, refers to the extent to which a staff member makes explicit the consequences of adherence or non-adherence to staff expectations as well as whether sanctions applied are positive or negative. This broadly includes any evaluation of boys' behavior to the extent that it is labeled good (praised, which is equivalent to symbolic reward) or bad (symbolically punished).

Question 22 attempts to assess whether the request or requests were fully granted, whether it was completely denied, or what method of circumventing either of the former two was used. The alternative "ignore the request" is applicable in cases where the observer is judged to have been aware of a request but did not respond and would include a case where a staff member talked about something else—that is, did not ignore the child but ignored the request itself. The reference point is the situation of *physical* reality—a request is "granted" if the staff member did what he could at the time to grant it. However, a boy's request to be exempted from rules, if turned down, is a denial nonetheless. Similarly, a promise to do something in the future is a delay if it seems objectively possible for the staff to act now. If the promise is objectively the most that the staff member *can* do at present, it should be regarded as "granting fully," though the boys may not perceive it as such.

Item 23. The observer should rate the overt feeling tone expressed by the staff member. This is our effort to get at pure feeling underlying our response. It is especially important to emphasize here that the observer should be oriented toward direct evidence. For example, anger should be indicated by a look of anger or a tone of anger or hostile words but not by how the observer thinks the staff member should feel given the circumstances.

In item 24, the objective standard should also be emphasized; the staff member's observed typical mode of response should *not* be taken into account here. The observer might feel or think that a staff member, who normally expressed no feeling, had very strong feelings when he displayed only a moderate feeling, but if he displays moderate feelings, "moderate" should be the alternative checked.

Item 25 should be seen in relation to item 18. That is, given the context of the roles which the boys assumed or were acting out with the situation, did the staff member deal with problems related to just those role relationships, did he select from among them and deal with a portion of the role systems which were in the context of the situation, or did he deal with role relationships which were not previously expressed in the situation? Here again the possibility that the staff member dealt with a conflicting or related roles means that it will be meaningful in some cases to check more than one alternative for this question. In general, the same instructions for coding item 18 are applicable here.

Item 26 requires the judgment of the staff member's assertion of power *vis-à-vis* the boys in the situation. What is important here is for the observer to make the rating independently of any judgment as to the appropriateness of a given kind of behavior in relation to the situation. "Dictatorial" means a commanding mode of relating without any softening or attempt to disguise the fact that the staff member was telling the children how to behave. "Supervisory" refers to a mode of relating in which the staff member does not overtly command; that is, he phrases the direction in the form of a request or a suggestion, but it is clear that he is in a position of authority over the boys. The third alternative, the staff member's adopting a position of equality, is indicated by the absence of behavior by which the staff member expressed his authority position. A prototype of this situation would be one in which the observer would not be able to judge from a description of the staff member's behavior whether it was a staff member or a boy engaging in that behavior. The fourth alternative indicating subservience to boys would be indicated by a situation where the staff member seemed not his own master but rather controlled by the boys, or buffeted around by their requests, demands, or behavior.

In item 27, the observation of whether certain boys received special treatment from the staff member should be evaluated on the basis of the general standards for a boy's behavior in the institution. However (and here is the only exception to the principle of using an external standard of objectivity in coding), if a given staff member is known to have especially high standards in some area—cleanliness for example—then his requiring a boy or boys to come up to this standard would not be regarded as discrimination, provided he enforced this standard among all boys.

Item 28 aims at recording any explicit reference made by the staff member to the source of the standards he uses in his actions, decisions, or evaluation. This is a more explicitly elaborated way of getting at some of the kinds of things aimed at question 24, but such explicit data may be less frequently observed; the residual category 8 will more often be coded here because there will be many cases in which the source of the standards are not clearly articulated.

For the first event in each observation period, the observer should indicate, in item 29, the staff member's predominant activity during the total time span of the observation.

The observer should record his name in item 30. In item 31 he should indicate when he finished coding the observation on the schedule.

Elaboration of Instructions for Coding Functions of Boys' Behavior and Function to which Staff Members Address Themselves— Items 15 and 20 of Systematic Observation Schedule.

Since this part of the analysis of staff-child interactions centers around classifying boys' behavior and staff behavior according to the function it serves in relation to the peer-group system, it is important that we try to achieve the highest reliability possible in this coding. At the same time, we recognize that the problems of coding these functions are extremely difficult.

Accordingly, in this area we shall try to set down in some detail examples of behavior that can be placed in each category, along with some of the reasoning underlying the categorization.

A. *Functions of Boys' Behavior.* / Here we are dealing with question 15—the assessment of the functions being carried out in the boys' behavior before the staff member intervenes in each event. The first category, "meeting institutional, staff requirements," includes all those actions which, in the observer's judgment, the boys are carrying out because they are required to do so by the staff member or institutional regulations. This includes maintaining institutionally acceptable standards of personal cleanliness and room cleanliness; it also includes carrying out assigned tasks within the cottage—"house jobs." It also includes meeting the expectations of segments of the institution other than the cottage, for example: homework, attending religious services, work in the dining hall alcove, keeping one's psychotherapy appointments, carrying out tasks assigned as punishment by higher administrative authority.

Boys' behavior in response to staff members' requests should also be put in this category when the requests of the staff members are related to fulfilling institutional goals, even when the procedures for boys to pursue these goals are not prescribed. Thus, if a staff member asks a child to do him a favor and empty a waste basket, even though it is not that boy's job, or if the staff member asks a boy to carry out some function of the staff member's duties— for example, waking another boy—we regard the goal as adapting to external requirements of the institution; boys' compliance with these requests are coded in category 1.

The second category, "organizing for and carrying out cottage group or subgroup goals," refers to attempts by the boys to plan for, assign roles in, and carry out activities that are primarily directed toward ends which are shared by the cottage as a whole or by some subgroup within the cottage—gardening, when it proceeds beyond general care of the grounds; attempts by a room of boys to refurbish their room, when their attempts go beyond normal cottage maintenance expected of everyone; participation in cottage athletics; working to get out a newspaper; having a meeting to plan a party.

Boys' satisfaction of their own individual needs, a third category, includes meeting such basic needs as eating and getting food, personal grooming above and beyond institutional requirements, and the satisfaction of personality needs: seeking approval, venting aggression, self-disparagement, autocratic behavior which is primarily self-enhancing rather than goal-directed.

The fourth alternative—"promoting harmonious relations among themselves"—refers to behavior in which boys are attempting to establish solidarity with other individuals or within the total cottage group, as an end in itself. Generally, joking among boys, expressions of approval of one boy for another, expressions of cottage spirit, and gossiping about other cottages belong in this category. Also appropriate here are instances where aggression is expressed among a subgroup against another subgroup or individual within the cottage, when the observer judges that the primary function of this behavior is the promotion of good feeling within the subgroup.

Since the greatest problems of coding arise when there are elements of each function in a situation, and the observer is expected to make a choice of what is primary, we shall offer some guidelines about the selection of alternatives.

Suppose, on the surface, behavior seems to be related to carrying out institutional or staff requirements or expectations. If a boy is simply doing what all boys are expected to do by staff and no more—that is, there is no evidence that he is doing it because he himself enjoys it, or because the cottage group or subgroup has made some investment in this goal, then it is to be coded simply as category 1. If he appears to be getting some personal satisfaction out of it but is still primarily doing it because he is expected to do it, the first alternative is still appropriate. However, if he seems to be deriving a great deal of personal satisfaction from the activity or if he is going far beyond the expectations of the institution in general or staff members in particular, then it should be regarded as satisfying his individual needs, category 3. If there is evidence to show that his behavior is primarily based on the achievement of some cottage goal—for example, if the boy or boys indicate that their cleaning up will make their own cottage more attractive than some other cottage, it is appropriately coded as category 2.

Another possibility is that there will be joking or talking in the course of carrying out required tasks. If the boys are primarily working and joking incidentally, category 1 is appropriate. However, if they are primarily talking and playing around and only incidentally doing a little work, category 4 is appropriate. The observer should take into consideration the intensity with which the boys are applying themselves to the job and the actual work which is getting done as evidence for choosing category 1; the absence of constructive accomplishment, plus the amount and intensity and interest in fooling around or the feeling of just being one of the boys should be taken as evidence for category 4. However, be careful not to assume that a particular activity automatically falls in a particular category by its very nature. We have said that cleaning up, maintenance of the cottage, etc., normally falls in category 1, whereas some cottage athletic activities, planning for an auction, going on trips, if there is no contradictory evidence, are similarly assumed to fall in category 2. However, a staff member may feel that all boys or particular boys in the cottage should engage in certain activities—athletics, gardening, newspaper —which are not specifically requirements of the institution for every boy to participate in. Where boys are engaged in these activities and there is evidence that they are primarily engaging in the activity in order to satisfy the staff member rather than because they have internalized the goal as a group, the behavior should be placed in category 1. And, if the boy gives evidence that his primary aim in engaging in group activity is some personal need to lord it over other boys or achieve recognition for himself, then the behavior is appropriately placed in category 3. Finally, if the athletic endeavor is directed not so much toward attaining a goal, that is, winning a game, but if there is considerable fooling around or the game is being played in such a way that the observer judges the group experience rather than the goal is an end in itself, category 4 is appropriate.

In category 3, a boy's statement of a personal desire, behavior which can be viewed only as satisfying some pathological motive and not falling into any other category such as provoking aggression, would be coded here. However, if the observer judges that a boy, who is simply brushing his teeth or engaging in other routine personal matters, is doing so in order to please staff rather than because he has a personal desire to be clean, then have this behavior placed in category 1. We shall be arbitrary in saying that taking care of one's person, in the absence of other evidence, is satisfying an individual need, whereas taking care of rooms and doing house jobs is meeting institutional requirements. We should emphasize that we are talking here about prima facie evidence which may be overruled if the observer sees evidence which would indicate the contrary. A boy who draws for his own pleasure would, in the absence of other evidence, be seen as satisfying an individual need. However, if he is doing the particular drawing as part of a cottage project—say publicity for a cottage party—then this would be placed in category 2. Similarly, if he were drawing a chart for house jobs at the staff member's request, this behavior would be placed in category 1. The rule is that the specific behavior being categorized should be seen in the light of the functional scheme. That is, apart from the general interests, if he is at the moment drawing a schedule of house jobs rather than something else, the function of this is meeting institutional requirements.

On the surface, what is ostensibly any informal joking or discussion without an ostensible goal belongs in category 4 in the absence of contrary evidence. However, if meeting staff expectations is the goal of the discussion, it should be placed in category 1. If some cottage group or subgroup is central to the discussion, the discussion may be instrumental to attainment of the goal and category 2 is appropriate. A discussion about baseball in a cottage living room might fall in categories 2, 3, or 4, although it is not likely to fall in category 1. If the discussion was about the cottage's own baseball team, where discussion centered around who had done what in a previous game or how the team might be improved, it would belong in category 2. If it developed into a contest among boys in which each was trying to show the other that he knew more than the other boy, it would belong in category 3, and if it was the more usual friendly chat about scores, team standings, it would belong in category 4. Some friendly disagreement might be considered appropriate and within the realm of still promoting harmonious relations, category 4; however, if the behavior is more disruptive than conducive toward promoting harmonious relations, it would be seen as satisfying individual needs. Finally, it should be noted that some kinds of behavior may not fit any of the above categories. For example, boys fulfilling requirements or expectations growing out of some completely non-institutional relationship—doing something because their parents required them to, for example—would belong in category 5.

B. Function to Which Staff Member Addresses Himself. / The first most general judgment that the observer should make in coding the function which the staff member addresses himself to, item 20, is whether he proceeds along the lines of the function to which the boys are addressing themselves or whether he focuses on something else.

If the boys are working at house jobs and the staff member addresses the boys with reference to that task—commending, or criticizing, making suggestions for improvement—we would see his behavior as further promoting the function the boys were addressing themselves to and it should be coded category 1. For purposes of this item, we generally take staff requirements as the announced standards of the staff member, making no judgment about whether his perception of expectations conforms with larger institutional expectations. From the point of view of the boys, the staff member has the power to interpret institutional requirements; since higher authorities back up the individual staff member's judgment, that is delegate authority to him, his judgment may be said to be the institutional expectation in matters relevant to institutional goals.

The staff member's function may be seen as a facilitating role in relation to organizing for and carrying out group or subgroup goals. The goal in this case is one which the boys have themselves set; the staff member provides information, advice, or physical resources to enable the boys to carry it through.

In satisfying individual boys' needs, the staff member will be addressing himself to meeting some wish or unexpressed need which a boy himself has. Giving support or advice or something material to an individual which has nothing to do with the boys' needs is placed in category 3.

As for category 4, the staff member may promote harmonious relations by contribution to a discussion that is not goal-directed by telling a joke to two or more boys. We assume that friendly behavior directed toward a group of boys has not only the function of establishing a relationship of individual boys with the staff member but, when boys are having a good time together as a result of the staff member's behavior, we assume the consequence to be integrative solidarity among the boys. In category 5, none of the above will be behavior which is selfish on the part of the staff member but serves no use from the point of view of the boys, or behavior which, as in item 15, derives from some other system. Selfish behavior would be making fun of a boy or getting the boy to do something which is clearly for the staff member's convenience but has nothing to do with institutional goals. For example, the staff member who got a boy to wash his car when it was clear that this satisfied not even an individual need of the boy would be in this category.

Now let us go back and deal with marginal situations that might fall in one category or the other and see if we can arrive at some means for distinguishing them, as we did in item 15. Let us consider the case of a staff member coaching a baseball team. This kind of activity on the surface would probably belong in category 2. However, if the staff member is insuring conformance to a norm of having a good team when the boys appeared not to be that dedicated, if he indicated that he saw his job as making the best baseball team possible for the cottage, his behavior would belong in category 1. However, if he used the coaching as an opportunity to help boys meet their individual needs, for example indicating to a boy that he would feel better if he could get a hit or succeed, or indicating to another boy that learning from this experience would help in his occupational aspirations to be a professional ballplayer, we would consider it falling in category 3. If the staff member was not concerned with the goal as such but saw the game as an opportunity to help the boys relate positively to each other by making jokes, not taking mistakes seriously but rather focusing on the boys being on good terms with each other in a tense situation, the behavior would fall in category 4. Finally, if he indicated that his paramount interest was in winning the game because it would bring him prestige as the coach of a cottage which had a good ball team, his behavior would fall in category 5.

In the area of carrying out institutional requirements, the staff member who facilitates, enforces, encourages the boys to do the things mentioned above as belonging in the category, is normally considered to be behaving in a way falling in category 1. However, if he tries to couch the task in terms of the satisfaction a boy will achieve from doing the job, category 3 is appropriate as well as category 1. If he mentions the boys' needs as even more important than getting the job done, or if the staff member otherwise indicates that he is not so much concerned about the job itself but about the therapeutic effect on the boys, then category 3 is more appropriate. If his primary attention is focused on getting the cottage as a group to internalize the standards of the institution as a basis for carrying out some institutionally expected behavior, then category 2 is appropriate as well as category 1; and if the staff member shows greater concern about the boys' accepting the job as a group goal and less concern about getting the job done, category 2 is appropriate alone. If the staff member makes a game out of the job, the observer should try to judge whether the staff member is simply joking a bit because he sees that as an effective way to get the institutional expectations met. In this case only category 1 is appropriate. However, if he makes a game out of it in such a way as to indicate that the good feeling among boys associated with the cooperative adaptation to institutional expectations is as important as meeting expectations themselves, then both 1 and 4 should be checked. If the game, as a result of the staff member's behavior, becomes more salient than the job itself, where the staff member does not try to refocus attention on the job to be done, category 4 alone is appropriate.

Where a boy is expressing some matter of concern to him and the staff member attempts to cope with it as the expression of an individual need, or without the boy's requesting it, the staff member attempts to meet some need which he perceives the boy to have, and the behavior is appropriately placed in category 3. A criterion of meeting an individual need is not that other boys do not have similar needs but how the staff member deals with it. The staff member's response, whether the need is expressed individually or as a group, should be judged on the basis of whether he treats the needs one by one or as a collective. A group of boys may get together to try to persuade a staff member to change his policy about home visits, in which case we would see their confrontation as a group goal. However, if the staff member takes the boys one by one and discusses the particular considerations about his home visit with each boy, then we would say the staff member is dealing with needs as though they were individual.

Perhaps the simplest case of a boy's expressing an individual need and the staff member's responding in terms of institutional requirements is when a boy requests something he himself wants and the staff member says "you can't have it because of some rule." If he says "you can't have it because it wouldn't be fair to the other guys," his response would be in terms of category 4, or if he said it would interfere with some project that the cottage as a group was trying to carry out, he would be responding in terms of category 2.

In deciding whether a staff member is expressing some personal need of his own that would belong in category 5 as opposed to expressing some requirement he is carrying out as the representative of the institution, the observer should first ask himself if it is reasonable on the basis of the request to think that it is the kind of thing which would serve the end of the role of a staff member functioning in the institution. If what the staff member asks or expects a boy to do or addresses himself to is the sort of thing that the institution might expect, and if there is no evidence to the contrary, this behavior should be placed in category 1. However, if the interest served has nothing to do with the institution—that is, if it doesn't have to do with maintaining order or maintenance of institutional property or the boys' caring for their own property but rather serves the staff member's own interest—it should be placed in category 5. Also, if what is requested is something that might serve institutional functions but which the staff member makes clear is really for the purposes of serving his own needs—for example, cutting the grass might be an institutional assignment, but if the staff member clearly indicates that his purpose in having the grass cut is so that he himself can play croquet—then category 5 is appropriate.

A general rule for the choice among alternatives is that the coder should always be alert to the fact that when we speak of functions we are concerned with the end results which the staff member is aiming toward rather than the means he chooses. Thus, as indicated above, when a staff member tries to promote good feeling among boys but clearly this is seen as directed toward the end of keeping the cottage clean, it should be coded in terms of that end. On the other hand, if the staff member sees working at some adaptive task as a means of promoting group solidarity the end—group solidarity, category 4—should be checked.

We should emphasize again the importance of the observer's objective viewpoint. It is often difficult to look beyond the simple content of what is being done and assess what are the consequences of the direction which the staff member's application of energy is likely to take even though expressed intention may often be the basis for our judgments. We are not concerned simply with intentions or even with what actually happens. For example, the boys may resist very much whatever the staff member does but that is not a basis for describing the staff member's behavior. We try to look at the action in terms of its probable consequences aside from the expressed motive and make our assessment of function on that basis.

Appendix C. "Guess Who" Questionnaire

In this questionnaire you are being asked to **guess who** the following descriptions fit among the boys in your cottage at the present time.

So that we can keep this anonymous, you have been given a list of boys in your cottage, with a letter, A,B,C, etc., next to each name.

For each description that fits a boy in your cottage, write his letter on the line next to the question. If any description fits two or three boys, write in their letters. But do not write more than three letters for each question. If the description applies to more than three boys, write the letters for the three boys it fits best.

If you honestly think that you yourself fit the description you may include your own letter.

Give your own best guess in each case, not the letters you think other boys will give.

There may be some descriptions that do not exactly fit any boy in your cottage. In that case, indicate who comes close to the description when possible.

Your answers will be kept confidential and known only to the research staff.

1. Wants everyone to take part in the cottage fun   ----------------------
2. Could beat anyone else in the cottage in a fair fight   ----------------------
3. Avoids making friends with other boys   ----------------------
4. Big joker   ----------------------
5. Gets around staff without actually breaking rules.   ----------------------
6. Does just as much as staff tells him to do in the cottage, but no more   ----------------------

7. Refuses to help other boys with house jobs ....
8. Has to be a leader, or he won't participate ....
9. Avoids getting involved in conflicts among boys ....
10. Tries to get special favors for himself from staff ....
11. Takes advantage of other boys who try to be nice to him ....
12. Talks to staff on behalf of other boys who have requests or complaints ....
13. Causes other boys to be blamed by staff for what he has done ....
14. Doesn't know how to do anything right ....
15. Is ignored by most boys in the cottage ....
16. Can be influenced by other boys to do things he's not supposed to do ....
17. Can't be trusted to stay out of other boys' lockers if no one is around ....
18. Keeps other boys from getting themselves in trouble with staff ....
19. Gets good grades with very little work in school ....
20. Stirs up arguments among boys but stays out of it himself ....
21. Gets other boys to do his job around the cottage ....
22. Plays his heart out on cottage teams, but wouldn't be a good captain ....
23. Never argues with staff ....
24. Tries to play one staff member against the other to get what he wants ....
25. Unwilling to lend things to other boys ....
26. Can get boys to work together in making things for the cottage ....
27. Is hardly ever asked to join other boys in activities ....
28. Knows the most about sports ....
29. Always does his share in house jobs ....
30. Doesn't care about doing his share of work in the cottage ....
31. Picks on boys weaker than himself, but not on anyone he's not sure he can lick ....
32. Cheers up boys who are feeling low ....
33. Always helpful to other boys in the cottage ....
34. Turns thumbs down on any new ideas or constructive suggestions from other boys in cottage meetings ....
35. Best all-around athlete ....
36. Ranks other boys but can't take it himself ....
37. Sticks with his own clique and doesn't pay much attention to other boys in the cottage ....
38. Other boys take orders from this boy because they're afraid of him ....
39. Always getting into fights with boys he can't beat ....

40. Will give up something he wants to help other boys ....
41. Other boys like to have this boy in on whatever they're doing ....
42. Argues with other boys about the least little thing ....
43. Tries to bum out of work all the time ....
44. Staff members like him more than any other boy ....
45. Is good at organizing boys to put their ideas for the cottage into action ....
46. Staff members ask this boy to get other boys to do things in the cottage ....
47. More friendly with staff than with other boys in the cottage ....
48. Very popular with girls at Hawthorne ....
49. Often picked on by other boys ....
50. **Often unites the boys in the cottage in whatever they're doing** ....
51. Has the best ideas for cottage group projects ....
52. Tries to help staff work with each other ....
53. Settles arguments before they break out into fights ....
54. Staff members dislike him more than any other boy in the cottage ....
55. Gets along very well with staff and other boys ....
56. Best all-around student in school ....
57. Seems to enjoy it when other boys don't get along with each other ....
58. Can get other boys in the cottage to do whatever he wants ....
59. Doesn't start fights but can take care of himself if anyone gets tough with him ....
60. Smooths over hard feelings between boys after a fight ....
61. Helps other boys with homework ....
62. Encourages other boys to get in arguments with staff ....
63. Argues the most with staff members ....
64. Does house jobs without ever being reminded by staff ....
65. Able to arrange for and carry through a ball game with no help from staff ....
66. Gets everyone to contribute his share for the cottage ....
67. Best all-around leader ....
68. Tries to sabotage co-operation among boys in the cottage ....

Appendix D. Opinion Questionnaire

Name ....

We want to find out about the kinds of behavior boys respect among their cottage mates and those they disrespect. Below are listed a number of kinds of behavior. Indicate how much respect or disrespect you personally have for each kind of behavior. Check the first column if you have **much respect** for that behavior, the second column if you have **some respect,** the third column if you have **some disrespect,** the fourth column if you have **much disrespect.**

Do not think about individuals in your cottage at present, whom you respect or disrespect. Give only your own opinion of **the kind of behavior** you respect or disrespect.

Since these are opinion questions, there are no "correct" answers. Your answers will be kept confidential and known only to the research staff.

Do not leave out any items. Give your own opinion on each one.

	Much respect	Some respect	Some dis- respect	Much dis- respect
1. Always getting into fights with boys he can't beat	....	....	....	....
2. Knows the most about sports	....	....	....	....
3. Tries to help staff work with each other	....	....	....	....
4. Is ignored by most boys in the cottage	....	....	....	....

	Much respect	Some respect	Some dis-respect	Much dis-respect
5. Other boys like to have this boy in on whatever they're doing	....	....	....	....
6. Never argues with staff	....	....	....	....
7. Argues with other boys about the least little thing	....	....	....	....
8. Smooths over hard feelings between boys after a fight	....	....	....	....
9. Plays his heart out on cottage teams, but wouldn't be a good captain	....	....	....	....
10. Tries to sabotage co-operation among boys in the cottage	....	....	....	....
11. Ranks other boys but can't take it himself	....	....	....	....
12. Turns thumbs down on any new ideas or constructive suggestions from other boys in cottage meetings	....	....	....	....
13. Argues the most with staff members	....	....	....	....
14. Doesn't care about doing his share of work in the cottage	....	....	....	....
15. Picks on boys weaker than himself, but not on anyone he's not sure he can lick	....	....	....	....
16. Best all-around student in school	....	....	....	....
17. Very popular with girls at Hawthorne	....	....	....	....
18. Can get other boys in the cottage to do whatever he wants	....	....	....	....
19. Is hardly ever asked to join other boys in cottage activities	....	....	....	....
20. Can get boys to work together in making things for the cottage	....	....	....	....
21. Tries to bum out of work all the time	....	....	....	....
22. Can be influenced by other boys to do things he's not supposed to do	....	....	....	....
23. Tries to get special favors for himself from staff	....	....	....	....
24. Does house jobs without ever being reminded by staff	....	....	....	....
25. Wants everyone to take part in the cottage fun	....	....	....	....
26. Unwilling to lend things to other boys	....	....	....	....
27. Doesn't know how to do anything right	....	....	....	....
28. Cheers up boys who are feeling low	....	....	....	....

	Much respect	Some respect	Some dis-respect	Much dis-respect
29. Gets around staff without actually breaking rules	....	....	....	....
30. Has to be a leader or he won't participate	....	....	....	....
31. Best all-around leader	....	....	....	....
32. Does just as much as staff tells him, but no more	....	....	....	....
33. Always helpful to other boys in the cottage	....	....	....	....
34. Avoids getting involved in conflicts with other boys	....	....	....	....
35. Takes advantage of other boys who try to be nice to him	....	....	....	....
36. Gets other boys to do his job around the cottage	....	....	....	....
37. More friendly with staff than with other boys in the cottage	....	....	....	....
38. Other boys take orders from this boy because they're afraid of him	....	....	....	....
39. Has the best ideas for cottage group projects	....	....	....	....
40. Could beat anyone else in the cottage in a fair fight	....	....	....	....
41. Gets along very well with staff and other boys	....	....	....	....
42. Able to arrange for and carry through a ball game with no help from staff	....	....	....	....
43. Helps other boys with homework	....	....	....	....
44. Always does his share in house jobs	....	....	....	....
45. Will give up something he wants to help other boys	....	....	....	....
46. Settles arguments before they break out into fights	....	....	....	....
47. Refuses to help other boys with house jobs	....	....	....	....
48. Big joker	....	....	....	....
49. Doesn't start fights but can take care of himself if anyone gets tough with him	....	....	....	....
50. Stirs up arguments among boys but stays out of it himself	....	....	....	....
51. Sticks with his own clique and doesn't pay much attention to other boys in the cottage	....	....	....	....
52. Best all-around athlete	....	....	....	....

	Much respect	Some respect	Some dis-respect	Much dis-respect
53. Keeps other boys from getting themselves in trouble with staff	....	....	....	....
54. Can't be trusted to stay out of other boys' lockers if no one is around	....	....	....	....
55. Causes other boys to be blamed by staff for what he has done	....	....	....	....
56. Gets good grades with very little work in school	....	....	....	....
57. Seems to enjoy it when other boys don't get along with each other	....	....	....	....
58. Tries to play one staff member against the other to get what he wants	....	....	....	....
59. Often picked on by other boys	....	....	....	....
60. Staff members dislike him more than any other boy in the cottage	....	....	....	....
61. Avoids making friends with other boys	....	....	....	....
62. Is good at organizing boys to put their ideas for the cottage into action	....	....	....	....
63. Gets everyone to contribute his share for the cottage	....	....	....	....
64. Staff members ask this boy to get other boys to do things in the cottage	....	....	....	....
65. Talks to staff on behalf of other boys who have requests or complaints	....	....	....	....
66. Staff members like him more than any other boy	....	....	....	....
67. Often unites the boys in the cottage in whatever they're doing	....	....	....	....
68. Encourages other boys to get in arguments with staff	....	....	....	....

Appendix E. Choice Questionnaire

Name ....

In the first part of this questionnaire you are asked to indicate the boys in your cottage you would personally choose for different kinds of activities, if you knew that your choice would come true.

In the second part you are asked to indicate which boys in your cottage you personally like and dislike most, and those you have the most respect and disrespect for.

In the third part, indicate which boys, of all boys you know at Hawthorne, you personally like and dislike most, and those you have most respect and disrespect for.

Indicate your first, second, and third choices in each case.

All answers will be kept confidential by the research staff.

Part I

1. Which boy in your cottage would you choose to be in charge of settling disagreements among other boys?
   1st choice ....
   2nd choice ....
   3rd choice ....

2. Which boy in your cottage would you choose to organize the other boys to work on projects that the boys want?
   1st choice ....
   2nd choice ....
   3rd choice ....

3. Which boy in your cottage would you choose to talk to when you are feeling low?
   1st choice ....
   2nd choice ....
   3rd choice ....

4. Which boy in your cottage would you choose to act as spokesman for the others if the boys in the cottage wanted a special favor from Mr. Helfer?
   1st choice ....
   2nd choice ....
   3rd choice ....

Part II

1. Which boy in your cottage do you personally like most?
   1st choice ....
   2nd choice ....
   3rd choice ....

2. Which boy in your cottage do you personally dislike most?
   1st choice ....
   2nd choice ....
   3rd choice ....

3. Which boy in your cottage do you personally have the most respect for?
   1st choice ....
   2nd choice ....
   3rd choice ....

Part III

1. Which boy at Hawthorne do you personally like most?
   1st choice ....
   2nd choice ....
   3rd choice ....

2. Which boy at Hawthorne do you personally dislike most?
   1st choice ....
   2nd choice ....
   3rd choice ....

3. Which boy at Hawthorne do you personally have the most respect for?
   1st choice ....
   2nd choice ....
   3rd choice ....

4. Which boy at Hawthorne do you personally have the most disrespect for?
   1st choice ....
   2nd choice ....
   3rd choice ....

Part IV In some cottages there seems to be more cottage spirit than in others.

Do you feel that your cottage has (check one)
.... a) a great deal of spirit?
.... b) a fair amount of spirit?
.... c) very little spirit?

Appendix F. Analysis of Questionnaire
Reliability and Validity

Reliability in our questionnaires is essentially item reliability. We tried to build the cottage comparisons by focusing on the content of individual role items evaluated and perceived by residents. Although it may be possible instead to develop empirical clusters of role-inventory items through factor analysis or scaling methods and thereby achieve higher reliability for factor or scale scores than for separate items, item reliability is most appropriate for our kind of application of the questionnaires.

Since we have no scales, it is not possible to measure concurrent reliability of role evaluations. We did have fourteen of our subjects return a week after they first took the evaluation questionnaire for a retest, under the same conditions. For each item, individuals' scores on the first questionnaire administration were correlated with their scores the next week. We thus got 68 correlation coefficients, one for each role item.

Of the correlation coefficients, 45 were above .43 and thus significantly different from zero at the 5-per-cent level of confidence. Of these 45, 15 r's were between .80 and 1.00, another 13 between .60 and .80, and the remaining 17 between .43 and .60. For all 68 items, the median correlation is .52. Because scale scores reflect underlying predispositions more stable than item responses, results appear low as compared with reliability coefficients for attitude scales. But, as item responses, the proportion of significant correlations justifies the conclusion that response variation is not entirely attributable to chance.

Since our primary interest in the "Guess Who" questionnaire was on role choices received, it is appropriate to assess reliability from this point of view. The reliability coefficient is based on correlating the number of choices received for a particular role item from one random half of cottage respondents with the number of choices received from the other half, corrected by the Spearman-Brown formula.[1]

Since the correlations represent, in part, actual differences in cottage structures, the reliability coefficients are given separately for each cottage. Corrected correlation coefficients range from −.05 to +.98 among Fairline roles, with a median of .84. Hearthstone's reliability correlations range from −.25 to +1.00, with a median of .76, and the correlations for Concord range from −.13 to .99, with a median of .85.

For the sociometric Choice Questionnaire, reliability has been computed in the same way as for the "Guess Who" instrument, by correlating number of choices received from one half of the boys in each cottage with choices received from the other half. Because only Parts I and II of the " 'Guess Who' Questionnaire" seek choices among cottage mates, reliability correlations to be reported include only the eight items in those two parts.

For Fairline these corrected correlations range from .34 to .97. Three of the eight are above .90 and another three between .80 and .90. The range in Hearthstone is from .40 to .95. Two are in the .90 to 1.00 range and three between .80 and .90. The highest coefficient for Concord is .98 and the lowest is .47, with four in the .90 to 1.00 range and another one between .80 and .90.

The general problem of questionnaire validity becomes especially salient for respondents like ours, who are residents in an institution that seeks, as a major goal, to change children's behavior from deviant to socially acceptable. Our evaluation questionnaire is particularly susceptible to the charge that boys might want to go on record as respecting certain kinds of behavior regarded as acceptable by adults whereas they in fact respect more negative behavior. Therefore, in spite of our impression that the boys accepted our assurance that responses would be kept confidential and so responded without dissembling, we also sought objective data

1. For a description of this application of split-half correlation, see Jane S. Mouton, Robert R. Blake, and Benjamin Fruchter, "The Reliability of Sociometric Measures," *Sociometry*, 18 (1950), 7-48.

to show that the social-desirability[2] variable had not distorted our results.

We asked respondents to sign their names to all questionnaires, as it was necessary to identify individual responses for some purposes—for example, in order to correlate personality factor scores on the HSPQ with choices received on the " 'Guess Who' Questionnaire." We reasoned that, if we obtained social-desirability biased evaluation ratings, giving the questionnaires under anonymous conditions would reveal a tendency for behavior which the institutional authorities consider positive to be rated lower, and institutionally disapproved behavior to be rated higher. Thus, the respect questionnaire was given a second time. Seven boys filled it out without signing names, in addition to the fourteen who did sign their names.

Compared with the original group of respondents, boys who took the questionnaire anonymously the second time showed somewhat greater differences. Inspection of items in which differences are observed does not, however, reveal any evidence that boys subscribe to socially approved values "for the record" and delinquent values when responses are anonymous. Greater variability on the retest, but not systematic bias, appears to account for the greater change in means. Boys seem to take the questionnaires more seriously when they are required to sign their names. Thus, it appears that having boys identify themselves does induce greater co-operation, but from our evidence this compliance seems to consist of accepting the instructions to answer frankly, rather than giving socially desirable responses.

Now we shall address ourselves to validity in broader scope, namely, whether the role-inventory items and the ways we have used them in peer nomination and evaluation questionnaires do tap the cultural and social systems of the cottage. Does the aggregate of role descriptions incorporated in the evaluation questionnaire in fact indicate the behaviors on which respect in the peer group is based? Does number of choices on these items indeed reflect role incumbency?

If there is validity in our conceptualizing the cottage group in terms of role evaluation and nomination, an individual's status position should be predictable on the basis of nominations received for a role and group evaluation of the role. To be seen by many of one's peers as occupying a highly evaluated role makes a positive contribution toward one's general status in the group; similarly, to be selected for a disvalued role detracts from one's status. The effect of an individual's enactment of a given role on his total

2. Allen L. Edwards, *The Social Desirability Variable in Personality Assessment and Research* (New York: Dryden, 1957).

esteem or disesteem in the group is, then, a function of the number of people who perceive him in that role and the group evaluation of that role. And the total esteem or disesteem in which he is held is a function of each role's valuation by the group and the nominations he received for that role.

Thus, a Composite Role-Evaluation Score has been computed for each boy. The mean evaluation scores attributed by each cottage to each role were converted to plus or minus scores. The possible range of this scale is from −2.00 to +2.00; a sum of −2.00 would indicate that all boys had given an evaluation of "much disrespect" to that kind of behavior. An average evaluation of −1.00 indicates "some disrespect," zero is the indifference point, "some respect" is +1.00, and +2.00 would indicate that all boys had "much respect" for that kind of behavior. The number of times a boy was chosen by others as incumbent of each role was multiplied by this evaluation score, and these products were summed algebraically to yield this Composite Role Evaluation Score.

Now, if our questionnaires had done what we have hypothesized, these Composite Role-Evaluation Scores should identify those boys who were most frequently mentioned by their peers when the questions "Which boy in your cottage do you personally have the most respect for?" and "Which boy in your cottage do you personally have the most disrespect for?" are subsequently asked; these two items serve as our validating criteria.

Table 1 shows the Composite Role-Evaluation Scores and the number of choices on each criterion question. In all three cottages the Composite Role-Evaluation Score identifies the two individuals with most choices on the "respect" item. In Fairline, H, who was much higher than any others with a Composite Role-Evaluation Score of 230.19, also greatly exceeded anyone else as the boy for whom others had the most respect (with eleven nominations for that role). E, ranking second with a score of 69.91, is far below the top individual; he also had the second highest number of choices as most respected (named four times). In Hearthstone, there was a relatively smaller gap between the top two boys on the Composite Role-Evaluation Score. K had a score of 148.57 and A a score of 102.07. Between them the ranking of choices was reversed on the two measures; A, lower on the Composite Role-Evaluation Score, was chosen one more time, with seven choices, than K, as most respected, so that here the composite score identifies the top two boys in peer respect, but in reverse order. In Concord the first three boys were clearly identified and differentiated in 1–2–3 order by both Composite Role-Evaluation Score and "respect." F, with a Composite Role-Evaluation Score of 321.61 and thirteen "respect" choices, is far above the others. P, who has a Composite

Table 1. Comparison of Composite Role-Evaluation Score with Number of Respect and Disrespect Nominations.

Boy	CRES	Number of Respect Choices	Number of Disrespect Choices
Fairline			
A	5.58		
B	− 90.50		9
C	−166.98		7
D	4.45	1	
E	69.91	4	
F	54.54	2	
G	4.45	2	1
H	230.19	11	
I	5.52		1
J	7.40		1
K	−130.38	1	7
L	− 46.13		2
M	− 6.30	2	
N	39.30	3	
O	− 1.74	2	
P	−124.68		2
Q	40.06	3	
Hearthstone			
A	102.07	7	
B	14.13	2	
C	− .71		
D	29.55	1	
E	− 8.17		7
F	− 16.94	1	3
G	− 40.33		3
H	− 7.33	1	
I	11.18	1	
J	4.46		
K	148.57	6	
L	−103.21		10
M	13.31		
N	− 7.55	1	6
O	− 23.76	1	
P	5.88		
Q	7.85	4	1
R	29.56	2	
Concord			
A	− 3.06		
B	− 69.60		3
C	− 12.71		1
D	−124.05		6

Table 1. (Continued)

Boy	CRES	Number of Respect Choices	Number of Disrespect Choices
E	— 68.40		4
F	321.61	13	
G	— 49.07	1	5
H	— 14.58	1	
I	— 6.45		
J	— 15.06		
K	— 23.26	1	2
L	1.42		4
M	80.26	4	1
N	— 46.42		4
O	37.04	1	
P	226.85	7	
Q	— 37.61	2	1

Role-Evaluation Score of 226.85 and seven choices on "respect," was clearly below F but clearly above the others, and M is third on both measures. On the basis of these comparisons, our assumption that Composite Role-Evaluation Score does reflect the boys' overall perception of whom they respect seems well supported and lends credence to the meaningfulness of the questionnaires from which the role-evaluation score was computed.

The negative Composite Role-Evaluation Scores can be compared with the last columns in Table 1, which indicate the number of choices received for "most disrespect." In Fairline, of the four boys with lowest Composite Role-Evaluation Score, B, C, K, and P, three were most frequently chosen as most disrespected by their peers. However, P, who was third-lowest on the Composite Role-Evaluation Score, did not receive as markedly great a number of choices on "disrespect" as the other three. Furthermore, B, who had the most choices on "disrespect," ranked fourth from the lowest (with a score of —90.50) on the Composite Role-Evaluation Score. Taking the five boys with lowest scores, N, C, K, L, and P, these were the same five with most choices on "disrespect," but L and P have only two choices on "disrespect," whereas the Composite Role-Evaluation Score placed them more noticeably below the others. For this cottage, although both the Composite Role-Evaluation Score and number of choices in "disrespect" agree in identifying the group who ranked lowest in their peers' esteem among that group, the order was not in agreement. The data for P represented the major inconsistency here. He was an individual who had an extremely negative attitude within the cottage toward meeting adult expectations, and he did engage in some delinquency against other boys, but he managed to stay sufficiently aloof from most boys in the cottage so that his behavior did not incur as much hostility as might be expected on the basis of many of his objective shortcomings.

In Hearthstone, L, the boy who was by far lowest on the Composite Role-Evaluation Score with a score of −103.21, also received appreciably more choices as "most disrespected," ten, than any other boy. However, two other boys, E and N, who received six and seven choices respectively as "most disrespected," were only slightly below the mid-point in the composite role evaluation score. From our observations of these two individuals, we believe that they were disrespected for rather subtle negative qualities which were not embodied in our inventory—N because of an attitude of snobbishness and aloofness and E because he was guilty of false bragging to the others.

In Concord, D, who had the lowest Composite Role-Evaluation Score (−124.05), also received more nominations as "most disrespected" than any other boys. B, D, E, G, K, and N all received three and more nominations as "most disrespected." These correspond to six of the seven lowest of the Composite Role-Evaluation Scores (Q was in the low group on the composite score but received only one nomination as "most disrespected.")

In sum, then, the high Composite Role-Evaluation Scores corresponded to peer choices for most respected boys in each cottage, identifying highest status boys in similar order, for the most part. Low scores on the Composite Role-Evaluation Index also identified boys chosen as disrespected, but the ranking on the two measures did not correspond so well at the lower end of the continuum. Apparently, when disrespect nominations are used as the validating criterion, some of the finer distinctions are not reflected in the composite role scores.

As for the broader question of construct validity raised initially, by and large these findings support our assumption that the role inventory and procedure do represent meaningful aspects of the social and cultural systems. We suggest that extension of the procedure used here to validate an already selected inventory would be useful for selecting role items in order to measure the representativeness of role inventories in future studies.

Index